Bristol Public Library

It Seems to Me

It Seems to Me

Selected Letters of Eleanor Roosevelt

Edited by Leonard C. Schlup
AND Donald W. Whisenhunt

THE UNIVERSITY PRESS OF KENTUCKY

Publication of this volume was made possible in part
by a grant from the National Endowment for the Humanities.

Scholarly publisher for the Commonwealth,
serving Bellarmine University, Berea College, Centre
College of Kentucky, Eastern Kentucky University,
The Filson Club Historical Society, Georgetown College,
Kentucky Historical Society, Kentucky State University,
Morehead State University, Murray State University,
Northern Kentucky University, Transylvania University,
University of Kentucky, University of Louisville,
and Western Kentucky University.

Editorial and Sales Offices: The University Press of Kentucky
663 South Limestone Street, Lexington, Kentucky 40508–4008

05 04 03 02 01   5 4 3 2 1

Frontispiece: Eleanor Roosevelt with her mail on the USS *Sequoia*.
(Courtesy of the Franklin D. Roosevelt Library)

Library of Congress Cataloging-in-Publication Data

Roosevelt, Eleanor, 1884-1962.
    It seems to me : selected letters of Eleanor Roosevelt / edited by
    Leonard C. Schlup and Donald W. Whisenhunt.
        p. cm.
    Includes bibliographical references (p.   ) and index.
    ISBN 0-8131-2185-X (cloth : acid-free paper)
    1. Roosevelt, Eleanor, 1884-1962—Correspondence. 2. Presidents'
    spouses—United States—Correspondence. 3. Roosevelt, Eleanor,
    1884-1962—Political and social views. 4. United States—Politics
    and government—1945-1989. I. Schlup, Leonard C., 1943-
    II. Whisenhunt, Donald W. III. Title.
E807.1.R48 A4   2001   00-012277
973.917'092—dc21

This book is printed on acid-free recycled paper meeting
the requirements of the American National Standard
for Permanence in Paper for Printed Library Materials.

∞ ✪

Manufactured in the United States of America.

*This book is dedicated
to the memory of* ELEANOR ROOSEVELT,
*first lady of the United States (1933–1945)
and first lady of the world (1945–1962).*

Contents

Foreword   vii

Introduction   1

Letters   13

Bibliography   283

Index   284

Foreword

Eleanor Roosevelt, arguably the most important woman of the twentieth century, has been the subject of considerable scholarship in recent years that focuses on the tensions between her public and private life. Examination of her close personal relationships, however, may tend to obscure the significance of her role as a stateswoman and professional political leader. This volume of selected letters is valuable because it shows a dimension of Eleanor Roosevelt lost in construction of a portrait that emphasizes her emotional life. Here we have her correspondence to a stunning array of individuals whose decisions affected the course of world and national affairs—Truman, Eisenhower, Churchill, Marshall, Harriman, Stevenson, Kennedy.

These letters, most of which were taken from the vast collection of Eleanor Roosevelt papers at the Franklin D. Roosevelt Library, Hyde Park, New York, have been available to scholars for years but never before published in a single volume. They picture Eleanor Roosevelt as a canny and astute adviser to presidents and would-be presidents, as a resourceful diplomat at the United Nations closely attuned to the currents of the Cold War, and as a powerful force in the Democratic Party. They show her lecturing President Truman, attempting to persuade Eisenhower to appear on her public affairs broadcasts, and critiquing Kennedy's television performance. What emerges is the voice of a shrewd, self-confident individual committed to both the Democratic Party and a democratic way of life.

Not all of the selections, however, are letters addressed to famous figures. The volume includes some correspondence with ordinary citizens to whom

Eleanor Roosevelt expressed her views on controversial topics such as the conviction of Alger Hiss. Letters concerning her service on the board of the National Association for the Advancement of Colored People demonstrates her commitment to civil rights. We also find references to her dispute with the Catholic church over aid to parochial schools.

Unlike some of her biographies, the letters do not present Eleanor Roosevelt as a saint. They picture her as a very down-to-earth individual—making recommendations for political appointments, trying to arrange for Bernard Baruch to have access to the White House, refusing to loan money to the grandson of an old friend. Although the editors wisely have decided not to include letters to family members, nevertheless, elements of Eleanor Roosevelt's personality flavor this volume of what essentially is a collection of political views by an important participant in the post–World War II scene.

Scholars and general readers alike should be grateful to the editors, Leonard C. Schlup and Donald W. Whisenhunt, for this fascinating volume that makes the study of Eleanor Roosevelt more accessible to the public. What is presented offers rich insights into a remarkable woman's life and times.

Maurine H. Beasley
University of Maryland

Introduction

*E*leanor Roosevelt ranks among the most remarkable women of the twentieth century. As the wife of an American president and his partner in a successful political combination, she defined the role of activist first lady. Her path broke barriers and set new standards for modern women. A pragmatic player in the American political landscape for three decades, she embraced coalitions and championed compromise while retaining her reverence for individual rights and dedication to progressive ideas. After the death of President Franklin D. Roosevelt in 1945, Mrs. Roosevelt emerged as first lady of the world, functioning as an ambassador of good will. "We have to prove . . . that democracy really brings about happier and better conditions for the people as a whole," she insisted. "She was a living symbol of world understanding and peace," said President John F. Kennedy, "and her untiring efforts had become a vital part of the historic fabric of this century." Gov. Adlai E. Stevenson of Illinois observed that ER would rather "light a candle than curse the darkness." He was right, for throughout her public life she lighted candles of courage. From 1932 until her death thirty years later, she evolved into the conscience of her generation and the voice of a common humanity yearning for decency and self-respect. An emblem of the American aspiration, ER stood for compassion, hope, and belief. She spoke her own mind in her own way, often using the words "it seems to me."

A passionate reformer and humanitarian who despised the politics of avoidance, Eleanor Roosevelt vigorously defended the causes and ideals she deemed just and worthy. An unofficial ambassador for justice who gave voice to the voiceless and hope to the hopeless, she accepted personal responsibility for her country. Roosevelt took self-government seriously and would not rest until she had done what she felt she had to do and what her conscience demanded that she somehow accomplish. "What one has to do usually can be done," she reasoned. Life for her was an ongoing adventure, an opportunity to learn, and an invitation to fulfill obligations. Throughout this process, with her ceaseless movements and measureless energy, ER developed into an American legend. She advocated women's rights, civil rights, and world peace. Envisioning a better world, she surfaced as a national representative for causes that helped shape the liberal movement in the 1940s and 1950s. In certain ways, Mrs. Roosevelt, the mother of the postwar Democratic Party, commanded more attention and proved more effective in proclaiming its message than did the leading male politicians of the era. Her understanding of her own time seems more sound in retrospect than that of many New Deal administrators, who thought in terms of policies. ER thought in terms of people. For the first lady, the real question was the human question, and her mission sought to keep the human perspective. ER's greatest talent was her ability to reduce the quarrels of doctrine and dogma to human differences to be discussed in human terms. "Where after all do universal human rights begin?" she asked. "In small places close to home, so close and so small that they cannot be seen on any maps of the world." ER also stated: "Human rights will become a reality only when people really believe in human rights and want to live for human rights."

Eleanor Roosevelt practiced her own brand of freedom from fear. She was first lady for twelve years in an era when Americans endured the worst depression and the most horrific war of all time. Roosevelt sought security and stability. She projected hope to a despondent, dispirited America. She felt an obligation to do something, to care, to feel, and to instill expectations. Her aim was to sow love and faith, and she did so with a rare grace and eloquence. Throughout these years, the first lady practiced the power of belief. She said, "Believe in yourself. You gain strength, courage, and confidence by every experience in which you stop to look fear in the face. . . . You must do that which you think you cannot do. . . . The future belongs to those who believe in the beauty of their dreams."

Intelligent and compassionate, Roosevelt remained decidedly outspoken in her beliefs. Because of her views and forthright stands, she not surprisingly confronted vicious verbal and written attacks and assassination threats, while earning the enmity of the Ku Klux Klan. Perceiving early the dangers of fascism, she labeled Adolf Hitler and Benito Mussolini as perverters of humanity. The Italian duce was so furious with the American first lady that he attacked her as a nuisance who should be embargoed. Mrs. Roosevelt quickly dismissed the autocrat's verbosity, countering with her own analysis of the explosive international situation. "All of us have an equal responsibility in the one great country that is free to the rest of the world wherever there may be people who are not free to become free again," she affirmed. In the postwar United States, she strongly opposed the investigative nature of the House Committee on Un-American Activities. Roosevelt abhorred the detrimental tactics and grandstanding of Republican senator Joseph R. McCarthy in his capacity as chairman of the Committee on Government Operations and its Permanent Subcommittee on Investigations, a congressional group that endeavored to document charges of Communist influence in government. She detested the politics of fear and character destruction. Long before many national leaders, she perceived the clandestine side of Richard M. Nixon. ER expressed doubt in 1956 whether President Dwight D. Eisenhower could survive a second term because of his earlier heart attack, and she firmly adhered to her contention that the country could not stand Nixon as chief executive. In 1960, prior to the Democratic National Convention in July, Eleanor Roosevelt openly questioned Sen. John F. Kennedy's experience for the presidency, basing her opinion partly on Joseph P. Kennedy's conduct during the Second World War, Robert F. Kennedy's association with the McCarthy hearings, and Senator Kennedy's overall moderation in strategic areas she valued highly.

Eleanor Roosevelt welcomed letters from people. In her first contributory essay that appeared on "Mrs. Roosevelt's Page" in the August 1933 issue of *Woman's Home Companion,* she entitled her piece, "I Want You to Write to Me." She wished to establish a clearinghouse for information and a discussion room for millions of Americans. They could turn to her with their puzzling problems as well as inform her of events that had brought joy into their lives. Inviting individuals to write freely while promising not to betray their confidence, the first lady concluded that it was often easier to write to someone than bear the burden alone. Frequently she gave of herself in her letters, for in the process of responding to strangers or friends, she found an outlet to express her own emotional needs, offer sympathy, or give an admonition. She could write detailed letters on domestic and foreign affairs to ordinary citizens or national leaders. In one case, to a close friend in 1956, ER confided that she considered strange the policy of brinkmanship advocated by

Eleanor Roosevelt at her desk. (Courtesy of the Franklin D. Roosevelt Library)

Secretary of State John Foster Dulles that frightened American allies. She went on to say that she hoped for a change in State Department attitudes under a Democratic administration.

No person was too prominent or powerful to escape ER's scrutiny. The list included generals, prime ministers, chief executives, and social leaders. Undeterred by controversy, she chastised presidential candidates and archbishops as easily as ordinary citizens. When, for example, in July 1949 Cardinal Francis Joseph Spellman, archbishop of New York, the nation's principal diocese, caustically accused Mrs. Roosevelt of anti-Catholicism and discrimination because of her opposition to federal aid for parochial schools, the former first lady swiftly responded to his attacks. Emphasizing that she harbored no bias against the Roman Catholic church and mentioning her endorsement of New York governor Alfred E. Smith for president in 1928, Roosevelt reiterated her intention to speak out on public issues and stand for those matters in government that she considered correct, regardless of what opposition developed from individuals or groups. In a letter printed in the

New York Times on July 28, 1949, ER informed Spellman, a theological conservative, that the final judgment of the worthiness of all human beings rested with God and not with cardinals. She reminded him of the lessons of European history regarding the domination of education and government by any one particular religious faith and how they had never resulted in a "happy arrangement for the people." Pointing out that spiritual leadership must be distinct from temporal power, she called attention to the fact that in the United States no rigid government-mandated religious beliefs were taught to children in public schools supported by tax dollars and that public school children normally were granted free textbooks, but asserted that it would be fallacious to think that these same things must be given to children attending private schools where parents pay tuition and expenses. Disavowing prejudicial attitudes, ER bluntly informed Spellman that she had never thought of the religion of the "boys" she visited in hospitals. "If you carefully studied my record," she concluded, "I think you would not find it one of anti-Catholic or anti-any religious group."

Another case involved Roy Wilkins, executive secretary of the National Association for the Advancement of Colored People. Outraged in 1956 by Adlai Stevenson's emphasis on moderation in civil rights, Wilkins berated the Democratic presidential contender for a squeamish stand. A surprised ER distanced herself from Wilkins's poorly construed and "hot-headed statement," professing that it was misguided behavior to tear down Stevenson, the only real hope that year for African Americans. After maintaining that African Americans were not bound to the Democratic Party, Wilkins received a cutting letter from an angry ER in which she alluded to his "unwise" remarks while warning him of the consequences of reactionary Republican rule. In this terse manner, Eleanor Roosevelt quickly put Wilkins in his place.

Born Anna Eleanor Roosevelt in New York City on October 11, 1884, the daughter of Elliott and Anna Hall Roosevelt and the niece of Theodore Roosevelt, twenty-sixth president of the United States, Eleanor experienced a troubled and unhappy childhood because of a distant mother who lacked compassion and an alcoholic father, both of whom died before she reached ten years of age. This misfortune compelled the young girl to live with her maternal grandmother, Mary Ludlow Hall, and other relatives, who demonstrated little affection and thereby left her with feelings of insecurity and inadequacy. Almost at once she found comfort in helping other people to compensate for her own fears of rejection.

To further her granddaughter's education, Mrs. Hall sent Eleanor to a small school for girls in England. At Allenswood School near London, Eleanor came under the influence of the headmistress, Marie Souvestre, daughter of a French philosopher. Once back in the United States, the young Miss Roosevelt made her debut in 1902 and almost immediately thereafter plunged into reform work. She championed health and safety standards in New York and taught calisthenics to immigrant children in Manhattan, beginning her commitment to improve the lives of members of minority groups and the underprivileged.

Eleanor Roosevelt's marriage on March 17, 1905, to her distant cousin Franklin Delano Roosevelt resulted in six children, one of whom died in infancy. ER was overshadowed for years by the dominating influence of her formidable mother-in-law, Sara Delano Roosevelt, and this was compounded by her husband's infidelities. It proved a difficult marriage for a woman who craved affection. After her husband rejected her offer of a divorce in 1918, a deeply wounded Eleanor remained with him, ending marital intimacy but gradually rebuilding with FDR a respectful mutuality.

Following Franklin Roosevelt's entrance into politics in 1911 as a state senator and thereafter his service as assistant secretary of the navy during the Woodrow Wilson administration, Eleanor Roosevelt moved to Albany and Washington, respectively. When Theodore Roosevelt sought the presidency on the Progressive "Bull Moose" ticket in 1912, his niece fumed that the newspapers had been "perfectly disgusting about Uncle Ted" and that she longed "to contradict them all." During World War I she busied herself with Navy Relief and the Red Cross. The postwar period and her husband's paralysis in 1921 opened opportunities unknown in her shy youth. She became active in the League of Women Voters, Women's Trade Union League, and the Democratic Party. After FDR's defeat for vice president in 1920 and his crippling fight with polio, Eleanor Roosevelt served as her husband's political legs and spokesperson. She fought energetically for her ideas while encountering family heartaches over the troubled lives of her children and their spouses.

In 1927, as part owner of the Todhunter School in New York City, ER taught history, literature, and government. The next year her husband won election as governor of New York at the time that Democratic governor Alfred E. Smith lost the presidential contest to Herbert Hoover. In 1930, one year after the stock market crash and at the beginning of the Great Depression, Governor Roosevelt secured reelection and immediately became a contender for the Democratic presidential nomination in 1932.

When her husband captured the presidential office in 1932 in a landslide victory, Eleanor Roosevelt at first privately expressed reluctance to move into the White House, where she feared she would become a prisoner in a glass cage. Yet she successfully handled her new role, emerging as the most active first lady up to that time and in the process establishing precedents for her successors. Mrs. Roosevelt held weekly press conferences with women reporters, traveled throughout the country, and starred on her own radio program to articulate her messages and challenge Americans to accept their responsibilities as citizens. She even visited a coal mine, where a startled miner exclaimed: "My Gosh. It's Mrs. Roosevelt." Her syndicated newspaper column, "My Day," appeared daily from 1936 to 1962. The first lady briefly served as assistant director of the Office of Civilian Defense during World War II, touring military bases abroad in this capacity.

The New Deal transformed the nation, and Franklin Roosevelt strengthened the presidency. At the same time, Eleanor Roosevelt played an influential role in policy-making, trying in the process to balance her interests with her husband's political realities. If FDR saw what could be done, ER visualized what should be done, often badgering the president when he caved in to political necessity. She was willing in some instances to follow expedient courses, as when she often muted her own views about African Americans to harmonize with FDR's southern strategy in courting conservative Democrats. During her White House years, ER made history by being the first wife of a president to hold a governmental position in her husband's administration and to receive an official diplomatic assignment. She also was the first to travel in an airplane to a foreign country and to have a news conference in the executive mansion. The White House exposure toughened her resolve. In 1994 First Lady Hillary Rodham Clinton remembered something that her predecessor had said: "A woman is like a tea bag; when she is in hot water she just gets stronger."

President Roosevelt's death on April 12, 1945, closed one part of ER's life and opened another. Refusing to retreat into retirement, the former first lady stepped out of the penumbra of FDR and evolved on her own, constantly ascending in importance and prestige. Her time had arrived. "Franklin's death ended a period in history," she said, "and now in its wake for lots of us who lived in his shadow ... we have to start again under our own momentum and wonder what we can achieve." Contending that it was a cowardly evasion to remain aloof, ER exhibited the qualities of an astute observer and savvy politician who learned from successes and mistakes and promoted an agenda prioritized by results.

Her achievements from 1945 until her death were numerous. President

Harry S Truman appointed her as a U.S. delegate to the United Nations General Assembly. She served in 1945, again from 1949 to 1952, and once more in 1961 and 1962 under President Kennedy. Eleanor Roosevelt chaired the Commission on Human Rights of the Economic and Social Council in 1946, helping to draft the United Nations Declaration of Human Rights. She occupied herself with family and friends, visited several nations, lectured across the country, published articles, and supported Adlai Stevenson for president. Had he been elected the nation's chief executive, he surely would have found a place for her in his administration where she could have continued her work.

Six months before her death, Roosevelt offered sound advice for future presidents and first ladies when she spoke of the importance of having White House occupants who understand the value of social justice. "Both the President and his wife can never give way to apprehension," she explained, "even though they are probably more aware than most citizens of the dangers which may surround us. If the country is to be confident, they must be confident. They cannot afford to harbor resentment, or to have enemies where it is possible to turn these enemies into friends. This demands from both the President and his wife a high order of intelligence, of self-discipline and a dedication to the public good."

After a period of failing health, Mrs. Roosevelt passed away in New York City on November 7, 1962. Numerous dignitaries attended her funeral. Her body was interred next to her husband's grave in the rose garden of the Franklin D. Roosevelt Library in Hyde Park, New York, not far from Val-Kill, the home she loved dearly. Roosevelt's death brought to a close the life of an inspiring person who fearlessly endorsed progressive causes, earned an enduring legacy, and achieved a reputation as perhaps the most respected American woman of the twentieth century.

Numerous biographies have stressed Eleanor Roosevelt's indomitable spirit, while three edited collections of her letters to family members and close friends, as well as a published assortment of her political writings, have revealed her personal relationships. Missing from this portrait of her life is a volume of selected letters to public figures, world leaders, and other individuals outside her family with whom she corresponded and to whom she expressed her views on particular matters and issues of domestic and international concern. These letters merit attention, for they reveal much about ER as a politician, diplomat, and reformer. Included among the recipients of her letters were Bernard Baruch, Mary McLeod Bethune, Pearl Buck, Ralph J.

Bunche, Carrie Chapman Catt, Madame Chiang Kai-shek, Winston Churchill, William O. Douglas, Dwight D. Eisenhower, Isabella Greenway, W. Averell Harriman, Oveta Culp Hobby, Harry Hopkins, Lyndon B. Johnson, John F. Kennedy, Robert F. Kennedy, Martin Luther King Jr., Herbert Lehman, George C. Marshall, Agnes Meyer, Frances Perkins, Samuel T. Rayburn, Walter P. Reuther, Adlai E. Stevenson, Harry S Truman, Robert F. Wagner, Henry A. Wallace, Walter White, and Edith Bolling Galt Wilson.

Such a book on ER has long been needed. This collection fills a gap in historical scholarship, covering a selection of her letters during a fifty-year period from 1912 to 1962. On its own merits, this single volume serves as a convenient primary reference source for historians, political scientists, librarians, social scientists, scholars of women's studies, the general public, and undergraduate and graduate students.

Letters usually disclose the direction of a person's life. They capture in some way the character of the writer as well as her relationships, hopes, and disappointments. Usually they command greater value as primary source material than diaries or sanitized autobiographies, for each letter was written on a particular day under a specific impulse, generally without thought that it would later be published for others to read or be judged in a larger context. "I never did like to be where I no longer belonged," Roosevelt confessed in a letter to her dear friend Joseph P. Lash on her last evening in the White House, "but the Trumans have been very nice. The upstairs looks desolate with all the things gone that make a home." Historians can also learn about a person by what she decided to conceal. Letters are, therefore, expressive in both their revelations and their evasions.

As one of the most important first ladies in American history and as a woman who found her own place on the world stage, Eleanor Roosevelt deserves scholarly attention for every aspect of her varied life. A selected compilation of her letters is one useful way to introduce her to a current generation of readers while providing seasoned Roosevelt scholars with more trenchant passages to enrich their understanding of her personal complexities and political insights. "The Republican ticket is a strong one," she revealed in the summer of 1948 to her close friend and personal physician, A. David Gurewitsch, "and I feel Eisenhower will be drafted and I don't think Truman can win against it. I feel sure he will be nominated, however. I expect a fair foreign policy from the Republicans if they win, tho' the Progressives will have to fight the reactionaries. In domestic things I expect reaction as far as they dare."

Although ER was not as reflective or exciting a letter writer as her uncle Theodore Roosevelt, she left historians with documents that illuminate her story and serve as a chronicle of her life, offering glimpses that range widely in subject and tone. Certainly her own writings, engaging and revealing, constitute one of the most important sources of information in reconstructing her life in print. Her voice emerges from these pages, portraying an intriguing picture of the times and of ER, a woman of contradictions and an outspoken advocate for social causes who secretly yearned for a personal passion. Reflecting her personality and broad interests, her voluminous letters are indispensable to understanding and appreciating her life's work. Numbering approximately two million pages, Eleanor Roosevelt's papers at the Franklin D. Roosevelt Library, the main repository of her correspondence, constitute the second-largest collection of materials at Hyde Park.

Unlike other published volumes of Eleanor Roosevelt's letters that concentrate solely on personal matters or combine personal and public life, the letters selected for this book focus on the public persona. This conception allows readers to develop an appreciation of the depth of ER's knowledge of public affairs. A compelling story of a towering woman of her century arises from these written self-portraits. More than 80 percent of the letters in this volume were written after FDR's death. Focusing on this material constituted a deliberate effort by the editors to concentrate on ER as an independent woman in her own limelight without the constraints imposed on her before 1945. They corroborate her increasing involvement in world affairs during the post-presidential period. These representative letters, comprising only a small percentage of her vast materials, tell the story in Eleanor Roosevelt's own words. Through these chronologically arranged letters, readers can track ER's thoughts at particular times, her expanding commitments and responsibilities, and her augmentation as a politician and maturation as a person.

Criteria for choosing the letters for this book involved a thorough examination of Eleanor Roosevelt's extensive correspondence, the elimination of previously published personal and family letters, and a comprehensive sampling of letters to various individuals expressing her views on particular topics. Often she digressed into other matters, but the purpose was to present her stand at a particular time. These letters show Roosevelt as she really was— a diverse personality—complex, generous, and judgmental. They portray a vivid picture of the young wife of FDR in the early twentieth century through her role as first lady of the nation and of the world until her death.

Most of the letters were typed carbon copies or drafts, completed by secretaries, but ER typed many of them herself since she carried a typewriter while traveling. Mrs. Roosevelt penned other letters by hand. Her handwriting was difficult, and in a few instances words could not be deciphered by the editors; nor could the staff at the Roosevelt Library interpret them. These letters were too important to be eliminated because of unreadable portions. In a few instances, blank lines indicate illegible words.

A number of errors, mostly typographical mistakes, occur throughout Mrs. Roosevelt's letters. There exist some inaccuracies, however, that reflect her limitations with grammar and syntax. Because it would detract from the book to insert the usual [*sic*] after every error, typographical mistakes have been corrected without additional notation. These editorial decisions in no way change Mrs. Roosevelt's meaning or reduce the importance of the letters. Grammatical and punctuation errors remain as she wrote them. Despite attempts to identify each name in ER's letters, various people could not be identified due to the wide array of correspondents and individuals she knew personally.

Fortunately, the editors received much help in this project. All staff people at the repositories from which the letters came were extremely accommodating, especially when dealing with us by long distance. They are too numerous to mention, but we would be remiss not to acknowledge some of those who provided the most cooperation. First to Supervisory Archivist Raymond Teichman and other anonymous members at the Roosevelt Library, we convey a heartfelt thanks. Without them, this project would not have been possible. Carol Briley, archivist at the Harry S Truman Library, was also of invaluable assistance.

Don Whisenhunt would like to take this opportunity to acknowledge and express appreciation for the financial support for this project provided by the Bureau for Faculty Research at Western Washington University. This agency has always been there when needed to assist in scholarly activities.

Readers of *It Seems to Me: Selected Letters of Eleanor Roosevelt* will study ER as a person from the Progressive Era to the New Frontier, revealing her individuality, workaholic schedule, and allegiance to social justice. The selections in this book will enable students of the Roosevelt era to discover a rich reflection and spontaneous self-revelation of an American personality who was indefatigable yet vulnerable, self-righteous and at times irritating, but compassionate and possessed of an imaginative humanity.

To cite each letter in the usual fashion would unnecessarily clutter this book and depreciate its readability. The 222 of the 272 letters that come from the Eleanor Roosevelt Papers at the Franklin D. Roosevelt Library are not specifically cited. The other fifty selections, located in a number of places, have a small code in brackets at the end of the letter:

AHS	Arizona Historical Society
Columbia	Columbia University, Frances Perkins Papers
DDEL	Dwight D. Eisenhower Library
HSTL	Harry S Truman Library
JFKL	John F. Kennedy Library
LC-Wilson	Library of Congress, Woodrow Wilson Papers
NYPL-Catt	New York Public Library, Carrie Chapman Catt Papers
SRL	Sam Rayburn Library

Eleanor Roosevelt to Isabella Selmes Ferguson

September 28, 1912

Isabella Ferguson and Eleanor Roosevelt were close friends from their girlhood days. An Arizona cattle rancher and businesswoman, Isabella, a native of Kentucky, established the Arizona Inn in Tucson in 1929 and served in the United States House of Representatives from 1933 to 1937. There she endorsed New Deal programs that benefited her state. Isabella's husband, Robert Munro Ferguson, whom she married in 1905, gained fame as one of the Rough Riders under Col. Theodore Roosevelt during the Spanish-American War in 1898. Mrs. Roosevelt corresponded frequently with the Fergusons over the years, discussing their myriad of mutual acquaintances, children, family members, neighbors, and other people with whom they shared memories. After Bob Ferguson died in 1927, Isabella married Jack Greenway, a family friend. Still later she wed Harry Orland King. She died in 1953.

The year 1912 was particularly busy for Mrs. Roosevelt. Her husband campaigned successfully for reelection to the New York state senate during the gubernatorial administration of John A. Dix, while her uncle, former president Theodore Roosevelt, sought a nonconsecutive third term as president on the Progressive "Bull Moose" Party ticket, running against Democratic governor Woodrow Wilson of New Jersey and the Republican president, William Howard Taft. Mrs. Roosevelt planned to hear her uncle speak in New York as well as listen to his vice presidential running mate, Gov. Hiram W. Johnson of California, a progressive who later served in the United States Senate. This letter reveals how occupied Mrs. Roosevelt was that year with the campaign, family, and friends. It also allows her own voice to be heard as a member of the Roosevelt family as the family redefined American liberalism and democratic reform during the Progressive Era.

Isabella dearest.

Your letter has gone to Hall[1] & I'm sure he'll do all he can for the boys & be glad of the chance. Their home in Cambridge is 18 Ash Street & I hope to go on this week to see it. Franklin and I expected to go yesterday but he got cold & had a temperature & felt so ill that he gave it up but I hope he'll be fine again to-morrow. His campaign is not yet very active. This last week has been very lazy which perhaps was not very entertaining for "Geoff"[2] but it gave Franklin a chance to really know him. They had some really nice times together which made his few days here seem all too short. We expect Ronald to dine with us in town Monday night & "Geoff" too if he comes in from Mrs. Cutting's[3] that day. I tried to get someone else to meet Ronald but nobody is in town so he will have to put up with our Society alone! Franklin goes to

Syracuse & Plattsburg Tuesday & I go to Cambridge & then Portland for a night with Maude,[4] getting home Friday!

I'm so glad Bob[5] is doing better again & I'm so sorry Mr. & Mrs. Cooley have had a disheartening time. I am planning to go hear Uncle Ted & Gov. Johnson too the first time they speak in New York. Uncle Ted's progressive ideas have fired so many of the young men to real work in this State that even if he doesn't win this time I feel a big work will have been accomplished.

I am hoping to see Edie[6] somehow before she starts for Silver [City] & I am so glad you are going to have her soon.

As far as I know _____ is doing nothing politically but I have not seen Pauline yet. When I do I will write you all about them.

The chicks[7] are all well & Anna[8] rides daily & is getting to be a grown up little girl. Elliott[9] is going to be a prize fighter & I think has inherited all Uncle Ted's energy. He has James[10] completely subdued & terrified & even Anna is under his thumb.

So much love to Bob & the children & you dear in which Franklin joins.

Ever yours devoted,
Eleanor

[AHS, *John Greenway Collection.*]

Notes

1. Hall Roosevelt, Eleanor's brother.
2. Geoffrey Luttrell, Bob's nephew, from Quebec.
3. Mrs. Bronson Cutting.
4. Maude Gray, Eleanor's aunt.
5. Isabella's husband.
6. Edith Ferguson, Bob's sister.
7. children
8. Eleanor's daughter.
9. Eleanor's son.
10. Eleanor's son.

Eleanor Roosevelt to Franklin D. Roosevelt

June 10, 1915

Franklin D. Roosevelt served as assistant secretary of the navy from 1913 to 1920 in the administration of President Woodrow Wilson. Josephus Daniels, a North Carolina editor and statesman, was secretary of the navy from 1913 to 1921. Mrs. Roosevelt wondered how her husband's career might be affected if Daniels chose to leave the cabinet. The event that precipitated expression of her thoughts on the matter occurred on June 9, 1915, with the resignation of Secretary of State William Jennings Bryan, an unsuccessful three-time presidential standard-bearer of the Democratic Party. Wilson appointed Robert Lansing of New York to succeed Bryan as head of the State Department. Because war had broken out in Europe in 1914, Mrs. Roosevelt expressed concern over how Bryan's departure would alter America's foreign policy toward Germany. Interestingly, although Mrs. Roosevelt admired Bryan's dedication to principle and the cause of peace, she did question the impracticality of some of his notions about the training or lack of military training of American servicemen needed to fight a war successfully. This letter clearly reveals her early interest in the conduct of American foreign policy.

Dearest Honey,

No word from you since you left. I feel much neglected but I realize these must be stirring times. I'm glad Bryan is out but I can't help admiring his sticking to his principles. How about J.D.[1] I wonder & how would his resignation affect you! This all most exciting but above all how will this affect the German question[2]—Anna's sore throat is gone though she still has a little cold. The rest are well. Martha[3] arrived safely & tells me Uncle Fred[4] is with you.

Love always,

E.R.

June 10th

Notes

1. Josephus Daniels.
2. The war in Europe that began in 1914.
3. Possibly Martha Selmes, Isabella's sister.
4. Frederic Delano, Sara Delano Roosevelt's brother.

Eleanor Roosevelt to Isabella Selmes Ferguson

January 11, 1918

Ten months prior to the armistice ending the first world war, Mrs. Roosevelt dispatched a letter to Isabella Ferguson informing her of a recent conversation she had had with Henry Adams, great-grandson of President John Adams and a distinguished American historian whose autobiography, The Education of Henry Adams, *won a Pulitzer Prize in 1919, and her surprise over the retirement of Sir Cecil Arthur Spring-Rice, the British ambassador to the United States, whom she admired greatly.*

11 Jan 1918

Dearest Isabella. Just a line to thank you for your letter & say I will write Bob next week after your Mother has been here & I will give him what gossip I can. When I ask Mr. Henry Adams how he feels about things he says "I'm only glad I'm not responsible for them"! We are all feeling very sad over the Spring Rice's sudden departure. Governments are not kind, are they & again Mr. Adams "Jews are trumps"[1] just now!

I feel very said for poor Muriel,[2] her husband died on the 8th & her cable is heart broken. He arranged in spite of endless operations & suffering to make their life a living joy & I am very thankful she has the baby girl to take her constant care & attention.

My dearest love to you one & all. Devotedly,

E.R.

Jan 11th [1918]
[*AHS, Isabella Ferguson Papers, Box 15.*]

Notes

1. Henry Adams was probably referring to the replacement of Cecil Spring-Rice as ambassador from Great Britain by Lord Reading, who was a Jew, Rufus Daniel Isaacs.
2. A mutual friend, Muriel Robbins Martineau.

Eleanor Roosevelt to Bob Ferguson
January 23, 1918

In this letter to her close friend, Robert H. Munro Ferguson, Mrs. Roosevelt mentioned family matters and the activities of former president Theodore Roosevelt's sons during World War I. Seven months later, Quentin Roosevelt was shot down in aerial combat in France on July 14. Disappointed that Sir Cecil Spring-Rice, the British ambassador to the United States, had resigned his position, Mrs. Roosevelt questioned the wisdom of appointing a politician, Lord Reading, instead of an experienced diplomat. Indirectly, she seemed to be chastising British prime minister David Lloyd George. The last part of the letter refers to Secretary of War Newton D. Baker and Sen. George F. Chamberlain of Oregon, the Democratic chairman of the Senate Committee on Military Affairs who had criticized the Wilson administration by claiming that the United States military establishment had deteriorated and that inefficiency reigned in every military department. Apparently Mrs. Roosevelt agreed that changes were necessary for improvements.

My dear Bob, I am ashamed to write so rarely when I think of you all at the Homestead so often but this winter is busier than ever. Washington is invaded by all the inhabitants of all the other cities in the country. We all try to do work of some kind & see more people than we've ever seen before!

We were all very sorry to see the Spring Rice's go & it seemed very sudden & inconsiderate but I suppose governments can't bother about anyone's convenience now. What a change in British policy to send a politician, isn't it? Franklin says he is very clever & able & of course in close touch with the present government. Sir Cecil never was well known by many people in this country like his predecessor but those who knew him, loved him & will miss him & his wife.

Mrs. Selmes was here on Tuesday & she does not look very well yet though she seemed stronger than I had expected. It was a great joy to see her & I only wish she could have been here longer.

Aunt Edith[1] & Uncle Ted arrived at Alice's[2] yesterday & we went to see them at tea time. They are wonderful about the boys & so pleased that they've done so well. Archie[3] has just been made a Captain. Quentin has had pneumonia but Eleanor[4] has been looking after him in Paris & he seems nearly well. A. Edith says Kermit's[5] letters are the most interesting of all of local colors. I suppose with Uncle Ted here exciting days are coming. I can't help feeling the President[6] has hurt himself in trying to support Baker blindly in every thing when we all know so much is wrong. Of course against the President Mr. Chamberlain can do nothing & yet something ought to be done. It all seems a hopeless tangle, doesn't it? I am glad the navy is making a so much better showing but Franklin says if he were investigating it he could rip it although the _____ for delays & indecisive policy which at present seems to be our curse![7]

Much, much love to you all & write when you can.

Always & devotedly,
Eleanor R—

Jan 23rd [1918]
[*AHS, Isabella Ferguson Papers, Box 15.*]

Notes

1. Edith Kermit Carow Roosevelt, wife of Theodore Roosevelt.
2. Alice Lee Roosevelt Longworth, daughter of Theodore Roosevelt by his first wife.
3. Archibald B. Roosevelt.
4. Probably Eleanor Butler Alexander Roosevelt, wife of Theodore Roosevelt Jr.
5. Kermit Roosevelt, son of Theodore Roosevelt.
6. Woodrow Wilson.
7. Franklin Roosevelt was assistant secretary of the navy at this time.

Eleanor Roosevelt to Sara Delano Roosevelt

October 19, 1920

In 1920 Franklin D. Roosevelt emerged as the Democratic nominee for vice president on the ticket headed by Gov. James M. Cox of Ohio, a Dayton newspaper publisher. Unlike the Republican presidential contender, Sen. Warren G. Harding of Ohio, who conducted a front porch campaign in Marion and promised a return to "normalcy," Cox waged an energetic effort in thirty-six states, traveling more than twenty-two thousand miles. Both Franklin and Eleanor Roosevelt copied this activist type of national campaign. In this letter to her mother-in-law, Mrs. Roosevelt outlined her busy itinerary. She found Harding's conservative philosophy disconcerting and worried about the disarray of the Democratic Party in the postwar period. One of the major issues of the contest was whether the United States should join the League of Nations, a world organization to mediate disputes that became a part of the Treaty of Versailles, which the United States Senate rejected three times. Mrs. Roosevelt favored United States participation in the league, for in her crusade against war, which she interpreted as a menace to civilization, she surfaced as one of the most prominent antiwar women in the United States in the 1920s. In fact, she established a woman's movement to support the Kellogg-Briand Pact in 1927 and 1928, the intent of which was to outlaw war. Fourteen days after sending this letter to her mother-in-law, Mrs. Roosevelt, in the first national presidential election after the Nineteenth Amendment permitting women's suffrage and in the first presidential election in which the returns were communicated on radio, Mrs. Roosevelt endured the sting of defeat when Cox and her husband lost overwhelmingly in the Harding-Republican landslide that year.

Dearest Mama,

I will come up from New York Friday & wire what train when I know what hour I can get hair & nails done. I feel sure you will want to go to Newburgh Sat. So we might go down in time to pay Aunt Annie[1] a brief visit. F will bring 6 men Sat. night & some arrangement will be made by him for motors as he knows only he & one other can go up with us. Will you ask Mary Howe[2] to come up on Sunday? F.[3] can get her before or after you go to church depending on whether they can get out before church. From present itineraries I think they will stay till Monday morning but such things are liable to change. The plan is to have him speak in Brooklyn Mon. eve. So he would sleep at the house that night in N.Y.

I enclose extracts from an old speech, also, itinerary & yesterdays schedule, only we got started at 8:30 & talk at 7:30. You can fill out the big schedule just like this for everyday only add when we are on the train streams of committeemen between every stop to keep F. talking! He made a fine speech last night. The hall was packed about 3000 I should say, but of course Michigan is hopelessly Republican. It is becoming almost impossible to stop F. now when he begins to speak. 10 minutes is always 20, 30 is always 45 & the evening speeches are now about 2 hours!

The men all get out & wave at him in front & when nothing succeeds I yank his coat tails! Everyone is getting tired but on the whole the car is still pretty good natured! They tell us Gov. Cox is all on edge.

I will wire Harriet[4] when I arrive.

Love to all,
E.R.

Oct. 19th.

Notes

1. Anna Bulloch Gracie, a great-aunt.
2. Louis Howe's daughter.
3. Franklin Roosevelt.
4. Harriet Howland Roosevelt.

Eleanor Roosevelt to Franklin Roosevelt

February 6, 1924

Three days after the death of former president Woodrow Wilson, who had been in declining health since his stroke in 1919, Mrs. Roosevelt sent a letter to her husband in which she discussed Wilson's death, intense partisanship in the nation, family matters, Gov. Alfred E. Smith of New York, her activities with women's groups and the Democratic Party, and other matters. Once again Mrs. Roosevelt showed that she wanted results rather than publicity and that she was an astute observer of the political scene and a savvy politician. William Gibbs McAdoo, secretary of the treasury under Woodrow Wilson, failed in his quest to secure the Democratic presidential nomination in 1924. The letter underscores the fact that Mrs. Roosevelt learned from her successes and failures and that she energetically mobilized support for political and economic reform. She also mentioned the impressive speech of John W. Davis of West Virginia, who captured the Democratic presidential nomination in 1924 after a bitterly divided convention. His address occurred on February 4 in Philadelphia upon the presentation of the Bok Peace Award, which had been established in 1923 by Edward Bok, former publisher and editor of the Ladies Home Journal. Dr. Charles H. Levermore, a history professor, secretary of the New York Peace Society, and secretary of the World Court League and League of Nations Union, won the Bok honor in 1924, which pleased Mrs. Roosevelt.

Dearest Franklin,

It was good to get your letter to-day. Your sound sunny, healthy & satisfied. I am so glad.

Poor Mr. Wilson lingered some time & it must be relief even to Mrs. Wilson[1] to know he is at last out of pain & miseries. The tributes to him everywhere have been fine but I must say if I had been Lodge[2] I would not have made his speech[3] in the Senate, would you? I hope, as you say his death may be at a good time but we seem so seething in partisan politics just now, it would seem hard to lift any subject out of them.

Monday I went over to Philadelphia after having Maude[4] & Anna & all to lunch. Maude went back to Portland to-day but returns the 12th & after 3 days with Alice Winthrop will come here for a time. David[5] may have operation for his rupture but isn't sure, if he does she'll be here till he is well I suppose. Did I tell you Hall was down last weekend, but he says he won't be back for a month.

The presentation of the Bok Award was quite impressive & Mr. Davis[6] made a fine speech. This time it was won by the kind of man Levermore is.

Yesterday morning Mrs. O'Day[7] & I went to Albany. Had a pleasant lunch with Mrs. Rice, with whom Mrs. O'Day & I stayed while Nancy went to Mrs. Green's. We saw the Governor[8] who asked us to get after the legislators on his programs. Louie[9] & I have to go up for a day soon. The driver in the evening was remarkable, 600 women from Albany & nearly all workers! Mrs. Colbert's a wonder. Nan & I came down this a.m. & I lunched with Mama[10] as Alice Carter was there but I had to leave at 2 as Anna & I went with the mem[orial] service at Mad[ison] Sq[uare] Garden group got up by the Wilson Foundation. The place was almost entirely filled even in the upper galleries & there was real feeling in the speeches in the audience. They have begged me so hard to go over for the service in Phil.[11] on Sunday a.m. that I had to say I'd go tho I hate to do it. They want your name really. Several people to-day spoke of you & wished you were there.

Well, McAdoo[12] seems out of the race[13] & Ted[14] also, how fast things change!

Elliott is better but only out of the infirmary by day. have you ever known such a long cough? You may have to let him go to you in March.

I'm up to my eyes in work for the convention[15] preparations & trying to raise our budget which is going to be an endless job.

Everyone well here & Anna the boys send their best love. Mama's knee seems better. We all miss you dreadfully. You need not be proud of me dear, I'm only being active till you can be again. it isn't such a great desire on my part to serve the world & I'll fall back into habits of sloth quite easily! Hurry up for as you know my ever present sense of the uselessness of all things will overwhelm me sooner or later! My love to Missy,[16] & to you.

Devotedly,

E.R.

Feb. 6th

Notes

1. Edith Bolling Galt Wilson.
2. Sen. Henry Cabot Lodge, a Massachusetts Republican.
3. Lodge paid tribute to Wilson in a Senate speech on February 4, but he was unable to attend the funeral because of illness. Lodge died nine months later.
4. Maude Gray.
5. David Gray.
6. John W. Davis, later Democratic nominee for president in 1924.
7. Caroline O'Day.
8. Gov. Alfred E. Smith of New York.
9. Louis Howe.
10. Sara Delano Roosevelt, Franklin Roosevelt's mother.
11. Philadelphia.
12. William Gibbs McAdoo.
13. For the presidential nomination in 1924.
14. Apparently, this was ER's cousin Theodore Roosevelt Jr., who was assistant secretary of the navy and ran for governor of New York in 1924.
15. New York Democratic convention.
16. Marguerite "Missy" Le Hand, one of Franklin Roosevelt's longtime secretaries.

Eleanor Roosevelt to Carrie Chapman Catt

April 14, 1924

As the elections of 1924 approached, Mrs. Roosevelt served as the chairman of the Finance Committee of the Democratic State Committee of New York. During this period, she emerged from her shyness because of the illness of her husband and became a political force in her own right. She contacted Mrs. Carrie Chapman Catt, the well-known supporter of women's rights, to solicit her help in writing a platform.

April 14, 1924

Dear Mrs. Catt:

Will you serve on the National Platform Committee on Social Legislation, of which I have been appointed Chairman by Mr. Hull.[1]

This Committee will try to get into touch with all Women's Organizations desiring to have planks presented to the Platform Committee of the Democratic Convention. When we have gone over these planks and have them in the best possible shape we will present them to the National Committeewomen at their meeting prior to the Convention in order that whatever goes from our Committee shall have the official backing of the democratic women.

Besides the democratic women serving on this Committee, I am having an Advisory Committee on each of the following subjects which is entirely non-partisan in character. The subjects will be "Women in Industry", "Public Health and Child Welfare," "Foreign Relations", "Law Enforcement", "Education," "Removal of Civil Disabilities", "Prison Reform", and "Public Control of Nation's National Resources."

Hoping you will be able to serve,

Very sincerely yours,

[*NYPL-Catt*]

Note

1. Cordell Hull, chairman of the Democratic National Executive Committee in 1924 and later secretary of state in the Roosevelt administration.

Eleanor Roosevelt to Carrie Chapman Catt

September 17, 1924

During the presidential campaign of 1924, the Democratic candidate, John W. Davis, failed to generate a great deal of enthusiasm among the voters. Mrs. Roosevelt, in her role with the Democratic State Committee of New York, attempted to stimulate interest. She wrote Mrs. Catt to persuade her to speak in behalf of Davis.

September 17, 1924

Dear Mrs. Catt:—

I do not know how you feel concerning Mr. Davis and the National Election. However, if you are thinking of supporting Mr. Davis, would it be possible for you to speak at a few of our meetings on the international situation? We do so need speakers at our larger meetings who can speak with conviction on the subject of peace.

Very cordially yours,

[*NYPL-Catt*]

Eleanor Roosevelt to Marion Dickerman

August 27, 1925

Marion Dickerman, an ardent suffragist, pacifist, and noted educator, and Nancy Cook, secretary of the Women's Division of the New York State Democratic Committee, were lifelong partners. Mrs. Roosevelt was one of their closest friends. Along with Caroline Love Goodwin O'Day, a future New York congresswoman, attorney Elizabeth F. Read, and consumer activist Esther E. Lape, Mrs. Roosevelt teamed with others to encourage the formation of Democratic women's clubs. During the Harding-Coolidge era, Mrs. Roosevelt gained a reputation as a woman of influence who spoke her mind. She expanded her level of commitment to the New York State Democratic Party, promoted certain candidates, championed the roles of women in the Democratic Party, and earned a reputation as a principled moral crusader. Her substantial activities in the 1920s as a writer and journalist demonstrated that she was a pragmatic politician and progressive who adapted to changing times while never wavering in her commitment to social justice. These years provided the foundation for the profound legacy she would leave for the nation.

August 27, 1925

Marion dearest,

Your letter of Sunday came yesterday afternoon & I have a horrible feeling my letter to Elmira[1] will never reach you. Well, I hope you got my night letter in Utica & you'll find a letter at Caroline's. I'm sending this to N.Y. as I expect you'll go there anyway for a few days. I'm so sorry you had to spend Sunday in Binghampton & you don't sound as though Delphi had been very for you. As I remember Miss Gerry gave Mrs. Roberts direct, not through me $50 for work in the County & last winter she gave me $50 for the Women's division. I doubt if she'll give us more but I'll write her when I get back.

The Meredith Inn sounds wonderful, sometimes when you & Nan[2] & I need a rest we'll take the car & go there! I'm curious about David Lee.

Today is glorious & Rose[3] & I are going to walk. I wish you & Nan were here. I feel I'd like to go off with you and forget the rest of the world existed.

Maude[4] left last night for Portland. At lunch we had a discussion on trade unions & I was left as I always am with the boys, feeling quite impotent to make a dent, because they regard me as a woman to be dutifully & affectionately thought of because I am their mother but even tho' I hold queer opinions they can't be considered seriously as against those of their usual male environment!

Marion dearest I love you & miss you & no amount of excitement could make me miss you less. I'll get to N.Y. the 10th & be anxiously awaiting your letter. Let me know your _____ route.

Much, much love, Eleanor

Notes

1. Elmira, New York.
2. Nancy Cook, Mrs. Roosevelt's friend and business associate in ValKill Industries.
3. Possibly Rose Schneiderman, a member of the Cap Makers Union in New York and director of the Women's Trade Union League.
4. Maude Gray.

Eleanor Roosevelt to Frances Perkins
March 6, 1929

Frances Perkins had been selected by Franklin Roosevelt as labor commissioner of New York after he won election as governor of the state. Early in the administration, Mrs. Roosevelt wrote her, asking for an article for the Women's Democratic News. Nelle [Nell] Swartz had been appointed by Roosevelt to the Industrial Commission.

March 6, 1929

Dear Miss Perkins:

Could you and Nelle Swartz write me an article for the Women's Democratic News telling of the work of the Labor Department and any particular things which you would like the women of the state to appreciate and have brought to their notice?

I would like to have this there at 66 East 80th Street by next Tuesday the 12th.

Very cordially yours,

Are there any new appointments in the Dept. you would like mentioned? Also I would like a photograph of Nelle.

ER.

[*Columbia*]

Eleanor Roosevelt to Carrie Chapman Catt
December 30, 1932

Mrs. Catt wrote Mrs. Roosevelt to inform her that she did not vote for Franklin D. Roosevelt for president in 1932. Mrs. Roosevelt responded in a courteous fashion and clearly tried to move Mrs. Catt toward support of President Roosevelt.

Eleanor Roosevelt, Katharine F. Lenroot, chief of the Children's Bureau, Federal Security Agency, in Washington, D.C., *center,* and Frances Perkins, *right.* (Courtesy of the Franklin D. Roosevelt Library)

December 30, 1932

Dear Mrs. Catt:

Thank you for your letter, it was very sweet of you to write to me. I quite understand your not voting for my husband. After all one must vote for the things one believes in and you undoubtedly feel that the international situation would be better handled by other people as I know that is your greatest interest.

I hope that you will find that my husband can be of assistance to you in the future and I am particularly anxious when you wish to talk to him, that you will let me know and I will arrange an appointment. I would like to be with you if possible.

With every good wish,

Very cordially yours,

[*NYPL-Catt*]

Eleanor Roosevelt to Walter White

May 2, 1934

After discussing the proposed lynching bill with her husband, Mrs. Roosevelt warned Walter White, executive secretary of the National Association for the Advancement of Colored People (NAACP), that he and the president might not agree on certain points. She urged White to visit Washington so that she and the president could converse with him on the controversial issue.

May 2, 1934

My dear Mr. White:

The President talked to me rather at length today about the lynching bill. As I do not think you will either like or agree with everything that he thinks, I would like an opportunity of telling you about it, and would also like you to talk to the President if you feel you want to. Therefore, will you let me know if you are going to be in Washington before long?

Very sincerely yours,

Eleanor Roosevelt to Bernard M. Baruch

June 13, 1934

The first lady was particularly interested in improving living conditions in rural America and raising standards so that people could live better lives and meet their expenses. She was especially grateful to Bernard M. Baruch, a financier and statesman, for his advice, support, and cooperation on this and other issues.

June 13, 1934.

Dear Mr. Baruch:

I got the copy of your note to Miss Jones[1] this morning. I had already written her as had Nancy.[2] I can not tell you how delighted I am to have this work made possible and that is one thing off my mind.

I have had a little difficulty because Miss Clapp[3] was out of town in getting the budget for the school in detail as I wanted it, but finally I am enclosing it. You can see the capital outlay for this year is for the interior fixings and for the extra buildings which would not go ordinarily into a rural community but which we feel will be a great demonstration of what can be done and should be done in rural communities. The running expenses for this year are less because I am taking care of Miss Clapp's salary. Next year and the year after they will have to be included. The other items are the items which the state is not prepared to carry. In the end if the whole set up proves its value, the yearly expenses will be carried by taxes on the people.

We are now busy figuring out, as we decided that it was better to drop the effort of putting through a post office factory for fear of having a great deal of "hot-air" in Congress and another attack on Reedsville[4] written into the record, what shall be the industry down there. The important thing from Dr. Wilson's[5] and my point of view is that a family shall have a sufficient means of livlihood and the assurance of an ability to pay their expenses covering a standard which we hope to establish as something to shoot at in all rural industrial communities. As soon as this becomes concrete at all I am going to ask you to give us the benefit of your advice.

My deepest thanks to you for your interest. You can not imagine what a pleasure it is to feel we may count upon you for advice and cooperation.

Very cordially yours,

Notes

1. Probably Olga A. Jones, director of the Coal Section of the American Friends Service Committee.

2. Nancy Cook, Mrs. Roosevelt's friend and business associate in ValKill Industries.

3. Elsie Ripley Clapp, a graduate of Vassar and Columbia and a colleague of John Dewey, she was principal of the schools and director of community affairs at Arthurdale.

4. At Reedsville, West Virginia, was located one of the subsistence homestead projects supported by the reform measures of the New Deal.

5. Milburn Wilson, head of the Division of Subsistence Homesteads, a forerunner of the Resettlement Administration in September 1933. Between July 1934 and February 1940, he was first assistant secretary of agriculture and then undersecretary of agriculture.

Eleanor Roosevelt to Bernard M. Baruch

July 14, 1934

Mrs. Roosevelt revealed how much it meant to her to have Baruch as an adviser and friend, while urging him to remain steadfast in their joint endeavors.

July 14, 1934

Dear Mr. Baruch:

Thank you very much for your letters. I gathered that you would sell the bonds,[1] so I told my young man if he could do so after he gets the August 1st interest that it would be wise.

Your letter on homesteads I am passing on to Mr. Pickett.[2] I do not think any money will be needed until you return and by that time I hope your ideas will help them to get the figures clear and fix the amount to be paid by the people.

I can never tell you how much it means to us to feel that we have you as an adviser and friend. I want you to be hard-boiled, for it is the kind of "hard-boiledness" which is helpful.

Miss Cook and I have learned a lot about handicraft on this trip and have enjoyed it all very much.

With my very best wishes, I am

Cordially yours,

Notes

1. Bernard Baruch, the financier, was a strong supporter of the subsistence homestead project in Arthurdale, New Jersey. He provided money for the project and helped to get others to assist.

2. Clarence E. Pickett, executive secretary of the American Friends Service Committee, a close associate of ER, and a supporter of many of her projects.

Eleanor Roosevelt to Walter White

November 12, 1934

In this clandestine letter to White, Mrs. Roosevelt disclosed some evidence she had gathered on the poor moral reputation of a man in Schenectady, New York, cautioning White to handle the problem delicately and leave her name out of the entire episode.

November 12, 1934

Dear Mr. White:

The man I spoke to you about lives at 414 Broadway, Schenectady, on the third floor. His shop is 601 Union Street and his name is Shakespeare Perique. He is employed in a garage. He has a wife, but whether there are any children I do not know.

My understanding is that the police will verify things for any one whom you wish to send, and that his reputation is evidently bad. I think he has had a number of white girls in school with whom he has been too intimate. If you have any one who could in some way manage to move him away from there to some other place, I think it would be an excellent thing. I should like very much to see this done in order to break up this whole situation.

I realize it is not easy now to find a new job, but think he should leave under the circumstances. Will you see what you can find out and do about it? Of course, do not bring my name into it.

Very sincerely yours,

Eleanor Roosevelt to Walter White
November 23, 1934

Disgusted with the refusal of the United States government to denounce twenty-eight lynchings of African Americans in 1933 and disturbed by the regrouping of the Ku Klux Klan in the South, Mrs. Roosevelt joined forces with Walter White, the executive secretary of the National Association for the Advancement of Colored People, in a crusade to promote the passage of federal antilynch legislation. On October 26, 1934, in Marianna, Florida, Claude Neal was brutally tortured and lynched before a crowd of several thousand people enjoying the event as if it were a community ceremony. Little children even waited with sharpened sticks to plunge them into the body of the victim. The complete failure of the state and county machinery to prevent this lynching convinced the first lady that it was imperative for Congress to pass the Costigan-Wagner antilynching bill (S. 1978). Introduced by Democratic senators Edward P. Costigan of Colorado and Robert F. Wagner of New York, this bill, which eventually died as a result of a southern filibuster, sought to hold local governmental officials responsible if they failed to protect its citizens regardless of race. The failure of Atty. Gen. Homer S. Cummings, a member of FDR's cabinet from Connecticut, to proceed against Neal's kidnappers under the "Lindbergh" law, or to act on the proliferation of lynchings, further angered Mrs. Roosevelt, who excoriated those who lacked the courage to apprehend the murderers. She vented her disgust in a letter to Walter White.

November 23, 1934

My dear Mr. White:

I talked with the President yesterday about your letter and he said that he hoped very much to get the Costigan-Wagner Bill passed in the coming session. The Marianna lynching was a horrible thing.

I wish very much the Department of Justice might come to a different point of view and I think possibly they will.

Very sincerely yours,

Eleanor Roosevelt to Walter White
November 28, 1934

During the early days of the New Deal, Harry Hopkins, director of the Federal Emergency Relief Administration (FERA), abolished a minimum wage scale of thirty cents per hour for work relief. In a letter to Walter White, Mrs. Roosevelt commented on this development. She believed it constituted an effort to conciliate Gov. Herman Talmadge of Georgia, a critic of the New Deal despite his being a Democrat. Mrs. Roosevelt trusted White because she vented her views critical of her husband's administration and of Hopkins regarding this matter.

November 28, 1934.

I most certainly do feel that the ruling by Hopkins of the FERA abolishing the minimum wage scale of thirty cents an hour for work relief was aimed at the Negro. It is significant that this ruling came immediately after Governor Talmadge of Georgia had visited the President recently at Warm Springs. Talmadge, as you know, has been the outstanding opponent of the thirty cents wage scale for work relief. Of course, he was not the only governor present at the Warm Springs conference but he was the particular one whom all the newspapers "played up" before the conference as one who was knocking the administration and particularly the FERA on the point of this thirty cents an hour wage scale, along with certain other features of the recovery program.

This thirty cents an hour has been almost a campaign issue with Talmadge for the last two or three years and for the last year or so he has not hesitated to link up the Negro in his statements concerning the ridiculousness of such a wage scale. Talmadge has been one of the two recalcitrant governors as viewed by the FERA and the governor who has given the FERA and the administration in general most trouble and this abolishing of the minimum wage scale looks like an attempt on the part of the administration to conciliate him.

May I state confidentially, and ask you not to reveal its source because the information was given to me in the strictest confidence, that Talmadge had planned up until a week ago (and may still be planning unless he has been fully conciliated by the President) one of the dirtiest anti-Negro campaigns that has been promoted in recent years in the South. Of course the real objective behind this is the United States senatorship. It is his idea, I understand, to oppose the present Senator Russell.[1] Talmadge's whole program has been, up until this last minute, anti-administration and as silly as it might seem to one in the North the theoretical favoritism shown the Negro in connection with the Recovery Program would be the biggest issue he would offer Georgia "Red Necks." His plan was and, in my opinion, still is to attack Russell not because he has shown any particular interest in the Negro but because Russell is a supporter of the administration and therefore by "reducto ad absurdem"[2] Russell is therefore in sympathy with giving an unusual amount of the benefits of the Recovery Program to the Negro.

This is all ridiculous because first of all the Recovery program has not functioned fairly among Negroes in the South. Secondly, Russell is no particular friend of the Negro. What I imagine will happen if and when Talmadge launches his campaign against Russell will be that Russell's defense instead of being a justification of giving the Negro an "alleged" square deal will be an attempt to exceed Talmadge in the bitterness of his attack on the Negro from some other front.

Of course Talmadge's opposition to the administration may be over come by such conciliatory measures as the abolishing of the thirty cents an hour wage scale for work relief and other measures that have not been announced as yet.

Very sincerely yours,

Notes

1. Sen. Richard B. Russell of Georgia.
2. *Reductio ad absurdum*, reducing an argument to an absurdity.

Eleanor Roosevelt to Ellen S. Woodward

December 20, 1934

On December 14, 1934, Ella G. Agnew, Virginia's director of women's work under the Federal Emergency Relief Administration (FERA), came across an attractive photograph of thirteen-month-old Franklin, Delano, and Roosevelt Jones, African American triplets from Prince Edward County, Virginia. She immediately sent the picture to Ellen S. Woodward, director of women's work under the FERA in Washington, who in turn mailed the item to Mrs. Melvian T. Scheider, secretary to Mrs. Roosevelt, with the hope that she would show it to the first lady. After seeing the photograph, Mrs. Roosevelt conveyed her appreciation in a letter to Mrs. Woodward. Her unfortunate choice of words in describing the infants as "pickaninnies," a derisive stereotypical term that depicted African American children as docile and domesticated young animals, caused an uproar when Mrs. Roosevelt's letter, enigmatically taken from Agnew's files, was published on

January 13, 1935, in the Richmond Times-Dispatch, along with a story about the "New Deal Triplets." A disconcerted Agnew and Woodward apologized profusely to the embarrassed first lady, who considered the word a term of endearment for any child. In a letter to a group of black Americans, Mrs. Roosevelt insisted that she meant no lack of respect.

December 20, 1934

Dear Mrs. Woodward:

Thank you so much for sending me the pictures of the little pickaninnies. They certainly are cunning and the President was very much amused by it.

I always have time for anything you care to send.

Very sincerely yours,

ER

Eleanor Roosevelt to Edith Bolling Galt Wilson

January 12, 1937

Mrs. Roosevelt always tried to be considerate of others. She took special actions to include former first ladies in appropriate events of her husbands' administrations. At the time of the inauguration for her husband's second term, she sent a special invitation to the widow of President Woodrow Wilson to sit with her for the concert on inauguration day.

Dear Mrs. Wilson:

There is to be a concert at Constitution Hall on Inauguration Day, January 20th, at nine o'clock.

If you have made no plans, it would give me the greatest pleasure to have you sit with my mother-in-law and me in my box that evening. Please do not hesitate to tell me if you have any other engagement, or if this hour is too early and you would like to come in later in the evening.

Sincerely yours,

[LC-Wilson]

Eleanor Roosevelt to Carola von Schaffer-bernstein

September 6, 1939

On September 1, 1939, Germany invaded Poland, and World War II began. Soon after he had become chancellor in 1933, Adolph Hitler embarked on a

*carefully crafted scheme to destroy the German constitution and build a dicta-
torship. He permitted only one political party—the Nazis, which under Hitler
as führer, controlled German life from 1933 to 1945, coinciding almost to the
day with the time that President and Mrs. Roosevelt lived in the White House.
In a revealing letter to Carola Schaffer, a close friend for many years and a
resident of Germany, the first lady, after briefly touching on the sudden illness
and death of Schaffer's son, expressed her views on Hitler and the outbreak of
war in Europe.*

September 6, 1939

Dear Carola:

Your last letter, written on August 19, has just come to me and I realize
even more how terribly sad you are, for evidently Arnold had meant a great
deal to both you and his father. Anything as sudden as his illness seems to
have been is a doubly hard blow.

I cannot say that I feel the present situation had a parallel in 1914. All of
us, of course, are appalled at plunging the European continent into war, but
I do not think there is any bitterness toward the German people in this country. There is an inability to understand how people of spirit can be terrified
by one man and his storm troops to the point of countenancing the kind of
horrors which seem to have come on in Germany, not only where the Jews
are concerned, but as in the case of the Catholics and some of the liberal
German Protestants.

I say this with knowledge, because I have actually seen many of the people
who have reached this country from concentration camps. I realize quite
well that there may be a need for curtailing the ascendency of the Jewish
people, but it seems to me it might have been done in a more humane way by
a ruler who had intelligence and decency.

The radio makes a tremendous difference because one can actually hear
these leaders make speeches, and I listened, knowing enough German, to Mr.
Hitler's speech to the Reichstag.[1] He never mentioned that there was a God
whom we are supposed to have, nor did he show the slightest sympathy for
the people whom he had plunged into war. There was a certain triumphant
note through the whole of it which was never heard from the leaders of other
nations.

You are wrong if you think the people of this country hate Germany.
That is not so, but they hate Hitler and Nazism because of the evidence that
have been placed before them. I do not think either France or England was
anxious for war and I think that was shown by the fact that their first planes
dropped no bombs but propaganda leaflets. They could easily have killed

women and children in the same way that women and children have been killed in Warsaw and other Polish cities.

You who believe in God must find it very difficult to follow a man who apparently thinks he is as great as any god. I hope that we are not facing another four years of struggle and I hope that our country will not have to go to war, but no country can exist free and unoppressed while a man like Hitler remains in power.

I shall be thinking of you and yours with great sympathy until these horrors are passed.

Affectionately,

Note

1. The Reichstag was the lower house of the German parliament, which was deprived of its power under Hitler.

Eleanor Roosevelt to Edith Bolling Galt Wilson
November 9, 1940

When Franklin Roosevelt won an unprecedented third term in 1940, Edith Wilson sent a congratulatory letter. Mrs. Roosevelt responded with a brief note of thanks for her good wishes.

Dear Mrs. Wilson:

You were thoughtful to leave that line of congratulations for my husband and me. It is gratifying to think that our friends remember us and we value good wishes, particularly when they come from such old friends as you. My husband joins with me in thanks and appreciation.

Very sincerely yours,

[LC-Wilson]

Eleanor Roosevelt to Pearl Buck
March 3, 1941

At times Mrs. Roosevelt could be very diplomatic. In 1941, as the war accelerated in Asia but before the United States entered the conflict, Pearl Buck, the noted China authority and author, wrote Mrs. Roosevelt requesting help. She wanted the first lady to invite Madame Chiang Kai-shek of China to visit America, claiming that it would be good if Madame Chiang could experience the unofficial warm friendship of Americans for China. Although Mrs. Roosevelt may have wanted Madame Chiang to come, she was somewhat terse in her brief response.

March 3, 1941

Dear Miss Buck:

I am sorry that I personally cannot invite anyone from another country. That is done through other channels.

If Madame Chiang Kai-shek were to come, I should of course be delighted.

Very sincerely yours,

Eleanor Roosevelt to Henry A. Wallace

January 12, 1942

Mrs. Roosevelt was asked regularly to help various groups with members of the administration with whom she was on good terms. Shortly after World War II began in December 1941, she contacted Vice President Henry A. Wallace, asking him to speak at a student conference on how to shape the postwar world. This assumed, of course, that the United States would have a role in determining what the world would be like after the war. Mrs. Roosevelt may appear to be flattering the vice president, but this more probably reflects her genuine respect for him.

January 12, 1945

Dear Mr. Vice President:

The International Student Service is planning, with certain universities, a great convocation in New York City of free universities.

I have been asked to ask you if you would be willing, on the invitation of Dr. Butler[1] of Columbia University, to speak at the convocation. It is to be held sometime in February, and the date could be February 10th, or anytime from the 16th to the 20th, or the 25th to the 28th of February. You can select the time which suits you best.

The subject which they want you to cover is "Our responsibility in shaping the post-war world."

I can think of no one who would carry more conviction and whose work fitted him better to give a ringing challenge to a great university audience, including students and faculty. The meeting will be in the afternoon. The place has not as yet been decided upon.

Very cordially yours,

Note

    1. Nicholas Murray Butler, president of Columbia University from 1902 to 1945, was the founder of Columbia Teachers College and a founder of the Carnegie Endowment for International Peace.

Eleanor Roosevelt to Mrs. Vanderbilt Webb

January 19, 1942

Wanting American arts and crafts to flourish during the second world war, Mrs. Roosevelt encouraged the sale of crafts and endorsed Webb's idea of bringing craftsmen together to discuss their problems. Aileen Webb was the daughter of William Church Osborn, a New York lawyer and former Democratic state committeeman, and the wife of Vanderbilt Webb, a prominent New York lawyer.

January 19, 1942

Dear Aileen:

    It is indeed difficult, at this moment when readjustment to a war program is resulting in serious temporary dislocations in many fields of productive activity, to see any one problem in a very clear perspective. I hope that as we are able to make these basic adjustments, our experience will follow that of England, where, as you know, support of the Arts developed on demand from the British people, who valued them as essential elements of the community they are fighting to preserve.

    It is clear, therefore, that our American art and crafts skills must be kept alive and vigorous, not only for their value in the task of rebuilding a peaceful world after the war, but as well for the services they can render during this present crisis.

    In addition to the openings for many specially skilled persons in defense industries, a number of interesting new outlets for crafts products and skills related to the war effort are evident. These include among others, recreational Art and Crafts Programs for enlisted men in Army camps and service centers, and the decoration and furnishing of recreation quarters for officers and enlisted men. We can, I think, also anticipate a growing need for crafts participation as therapeutic and morale-building activities among our civilian population.

    The Office of Civilian Defense, under the direction of Mr. Olin Dows,[1] is beginning to develop programs of volunteer participation of artists with local defense organizations. It seems to me that craftsmen can have opportunities for service here along with the artists.

I wonder also if some very good opportunities may not develop for the sale of crafts. Here the ingenuity of craftsmen in adapting simple and readily available materials to the making of attractive and useful articles, should operate as a distinct advantage in meeting demands that can be no longer supplied by other sources.

Your plan of bringing the craftsmen together to discuss their common problems appeals to me as an excellent idea. I am sure that by working together they can go a long way toward discovering for themselves how best to put their talents and skills to the most constructive use during the present crisis.

In this connection an idea was suggested recently, with which you may already be familiar. Nevertheless, I want to pass it on to you, since I feel it may have merit. This was a proposal to the effect that crafts groups and organizations unite in setting up a central clearing house which would conduct an exchange of information of particular interest to handicraft workers, which would keep them informed of new opportunities, developments, and trends in this field, and which would also be able to interpret their interests to the public.

I should be interested to learn what the results of this meeting may be.

Sincerely yours,

Note

1. Stephen Olin Dows, a prominent American painter and lithographer, was from Dutchess County, New York.

Eleanor Roosevelt to Aileen Webb

February 7, 1942

Eleanor Roosevelt had received numerous letters from craftsmen pertaining to their problems. She declined to fault the government because of the lack of facilities and staff to monitor the situation carefully. In a letter to Aileen Webb, the first lady praised the efforts and services of the Handicraft Cooperative League, which had been established to serve as a clearinghouse to help craft workers across the nation.

February 7, 1942.

Dear Aileen:

I am glad to know that my suggestions concerning the situation of Handicrafts at this time were of help to you in connection with your recent meeting.

I am also glad to learn that the Handicraft Cooperative is set up to serve as a clearing house.

Many craftsmen have written to me about their problems, and I understand many inquiries have come to the Work Projects Administration Art Program, the Extension Service of the Department of Agriculture, and other Government programs interested in crafts. They come from persons and groups in all parts of the country and bring up all sorts of problems—on techniques, where to go for instruction, sources of materials, marketing information, etc. You are no doubt quite familiar with them.

Although I know these offices do what they can, they lack the facilities and staff to give adequate attention to these problems. Miss Lenore Fuller, with the Department of Agriculture,[1] Mr. Adrian Dornbush[2] in the Work Projects Administration Art Program, Miss Mary LaFollette[3] in the Farm Security Administration, and others in the Government concerned, have been very much aware of this need for some time and hopeful that some clearing house be set up. Mr. Charles Hapgood,[4] I understand, developed some ideas for a clearing center of this sort. However, I do not believe anything has developed along these lines to date in the Government.

I am sure that the people I have mentioned would be glad to be helpful to you in any way they can be in this matter.

I know that the League, through its service, can do a great deal to help crafts workers in all sections of the country.

Sincerely yours,

Notes

1. With the Extension Service of the Department of Agriculture.

2. An artist discovered on the Public Works of Art Project who later supervised the art activities of the Resettlement Administration and then headed the WPA Technical Services Laboratory until 1939 when he was appointed director of arts and crafts in the national office of the Federal Art Project.

3. An official in the Farm Security Administration.

4. A WPA recreational leader in Massachusetts and supervisor of community recreation in Provincetown, Massachusetts. In the 1930s he made a report to Harold Ickes that led to the establishment of a Board of Indian Arts and Crafts.

Eleanor Roosevelt to Henry A. Wallace

May 1, 1942

Martin Dies, a congressman from Texas, had been head of an investigating committee of Congress that became known as the House Un-American Activities

Committee (*HUAC*). *Attacks were made on various government officials as communists or security risks. Knowing Mrs. Roosevelt's reputation as a defender of those who had little defense, Maurice Parmelee of Arlington, Virginia, wrote her about his situation. He said that he was an employee of the Board of Economic Warfare and was attacked by the Dies Committee. Vice President Wallace defended him, and the FBI cleared him of any wrongdoing. Then he said the board terminated his employment on the pretext of "reorganization." He told Mrs. Roosevelt this incident indicated that Dies had won a "victory" with the result that federal employees had no job security, federal employee morale had been threatened, and the war effort had been impaired. He asked for her support.*

May 1, 1942.

Dear Mr. Vice President:

It seems to me very unfortunate when these people are made to resign, because it gives Mr. Dies the satisfaction of saying he forced them out.

I understand from the President that no one had resigned except from their own free will. If this record is truthful, Mr. Parmelee was practically forced to resign. What can we do about such situations?

Very sincerely yours,

Eleanor Roosevelt to Pearl Buck
May 29, 1942

One of the most controversial acts of the United States during World War II was the evacuation of Japanese nationals and Japanese Americans from the West Coast to internment camps in the interior of the country. This occurred at first under executive order of President Roosevelt. Pearl Buck worried about the treatment of the relocated Japanese. She appealed to the first lady "as one American woman to another" about the conditions and mentioned many letters she had received from non-Japanese Americans about "the inhuman and cruel treatment" of these people. Pearl Buck also questioned "the effect upon our own people that is so evil." She asked Mrs. Roosevelt's advice about what should be done and said the way these people were "being treated is so much more German than it is American." Mrs. Roosevelt answered her briefly and mildly defended the action, encouraging Buck to visit some of the camps and indicating that she had offered to do so as well.

May 29, 1942

Dear Miss Buck:

I read your letter of May 22d with a great deal of interest. I regret the need to evacuate, but I recognize it has to be done. I hear high praise for the way in which the Army has handled this evacuation and I am told that the resettlement is being done as well as could be expected.

I think it would be very helpful if you were to visit some of these resettlement areas. I have offered to go later in the summer.

Very sincerely yours,

Eleanor Roosevelt's Memo to Harry Hopkins

May 31, 1942

Harry Hopkins served as one of the most important advisers to President Roosevelt, first on the domestic side in the war against the Depression and then in foreign policy during World War II. Considering the need for labor in war industries, Mrs. Roosevelt foresaw that women workers were going to be much more numerous. In May 1942 she wrote Hopkins with her ideas about the use of women so that they would be efficient workers and home life would be disrupted as little as possible. Her concern is obvious.

MEMO FOR MR. HARRY HOPKINS   MAY 31, 1942
FROM: MRS. ROOSEVELT
Subject: The Problems of women workers.

If great numbers of women are going to be used, undoubtedly many married women will be needed. This is going to have an effect on the way of life and on the homes in the United States, if we wish to have as little dislocation as possible, and we should plan ahead.

I suggest a meeting with the
    Heads of the Unions
    Dean Landis[1] and Jonathan Daniels[2] of OCD
    Miss Mary Anderson[3]—Labor Dept.
    Mrs. Ellen Woodward[4]
    Mrs. Florence Kerr[5]
I include all these people because they have had experience and will look at this problem of the future, with that background and with a knowledge of what are the techniques to be used.

I should judge that we would want to preserve as far as possible, because of the preference of our people:

1. A sense of home life and that centers very largely with us around eating in the home

2. We must preserve the health of our women as far as possible

3. For the sake of the home and efficient production, women must be as little tired as possible.

I see the possibility of chain restaurants, near plants; day nurseries; play schools, adjacent, and if possible, local schools attended by older children within walking distance, or the providing of transportation to both grade and high schools.

Mass buying will probably make it possible to serve food at a cost below that which the individual could buy it for. The whole feeding plan might be run as a cooperative thing so that people might feel that they owned these restaurants. These restaurants should serve breakfast and lunch, and have lunches packed where necessary which can be bought by workers and children. The evening meal could be packed in a container, ordered from a menu available in the morning and taken home by the family at the end of the working day in order to give the family one meal at home together.

On the day of rest or on any holiday, prepared or semi-prepared food should be available at the close of the day before and taken home, minimizing the work in the home as much as possible.

I think we should establish community laundries.

How much subsidy by the government would have to be granted to start these various things, including day nurseries and play schools, should be worked out. Eventually I think play schools and day nurseries should be included in the regular school systems in order that preparation for school life should be continuous from the earliest possible age.

As many methods as possible should be devised for selling to the people, this new mode of living and making the people aware of the possibility of more valuable home life with better education; less fatigue; better understanding of the training of children, and the type of family life that can be developed in leisure hours both through joint recreation and the sharing of necessary tasks.

This pattern may seem to be important only to the war effort, but it may be possible that we are going into a period where much more production will be sustained and many more women will be at work many ways. I am not at all sure that everybody in the future may not have to justify themselves either by working with their heads or working with their hands.

None of what I have suggested, of course, takes into account the changes which may have to come in rural communities. These changes may come for a number of reasons—the increased need for food production; the need of young people over a period of years in the Services or some production occupation; the need of making farm life more attractive in order to keep the population on the farms which is really needed.

Unionization of farm labor with changed standards will bring changes.

There seems to me to be a dearth of women on the higher planning boards. I think this is vital to the consideration of the whole problem of American life in the future.

There is also the problem of proper legislation to cover the medical side of the whole picture, but specifically the period allowed before a child is born and afterwards, the salary which must be paid, the medical care which must be provided and a general health check up before a woman returns to work.

Many more suggestions will be made by other people during the discussion. This seems to me a possible skeleton for a beginning.

Notes

1. James McCauley Landis, an early "brain truster" of the Roosevelt administration, chaired the Securities and Exchange Commission from 1935 to 1937, when he accepted an appointment as dean of the Harvard Law School.

2. Jonathan Daniels, son of Josephus Daniels, became head of the Office of Civilian Defense (OCD) after the Japanese attack on Pearl Harbor on December 7, 1941.

3. A native of Sweden, Miss Mary Anderson advocated special labor legislation to protect women. She had been head of the Women's Bureau of the Department of Labor since 1920.

4. As various federal agencies were established under the New Deal, Ellen Sullivan Woodward, a former member of the Mississippi State Board of Public Welfare, headed the divisions for women. Among these were the Civil Works Administration and the Federal Emergency Relief Administration.

5. Florence Stewart Kerr in 1935 was one of the regional directors of the Division of Women's and Professional Projects in the Works Progress Administration. In 1938 she was named assistant administrator of the WPA and director of Women's and Professional Projects.

Eleanor Roosevelt to Walter White

June 24, 1942

In a brief letter to Walter White, Mrs. Roosevelt expressed relief after hearing from Mary McLeod Bethune, an educator and director of the National Youth Administration, that Oveta Culp Hobby, co-editor and publisher of the Houston Post who was also appointed the first director of the newly created Women's Auxiliary Army Corps—later named the Women's Army Corps—was gradually changing her mind on integration.

June 24, 1942

Dear Mr. White:

Mrs. Bethune tells me that Mrs. Hobby is taking her on as an adviser and that, while she doubts if there will be complete integration, she will work toward that end, and there will be full representation both in officers and privates in the women's section.

I think this a good step forward and from what I hear Mrs. Hobby is gradually changing from being completely a Texan to a saner point of view.

Very sincerely yours,

Eleanor Roosevelt to Madame Chiang Kai-shek
July 3, 1942

In the early days after America entered World War II, Mrs. Roosevelt wanted to assure Madame Chiang, the wife of the leader of China, of the friendship of the United States. In this message, she indicated that she would send books to Madame Chiang, but she also took the opportunity to praise China.

Eleanor Roosevelt and Madame Chiang Kai-shek. (Courtesy of the Franklin D. Roosevelt Library)

July 3, 1942

My dear Madame Chiang,

I have just learned that Mr. Laughlin Currie[1] is paying another visit to your country and he has very kindly offered to take these books to you. I have autographed one to you, and signed the others in the hope that you will find them worth while putting in one of your libraries.

I am also asking Mr. Currie to take you my warm personal regards and to tell you that we in the United States are praying for the success of the United Nations before too long. We have the greatest admiration and appreciation for the valiant spirit of your people and are proud to be among your allies.

With every good wish, I am

Very cordially yours,

Note

1. Lauchlin M. Currie, a chemist and engineer.

Eleanor Roosevelt to Henry A. Wallace
July 31, 1942

Mrs. Roosevelt was always complimentary to Vice President Wallace, and that was the case in the summer of 1942 when she praised a speech he had made to a meeting of The People's Century.

July 31, 1942

Dear Mr. Vice President:

I wanted to tell you the other day, but I thought it would be easier to write how much I am impressed by the effect that your speech on The People's Century has had on young people. Last week I went to the International Student Service Summer Institutes in both Asheville and Campobello and found in both places that that speech was the basis for more real stirring of thought than anything else which has happened and, in a way, for more conscious desire to act, on the part of both boys and girls.

Therefore, I am more grateful than ever that you are going to speak for them in September at the Assembly.

Sincerely yours,

Eleanor Roosevelt to Madame Chiang Kai-shek
August 24, 1942

Shortly after Mrs. Roosevelt sent books and best wishes to Madame Chiang Kai-shek in China, she wrote her again, obviously in response to a message from Madame Chiang. Her statements about the "great majority of people in this country" who are deeply interested in China may well be an exaggeration, but with China as an ally in a time of war, the first lady utilized her diplomatic skills.

August 24, 1942

Dear Madame Chiang,

I am delighted to have your inscribed photograph and I am having it framed to hang among others of people whom I greatly admire.

I appreciate your very kind letter, but feel that anything I do is very insignificant as compared with all you do. I often wonder how you accomplish so much. My admiration for you is shared by the great majority of people in this country, especially the young people who are so deeply interested in China.

My very best wishes and warm personal regards go to you with the sincere hope that we shall be able to meet before long.

Very cordially yours,

Eleanor Roosevelt to Madame Chiang Kai-shek
September 16, 1942

During the first year of America's involvement in World War II, China was in its sixth year of fighting to drive out the Japanese. Mrs. Roosevelt wrote this letter to offer her sympathy and admiration for the bravery of the Chinese, but she also invited Madame Chiang to visit the United States and offered the White House for her residence while here. The first lady expressed her strong desire to meet personally Madame Chiang and mentioned her conversation with Dr. Lauchlin Currie, an economist and governmental official who headed the United States economic mission to China in 1941 as deputy administrator of the Foreign Economic Administration.

September 16, 1942

Dear Madame Chiang,

Thank you so much for your delightful photograph. What I am really anxious to see, however, is the original of the photo!

Dr. Currie tells me that you have been in wretched health this summer and he feels that, quite apart from and in addition to the benefit you would derive from treatment in the country, you would be benefited by a change of scene. I have discussed the matter with my husband and we both feel that a visit with us at the White House would not only enable us to get to know you better and to secure a better appreciation of China's problems, but would also, in large measure, serve the ends of publicity. You would henceforth be perfectly justified in keeping your public and social engagements to a bare minimum.

We could, of course, send a comfortable plane for you. Not feeling well you would doubtless wish to be accompanied by your sister, Madame Kung, and our cordial invitation, of course, embraces her. If, on the other hand, you do not feel up to the trip, do not hesitate to say so and we will quite understand.

My warmest sympathy and admiration go out to the Generalissimo[1] and to you as you lead China through her sixth year of hostilities.

Sincerely yours,

Note

1. Chiang Kai-shek.

Eleanor Roosevelt to Madame Chiang Kai-shek
September 17, 1942

In 1942 Mrs. Roosevelt corresponded frequently with Madame Chiang Kai-shek. She still had not met the wife of the Chinese leader, but she repeated her desire to do so. Mrs. Roosevelt also offered the White House as a place for convalescence. The Roosevelts were known for opening the executive mansion to various guests, foreign and domestic.

September 17, 1942

Dear Madame Chiang,

Mr. Lattimore[1] has very kindly offered to take this note to you, and I am very glad of this opportunity to write you again.

I have heard that you are not well, and that you are thinking of coming to the United States for medication. This is just to tell you that we will welcome you warmly, and that if you have to submit to hospital treatment, we will be happy to have you convalesce in the White House. I know that if you come, your sister will accompany you, and of course, our invitation includes her and we shall be happy to see you both.

I shall wait for word from you that you are coming, and look forward eagerly to knowing you in person, even though I have a warm feeling of friendship through our correspondence.

With deep admiration and my kindest regards, I am,

Very cordially yours,

Note

1. Owen Lattimore, a scholar of Far Eastern affairs.

Eleanor Roosevelt to Henry A. Wallace
October 16, 1942

Eleanor Roosevelt often tried to pave the way for speaking and other requests from organizations that she supported or thought were worthwhile. In this case, she asked the vice president to consider making a recording for broadcast to Poland during the war.

October 16, 1942.

Dear Mr. Vice President:

The group known as "America Speaks for Poland", are going to approach you with a request that you make a recording for them to use on a short wave broadcast to Poland on November 11th.

I know how very busy you are and I am only sending this note to tell you I have done two broadcasts for them and have been surprised to get word back that they had gotten through.

Very sincerely yours,

Eleanor Roosevelt to Walter White
November 23, 1942

Reciprocating to White's letter of October 28 dealing with the matter of segregation of African American WAACS at Fort Des Moines, Mrs. Roosevelt promised to journey there eventually to assist the cause of breaking down racial barriers.

November 23 1942.

Dear Mr. White:

I will try to go to the WAACS in Des Moines before too long. I did not go because I asked for a report on the segregation question and was told that on the whole the opportunities given for actual work and training were equal, and that the segregation only came in matters effecting their social lives. That barrier, I doubt very much can yet be broken down, though I will do what I can. I think my visit will be more worth while now that I know what is being done abroad.

Very sincerely yours,

Eleanor Roosevelt to Walter White
December 10, 1942

After receiving a letter from White on December 5 in which he proposed that Mme. Chiang Kai-shek speak at a biracial meeting on the matter of discrimination based on color, Mrs. Roosevelt responded that she liked the idea of such a meeting but would first have to discuss the matter with Mme. Chiang Kai-shek. She also suggested that he and President Roosevelt compromise on an antilynching bill.

December 10, 1942

My dear Mr. White:

I like the idea of the meeting you want, but before making the arrangements, I would like a chance to talk unofficially with Madame Chiang Kai-Shek and see how she feels about it and also to find out what she might be able to do while she is in this country. She will not do anything for two months as the doctors want her to spend that amount of time in the hospital and she may not feel she can do much after that. I will let you know what I find out.

The President told me the other night that if you are willing to give up the anti-lynching bill and accept the bill which he suggested to you, he felt sure he could get it passed. I think you should write a letter about it as it would be better to get what the President wants through, than to wait and try to get something passed which he feels might, in the end, be declared unconstitutional.

Cordially yours,

Eleanor Roosevelt to Clifton Searles
January 23, 1943

Early in 1943, nearly fourteen months after the United States entered the second world war, Mrs. Roosevelt received a moving, heartfelt letter from Pvt. Clifton

Searles, an unassigned African American soldier in the United States Army, written from Lincoln University in Pennsylvania. While visiting the nation's capital on January 11, Searles stopped at a People's Drug Store for a small soda. The clerk served him the soda in a paper cup and asked him to leave the premises, while a white man at the same moment was being seated and served a soda in a glass. Noting that his four brothers were in the service and that he would soon join them, Searles questioned that for which he would be fighting (a Jim Crow government). He stated he hoped that he would not remember this racial incident if he had to give a dying white man a drink of water on the battlefield. Although recognizing that Franklin and Eleanor Roosevelt were for the common people, he asked why the Chinese and Japanese were called "yellow" and speculated on possible black equality if Hitler and Japan won the war. Searles ended by enclosing the cup and praying that God would teach the white people something about brotherhood and democracy. Mrs. Roosevelt quickly responded to his letter.

January 23, 1943

Dear Mr. Searles:

I can quite understand how what happened to you made you feel as bitterly as you do feel. There are many things of that kind which many of us in this country deeply regret. The only thing I can say to you is that under the Germans or the Japanese you would have very little freedom, and you certainly would not have the freedom to write to me as you have. You are free to go on working as a people for the betterment of your people and you are gradually gathering behind you a larger and larger group of white people who are conscious of the wrongs and who are helping to correct them.

Very sincerely yours,

Eleanor Roosevelt to Madame Chiang Kai-shek
January 26, 1943

When Madame Chiang Kai-shek planned a trip to the United States, Mrs. Roosevelt informed her of the general interest in her speaking over the radio and accepting an award at the White House.

January 26, 1943

Dear Madame Chiang,

I have two requests that I feel I must pass on to you myself. One is from the League of Women Voters which is starting a campaign all over the country against isolationism. They want you if it would be possible, to make one speech in their series over the radio.

In addition, the National Achievement Award of the Chi Omega[1] asked me to find out if you would be willing to accept from them a medal of achievement. This is an annual award usually given to an American woman in some field of work. They feel that because you were educated in this country they would like to give it to you and it would be presented at a ceremony in the White House. As I am a member of the Awards Committee this has been done a number of times.

Very cordially yours,

Note

1. A social sorority founded in 1895.

Eleanor Roosevelt to Madame Chiang Kai-shek
February 11, 1943

In 1943, in the midst of World War II, Madame Chiang Kai-shek came to America partly to improve the image of her husband's government. Mrs. Roosevelt wrote to tell her that President Roosevelt thought she should address Congress at her convenience. As a social leader, she was also in demand by members of Congress.

February 11, 1943

Dear Madame Chiang,

The President thinks that you should, of course, address the Congress and that you can do it at your convenience. He also feels it would be better for you to have a joint press conference including all of his White House correspondents and my women correspondents. I will be glad to arrange this at any time you desire, if you will let me know ahead.

Very cordially yours,

P.S. Mrs. Edith Nourse Rogers,[1] a Member of Congress from Massachusetts, would very much like to have you lunch with the members of the Foreign Affairs Committee at the Capitol the day you speak there. This would mean about 25 people.

E.R.

Note

1. Republican member.

Eleanor Roosevelt to Madame Chiang Kai-shek
April 20, 1943

By the spring of 1943, Eleanor Roosevelt and Madame Chiang Kai-shek had met and had developed a friendship. Madame Chiang was planning a visit to the United States, and Mrs. Roosevelt suggested good dates for her to come, offering the White House again as a place of residence while in the United States. Gen. Joseph W. Stilwell, known as "Vinegar Joe," was chief of staff of Allied armies in the Chinese theater of operations. Maj. Gen. Claire L. Chennault, a specialist in fighter tactics, founded the American Volunteer Group (Flying Tigers) in China and trained pilots at an aviation school sponsored by Madame Chiang. Mrs. Roosevelt's cautious note referred to the problems of secrecy during wartime.

April 20th, 1943

Dear Madame Chiang,

I just sent you a rather guarded telegram, because the President said that not even over the telephone should I mention these gentlemen's names.

As you know, both General Stillwell and General Chenault are returning. The President says it will be impossible to be sure of the time of their arrival.

As he has a number of engagements, he hopes you will come from May 3rd to May 5th and stay with us in any case, as that would give him time for your talks together.

The President says, of course, General Chenault will want to see you and that can be arranged wherever you are.

I hope you are getting a real rest, and I shall be happy to see you again.

Affectionately,

Eleanor Roosevelt to Oveta Culp Hobby
May 6, 1943

After visiting a Japanese-American relocation camp in Arizona and learning of the desire of some young Japanese women to enlist in the Women's Army Auxiliary Corps, Mrs. Roosevelt wondered if Colonel Hobby, director of the WAAC, had given any thought to this matter.

May 6, 1943

Dear Colonel Hobby:

When I was out in Arizona, visiting one of the Japanese relocation camps, the young Japanese girls who are American citizens, asked me if it was going to be possible for them to enlist in the WAAC. They know, of course, that they have to be thoroughly investigated and that they may have to go into a unit made up of Japanese girls, but they are anxious to have the opportunity. Has any thought been given to this and has any decision been reached?

Very sincerely yours,

Eleanor Roosevelt to Francis Biddle

June 16, 1943

After reading a letter from Mike Masaoka, national secretary of the Japanese-American Citizens League, and visiting with him and others from the Japanese Student League, Mrs. Roosevelt was furious to learn that a bill introduced in the Arizona House of Representatives proposed to restrict the movements of certain persons. She thought such acts would be vicious and questioned their constitutionality in a letter to the attorney general.

June 16, 1943.

Dear Mr. Attorney General:

This boy has come to see me with a group from the Japanese Student League and has sent me this letter pointing out how utterly absurd this kind of law is. It is not only absurd but really vicious and while nobody will rise up against such a law now, in the future they will create great difficulties. I wonder if such laws could be prevented in any way or whether they could be declared unconstitutional because they abrogate the rights of American citizens.

Very sincerely yours,

Eleanor Roosevelt to Madame Chiang Kai-shek

July 26, 1943

After Madame Chiang Kai-shek returned to China, Mrs. Roosevelt sent her a personal letter. She indicated that she might visit China and the surrounding region in the near future—that is, if the president could arrange a trip for her that would not interfere with the war effort. She passed along several personal messages from herself and the president to Madame Chiang and her husband.

July 26, 1943

Dear Madame Chiang,

It was good to see Captain Shelton[1] and get first hand news of you. He seemed very much concerned with the effects of the heat on the ground, and the cold which you caught in your neck. I hope by now you are beginning to recover, though I realize the climate of Chungking will not make it easy for you for the next few months.

I gave the President your message and the silk and of course, he is more than delighted to have it. You are much too kind and all of us will enjoy the tea when ever we drink it, and we will think of your thoughtfulness.

How you could do anything immediately on your arrival is beyond my understanding. I should think you would have wanted to go to bed and keep everyone away from you.

I think I am leaving the middle of August for a short trip through the Islands of the Southwest Pacific and to Australia and New Zealand and Hawaii. There is always of course, a question about any of these trips. I will not be gone very long.

I talked to the President about getting out to you and he said just what he always says about so many other things—that I must not interfere with war plans. However he said he would try to arrange it as soon as it seems practical.

I hope the engagement pad which the President sent to the Generalissimo arrived safely, and that you have been able to retain yours because I want you to have it as a reminder of your busy days here. I am sure that your days are busier now that you are back at home and carrying on your many responsibilities.

Please tell the Generalissimo that we look forward, both of us, to having the pleasure of meeting him some day. Please remember me to Miss Kung and Mrs. Kung.[2] My very warm affection to you.

Notes

1. A mutual friend who apparently was a military aide who returned from China with items for President and Mrs. Roosevelt from Madame Chiang.

2. Educated in the United States at Oberlin College and Yale University, Dr. H.H. Kung was China's minister of finance. He often conferred with FDR and Treasury Department officials about economic and industrial development in the United States. Mrs. Roosevelt knew him, his wife, and his daughter.

Eleanor Roosevelt to Dwight D. Eisenhower
November 10, [1943?]

Mrs. Roosevelt had watched how much Dwight D. Eisenhower had accomplished as a military leader for the Allied forces during the Second World War. She admired his work and wrote this note to express her feelings. The Harry she refers to was probably Harry L. Hopkins, a close adviser to Franklin D. Roosevelt, who was on his way to Europe.

November 10, [1943?]

Dear General Eisenhower:

I have been thinking how much you have accomplished since we met about a year ago in London & I'm giving Harry this note to take to you just to tell you that I watch with interest & applause.

I saw a photograph of you with a dog & I hope it's the cute little puppy I saw with you now grown to companionable dogdom!

I found the southwest Pacific interesting & the men, all of them, in such fine spirits. The hospitals were moving because there one is proud of young America. I hope I may be allowed someday to visit you & your men when you think it might be a help.

In the meantime my congratulations & best wishes for good luck.

Sincerely yours,

[*DDEL*]

Eleanor Roosevelt to William O. Douglas
[1944]

In 1944, when Franklin Roosevelt chose to run for a fourth time, most Democratic leaders worried that he would not live to complete the term. Because of that, many were convinced that the vice president in the third term, Henry Wallace, was too radical and unpredictable to keep on the ticket since there was a good chance that the vice president would succeed to the presidency. Many names were floated as to an alternate vice presidential candidate, including that of Supreme Court Justice William O. Douglas. Roosevelt even suggested at one point that he was his choice, but he may have told more than one person that. Mrs. Roosevelt was interested in the matter, but she was very cautious in how she expressed her opinions in this memo. This is an undated, typed draft.

[1944]

Have just been told of the request to you to serve as running mate in the campaign. I feel you are the best judge of where your services are most valuable but you would be of great value and give some confidence in the party to liberals if you accept. My confidence in your good judgment prevents my urging you to do anything but I want you to know that your acceptance would give hope to many for the future of a liberal democratic party.

e.r.

Eleanor Roosevelt to Henry A. Wallace
July 22, 1944

Henry Wallace, who had served as vice president for Franklin Roosevelt during his third term, was not renominated for the position for a fourth term. Instead, little-known senator Harry Truman of Missouri was chosen. Mrs. Roosevelt wrote this note to Wallace to express her feelings about his not being chosen for the fourth term. She says she is told that Senator Truman is a good man and that she hopes so for the sake of the country. This is probably just a normal concern for national leadership, but some might read into the statement that Mrs. Roosevelt had some reason to believe that her husband would not survive the fourth term.

July 22, 1944

Dear Mr. Vice-President:

I am dictating this because my handwriting is so bad I do not want to take up your time in trying to read it.

I can not let another day go by without telling you how distressed I was to have you lose out in the Convention. I had hoped that by some miracle you could win out but it looks to me as though the bosses had functioned pretty smoothly. I am told that Senator Truman is a good man, and I hope so for the sake of the country.

Incidentally I realize that it must be a great relief to you and to your family to feel that you will not be in a position which I have always felt was an unsatisfactory one. Being Vice President, to me, has never seemed a very happy job.

With my best wishes to you and do tell Mrs. Wallace I thought of her all through the balloting, remembering four years ago.

Very cordially yours,

Eleanor Roosevelt to Winston Churchill
April 30, 1945

Shortly after the death of Franklin Roosevelt, Winston Churchill sent a telegram to Mrs. Roosevelt expressing his condolences and saying that President Roosevelt's influence was felt at the San Francisco conference, where the United Nations was being formed. Her answer reflected her interest in world affairs.

April 30, 1945

Dear Mr. Prime Minister:

I was very much touched by your wire from San Francisco, and your thought of me and my children when you have so much to engross your time.

It makes me very happy to know that you feel my husband's influence at the conference, and I pray that we will be given the courage and the wisdom to follow through on the objectives in which he believed and for which he worked so hard.

The news which we get day by day of the shocking behavior of the Germans, makes one realize the depths of degradation to which fanaticism plunges a whole people. We must pledge ourselves, with God's help, to prevent any recurrence of what we are witnessing today.

With my deep gratitude in which my children join, I am

Very cordially yours,

Eleanor Roosevelt to Harry S Truman
May 8, 1945

When Germany surrendered in May 1945, Mrs. Roosevelt hurried to write President Truman a note of congratulations on his proclamation ending the war. She must have had mixed feelings, since her husband had died on April 12, 1945, so close to the end of the war (in Europe) for which he had worked so long.

May 8, 1945

Dear Mr. President:

I listened to your Proclamation this morning and I was deeply moved. I am so happy that this Day has come and the war in Europe is over. It will in a small way lighten your burdens for which we are all grateful.

Eleanor Roosevelt and President Harry Truman. (Courtesy of the Franklin D. Roosevelt Library)

My congratulations to you on your Proclamation and on your birthday, and my best wishes that your future birthdays will be happier ones.

Very sincerely yours,

Don't bother to answer *please!* My warm regards to Mrs. Truman.
[*HSTL*]

Eleanor Roosevelt to Harry S Truman

May 14, 1945

Shortly after the death of President Franklin D. Roosevelt in April 1945, Mrs. Roosevelt wrote a note to President Truman assuring him of her support and wishing him well. Much to her surprise Truman responded on May 10 with an eight-page handwritten letter in which he explained some of the things he was facing, especially with the end of World War II approaching and the relations with Prime Minister Winston Churchill of Great Britain and Premier Joseph Stalin of the Soviet Union. Mrs. Roosevelt took him at his word and gave him some of her impressions, gathered through her husband, of Churchill and Stalin.

May 14, 1945

Dear Mr. President:

I was very much touched to have you take the trouble to write me that long letter in longhand about the Russian situation. Please if you write again, do have it typed because I feel guilty to take any of your time.

I am typing this because I know my husband always preferred to have things typed so he could read them more quickly and my handwriting is anything but legible.

Your experience with Mr. Churchill is not at all surprising. He is suspicious of the Russians and they know it. If you will remember, he said some pretty rough things about them years ago and they do not forget.

Of course, we will have to be patient, and any lasting peace will have to have the Three Great Powers behind it. I think, however, if you can get on a personal basis with Mr. Churchill, you will find it easier. If you talk to him about books and let him quote to you from his marvelous memory everything on earth from Barbara Fritche[1] to the Nonsense Rhymes and Greek tragedy, you will find him easier to deal with on political subjects. He is a gentleman to whom the personal element means a great deal.

Mr. Churchill does not have the same kind of sense of humor that the Russians have. In some ways the Russians are more like us. They enjoy a practical joke, rough-housing and play and they will joke about things which Mr. Churchill thinks are sacred. He takes them dead seriously and argues about them when what he ought to do is to laugh. That was where Franklin usually won out because if you know where to laugh and when to look upon things as too absurd to take seriously, the other person is ashamed to carry through even if he was serious about it.

You are quite right in believing that the Russians will watch with great care to see how we keep our commitments.

A rumor has reached me that that message from Mr. Stalin to you was really received in plenty of time to have changed the hour but it was held back from you. Those little things were done to my husband now and then. I tell you of this rumor simply because while you may have known about it and decided that it was wise just not to receive it in time, you told me in your letter that you did not receive it and I have known of things which just did not reach my husband in time. That is one of the things which your Military and Naval aides ought to watch very carefully.

Sometime when you have time, since my son, Elliott is in Washington now and then, you might like to let him tell you about what he learned of the Russians when he was there. He was in Russia quite a good deal and helped establish our airforce there and he has an old friend who is the only American who has flown with the Russians from the very beginning. Elliott gets on with them and understands the peculiar combination that can look upon human life rather cheaply at times and yet strive for an ideal of future well-being for the people and making the people believe in it. He has an understanding of their enjoyment of drama and music and the arts in general and he realizes what few people seem to understand—namely that when you telescope into a few years a development in civilization which has taken hundreds of years for the people around you to achieve, the development is very uneven.

I will, of course, keep confidential anything which comes to me in any letter from you and I will never mention it, and I would not use a private letter in any public way at any time.

I would not presume to write you this only you did say you would like me to give you some little personal impressions of these people, gathered from my husband's contacts, before you went to meet them and as I realize that may happen soon, I thought perhaps you would like this letter now.

If you or any of your family ever feel like getting away from formality and spending a few days with me in this very simple cottage, I should love to have you and I am quite accustomed to the necessary Secret Service protection.

With much gratitude for the trouble which you took, and with my kind regards to Mrs. Truman and your daughter, believe me,

Very cordially yours,

Note

1. Barbara Fritchie (1766–1862), a heroine in American history about whom John Greenleaf Whittier had written a poem.

Eleanor Roosevelt to Carrie Chapman Catt

June 11, 1945

Mrs. Catt contacted Mrs. Roosevelt to offer her condolences on the death of Franklin Roosevelt. She waited a while before writing because she knew Mrs.

Roosevelt would be flooded with letters and expressions of sympathy. Mrs. Roosevelt's response reflected the care with how she was assessing her future.

June 11, 1945

Dear Mrs. Catt:

I am so glad you waited to write until I could have the time to read your letter.

I deeply appreciate all that you say and prize very highly your good opinion. Your faith in me is a great help and I shall certainly try to be useful in the future.

There is so much to do in regard to my husband's possessions. I have decided that I would not undertake anything new for the next few months. By that time I should be able to decide what I think is the most useful thing or things to do.

With my warm thanks, I am,

Affectionately,

[*NYPL-Catt*]

Eleanor Roosevelt to Dwight D. Eisenhower
Telegram, June 18, 1945

Gen. Dwight D. Eisenhower was thrust into the limelight by his leadership in World War II. On his return to the United States following the surrender of Germany, he received a hero's welcome. Mrs. Roosevelt added her congratulations in this telegram.

June 18, 1945

GENERAL OF THE ARMY DWIGHT D. EISENHOWER:
    MAY I ADD A WORD OF WELCOME AND CONGRATULATIONS ON YOUR RETURN I KNOW YOU WILL HAVE THE GREATEST WELCOME EVER RECORDED ANY CONQUERING HERO I WISH MY HUSBAND COULD HAVE BEEN HERE TO GREET YOU BUT YOU KNOW YOU HAVE ALL MY GOOD WISHES.
ELEANOR ROOSEVELT
[*DDEL*]

Eleanor Roosevelt to Harry Hopkins

June 30, 1945

Shortly after her husband's death, Eleanor Roosevelt was contacted by Harry Hopkins, one of her husband's key advisers who continued to perform similar services for President Truman. Hopkins asked if she would be willing to go to the Soviet Union in September. Transportation posed a problem, but he said Averell Harriman had a good plane he could bring from Paris to Russia for her to use. He also told her that he had been offered a position, which he was seriously considering, by the Dubinsky union and the Women's Cloak and Suit Manufacturers. After Mrs. Roosevelt's response, he wrote again saying that he thought she should go as a correspondent but that she would be received as the widow of the president and there was nothing she could do about that status. He also stated that by the time she was ready to go she should probably be able to fly across Germany rather than having to detour by way of Teheran.

June 30, 1945

Dear Harry:

I could, of course, go to Russia in September if it is important that I go then and not wait until May.

However, when I do go I shall go as a correspondent for the United Feature Syndicate and use whatever transportation the other correspondents use. I would not want to use Averell's private plane.

Also, I would not want to do a lot of parties, etc., except of course, for calling on Marshal Stalin. I have not spoken to Mr. Carlin[1] of the Syndicate about going in September, and I do not know that he would want me to go that soon and I also want to know first what you think of my going purely as a correspondent and not as Franklin's widow.

I heard about the Dubinsky offer and I am very pleased.

Very cordially yours,

Note

1. George A. Carlin, editor of Mrs. Roosevelt's newspaper syndicate.

Eleanor Roosevelt to Winston Churchill

July 28, 1945

Shortly after World War II ended in Germany but before the Japanese surrendered, English voters turned out the government of Winston Churchill that had led the country through the dark years of the war. It was an abrupt change for Churchill, who was in Potsdam, Germany, at the time participating in the first Allied war conference attended by the new president, Truman. It was a more bitter defeat for Churchill because the voters had chosen the Labour Party, which was committed to taking England into a Socialist government. Mrs. Roosevelt wrote a brief note of condolence to Churchill.

July 28, 1945

Dear Mr. Churchill:

I know that you and Mrs. Churchill both are probably very happy and look forward to a few years of less strenuous life, and yet to those who lay down the burdens of great responsibility, there must come for a while a sense of being rudderless.

I hope that you will keep your health and vigor and continue to give of your great gifts to the people of Great Britain and the world as you have in the past.

With my affectionate regards to Mrs. Churchill and every good wish to you, I am,

Very cordially yours,

Eleanor Roosevelt to Harry S Truman

September 11, 1945

In the fall of 1945, Mrs. Roosevelt wrote President Truman to notify him of the interest in her hometown of Hyde Park in having the United Nations permanent headquarters placed there. To some this may have been a preposterous idea, but to others it seemed logical because of the facilities available that Mrs. Roosevelt describes in this letter. Truman responded that it was a good idea but that the decision of a permanent location would be made by the UN as a whole. He assured her that he had instructed American delegates to accept if the UN offered to come to the United States. Only then would they decide on a location.

Dear Mr. President:

The Rogers estate, which joins ours at Hyde Park, was, as you know, leased by the War Department for the Military Police school. Now that the Military Police are no longer there, there is a great interest in the Village in having all or some of the property owned by the government, selected as the permanent headquarters of the United Nations.

I have told those who came to me that a decision of this kind would have to be made by a majority of the nations and that our government could make no such decision alone.

The idea seems to me good, however and I wondered if our house and the Vanderbilt Mansion[1] couldn't all be used at times of meeting and make a very acceptable center.

You will get the local petition eventually, but I thought I'd pass the idea along now.

Very cordially yours,

Note

1. The neoclassical, opulent Vanderbilt mansion in Hyde Park, New York, close to FDR's home, was designed by the architectural firm of McKim, Mead, and White in 1896.

Eleanor Roosevelt to Harry S Truman
November 20, 1945

During 1945 Mrs. Roosevelt continued to write President Truman, offering advice and observations on national and world conditions. In this letter she once again promoted Bernard Baruch, a statesman and financier, as a valuable adviser and strongly encouraged Truman to consult with him. She also comments on various problems throughout the world. One of the more interesting concerned her view on Great Britain. Truman responded to her letter and commented upon each of the points except the Baruch matter.

November 20, 1945

Dear Mr. President:

I hope you will forgive my writing you this letter, but I, like a great many other citizens, have been deeply concerned about the situation as it seems to be developing both at home and abroad. I have a deep sense that we have an obligation first of all, to solve our own problems at home, because our failure must of necessity, take away hope from the other nations of the world who have so much more to contend with than we have.

It seems to me, therefore, that we must get to work.

The suggestion that was made the other day that a survey of our resources be made, on which we base not only our national economy, but what we lend to other nations, would seem to me sound, if the person making the investigation had sufficient standing to be accepted by management and labor as well.

In situations of this kind, my husband some times turned to Mr. Bernard Baruch, because of his wealth of experience and his standing with the industrialists of the country. At the same time, I think that even the young labor leaders, like Walter Reuther and James Carey, believe in his integrity. If it could be possible to get the Detroit situation[1] started up by giving both management and labor something so they would at least agree to go to work until, let us say, next October on condition that Mr. Baruch was asked to father a staff of experts, I feel he would consult with both sides as he always has in the past.

If there was a limit for the time of the report, I think labor would not feel that it was being taken for a ride.

When it comes to lending money, it seems to me that we should lend other nations equally. If we lend only to Great Britain, we enter into an economic alliance against other nations, and our hope for the future lies in joint cooperation. If we could only lend in small amounts at present, until we get into production we can not sell to any of these countries in great quantities and there is no value in their having the money unless they can use it, it would be helpful. They would also profit by this type of survey and we would be making no promises which we could not carry out.

If you talk to Mr. Baruch, I think you must do so only if you yourself, feel confidence in him, because once you accept him you will find, as my husband did, that many of those around you will at once, cast doubts upon whatever he does,[2] but that would be true even if the job were given to the Angel Gabriel.

I think Mr. Baruch has proved in the past, his ability to see things on a large scale, and where financial matters are concerned, he certainly knows the world picture which is what we need at the present time.

I am very much distressed that Great Britain has made us take a share in another investigation of the few Jews remaining in Europe.[3] If they are not to be allowed to enter Palestine, then certainly they could have been apportioned among the different United Nations and we would not have to continue to have on our consciences, the death of at least fifty of these poor creatures daily.

The question between Palestine and the Arabs, of course, has always been complicated by the oil deposits, and I suppose it always will. I do not happen to be a Zionist, and I know what a difference there is among such Jews as consider themselves nationals of other countries and not a separate nationality.

Great Britain is always anxious to have some one pull her chestnuts out of the fire, and though I am very fond of the British individually and like a great many of them, I object very much to being used by them. I am enclosing a copy of a letter bearing on the subject.

Lastly, I am deeply troubled about China. Unless we can stop the civil war there by moral pressure and not by the use of military force, and insist that Generalissimo Chiang give wider representation to all Chinese groups, which will allow the middle of the road Democratic League to grow, I am very much afraid that continued war there may lead us to general war again.

Being a strong nation and having the greatest physical, mental and spiritual strength today, gives us a tremendous responsibility. We can not use our strength to coerce, but if we are big enough, I think we can lead, but it will require great vision and understanding on our part. The first and foremost thing, it seems to me, is the setting of our own house in order, and so I have made the suggestion contained in the first part of this letter. I shall quite understand, however, if with the broader knowledge which is yours, you decide against it, but I would not have a quiet conscience unless I wrote you what I feel in these difficult days.

With every good wish, I am,

Very cordially yours,

Notes

1. This refers to a strike in 1945 at the Kelsey-Hayes Wheel Company in Detroit, which had created tension between labor and management even after it ended.

2. Bernard Baruch was always a controversial figure, beginning with his service to Woodrow Wilson during World War I. His wealth and his conservative views did not always sit well with Democratic presidents.

3. An article in the *New York Times* on June 30, 1945, reported on growing and disturbing anti-Semitism in France. Several Jewish leaders had spoken on this matter. Many returning Jewish deportees discovered that their homes, apartments, businesses, and other possessions had been seized in their absence, and they encountered much discrimination. The Joint Distribution Committee provided aid to suffering people, including Jews who desired to rebuild their communities. Naturally, Mrs. Roosevelt would be concerned about their plight. (Perhaps through the UN or other means England made its feelings known.) At least this article confirms that something was happening.

Eleanor Roosevelt to Frank P. Graham
November 24, 1945

Mrs. Roosevelt was never hesitant to speak her mind and to criticize people where she felt it necessary. In November 1945, Frank P. Graham, president of the University of North Carolina at Chapel Hill, wrote to Mrs. Roosevelt asking for her *support for a grant from the Julius Rosenwald Fund, of which she was a member of the board, to the Southern Conference on Human Welfare. The Rosenwald Fund was created in 1917 in honor of Julius Rosenwald "for the well-being of mankind." In 1945 grants totaling $88,500 were given to 46 people, including New Yorkers. Among the fellows were twenty-nine African Americans. Graham argued that the conference was a "vital necessity in this struggle to make political and social adjustment to economic change" in the South. Mrs. Roosevelt minced no words in her response to him.*

November 24, 1945

Dear Dr. Graham:

Your letter about the appeal made by the Southern Conference for Human Welfare[1] to the Rosenwald Fund, reached me after I had attended the semi-annual meeting.

The trustees of the Rosenwald Fund feel very doubtful of Clarke Foreman[2] and James Dombromskie's[3] leadership. They have offended many people and the trustees doubt the value of a contribution.

Very sincerely yours,

Notes

1. Along with Joseph Gelders, a former professor of physics at the University of Alabama and southern representative of the National Committee for the Defense of Political Prisoners, and Lucy Randolph Mason, the southern field representative for the Congress of Industrial Organizations (CIO), ER helped in 1938 to organize the Southern Conference for Human Welfare (SCHW), a radical biracial organization determined to challenge segregation, which dealt with southern matters, including the economy, civil liberties, voting rights, and poll taxes. That year ER addressed the meeting of the SCHW in Birmingham, Alabama.

2. Dr. Clarke Foreman, a member of President Roosevelt's National Emergency Council, helped in 1938 to study southern conditions and drafted the *Report on Economic Conditions of the South*, which portrayed the South's serious economic problems. Foreman was aligned with Joseph Gelders, Judge Louise Charlton, and others in the Southern Conference for Human Welfare in an endeavor to rehabilitate and transform the South's economy.

3. Along with Myles Horton, James Dombrowski ran the Highlander Folk School in Monteagle, Tennessee, a school that trained union organizers. Dombrowski was a leader in the Southern Conference for Human Welfare.

Eleanor Roosevelt to Harry S Truman

January 12, 1946

In early 1946 Mrs. Roosevelt went to London for a meeting of the United Nations. She expressed gratitude to President Truman for her appointment as delegate to the Human Rights Commission and said she understood that her presence would be a reminder of her husband and his policies. Mrs. Roosevelt also reported on what she had heard from some of the American servicemen in England, who were anxious to get back home. She informed Truman that she planned to send a similar letter to Gen. Dwight Eisenhower explaining the thinking of the men still in service.

London, January 12, 1946.

Dear Mr. President,

I want to thank you very much for the opportunity you have given me of being part of this Delegation. It is a great privilege and my only fear is that I shall not be able to make enough of a contribution. I do feel, however, that you were very wise in thinking that anyone connected with my husband could, perhaps, by their presence here keep the level of his ideals. Just being here, perhaps, is a good reminder, which I think is what you had in mind.

I feel that the meeting is starting off with good feeling though there was a little difference of opinion over the election of the President of the Assembly.

I am sending a little note to General Eisenhower about a group of men who came to see me, representing the soldiers in this area. They were very well behaved and, I thought, very logical. They said that the men with points below 45 realized that they had to stay here and were entirely reconciled; those with more than 60 had gone home; but those in between were very anxious to have a definite policy announced. A great many of them feel that more men are kept in the area than are really needed for the work and that this is done by officers who find their jobs not too unpleasant and like to have a good number of men under them. One boy said he would give anything to do one good day's work. I have had that said to me by a number of men, and written to me by a number of them; and of course their living conditions are not as pleasant as the officers'. I think, however, if it is possible for the War Department to give them some kind of a definite answer as to the plans made for bringing them home, it would make a great difference. One boy told me he had been six years in the Army; he had volunteered for a year, here, after being in the Pacific, but he had been here a great deal longer than that and was now anxious to get home. They do feel that there is some injustice in the way people are sent home and that I know is difficult to eliminate in any great big undertaking. But certainly a clear and definite policy could now be formulated, and therefore in my note to General Eisenhower I am giving him the same information I am giving you in this letter. They are good boys but if they don't have enough to do, they will get into trouble. That is the nature of boys, I am afraid, in any situation.

With thanks and best wishes, I am

Gratefully yours,

Eleanor Roosevelt's Report to Harry S Truman
n.d.

Mrs. Roosevelt provided a report to President Truman, probably in 1946, re-garding the situation as she saw it from the view of the United Nations. She detailed conditions in various countries and parts of the world and gave her opinion as to possible remedies. Her evaluations of Great Britain, the USSR, and Ireland were generally correct, but she was not correct about Germany be-ing a nonindustrial nation. An interesting feature of this report was her assess-ment that Europe would have to have massive aid to survive and resist Commu-nism. Her ideas seem very similar to what occurred in 1948 and became known as the Marshall Plan.

MEMO FOR THE PRESIDENT   n.d.

First—the economic situation in Europe.
I feel very strongly that it cannot be handled piecemeal. For the safety of the world, we have decided to change the center of European economy from Germany. Much of the coal and heavy industry emanated from Germany in the past. Now, as far as possible, Germany will be an agricultural nation. Unfortunately in giving Poland some of Germany's best land, we have com-plicated the industrial situation somewhat because she will have to have not only enough industry to meet her own internal needs, but enough industry to keep her people on a reasonable living basis which will mean a revival, at least, of the old toy industry and other light industries. When we made this decision, we also made the decision that Europe had to have in Great Britain, France, Holland and other countries, the things which Germany had once provided.

Owing to the fact that this second World War has done more than de-stroy material things, bad as that situation is in all these countries, a much greater responsibility is going to devolve on us not only materially but for leadership.

Great Britain is better off than the rest of Europe, but even in Great Brit-ain our help in the provision of goods is going to be necessary. In Europe it will not only be the provision of goods without which loans would be merely a farce, since you can not start a factory with money alone—you have to have machinery. We will also have to provide skilled administrators and skilled technicians. This will be necessary because Germany in over-running Europe wiped out one group of administrative officials, those who ran the towns and villages and cities, and those who ran the factories and businesses, etc. The Germans put in people whom they felt they could trust and they were usually efficient in large part. When we came and reconquered Europe we had to liquidate this second group and now there is no one left to take the leadership.

The young people returning from concentration camps and forced labor camps will nearly all of them spend some time in sanitariums, but they will not only have to rebuild their bodies. The suffering they have been through will have left a mark on their personalities.

I happen to remember the effect of unemployment and poverty in some of our mining areas in the depth of the depression. It took several years for people to regain self confidence and initiative, and that was not comparable to what these people in Europe have been through. That takes a large group out of the leadership area.

Amongst the resistance groups, you have young people who have missed out on five or six years of education which they must either now try to get or they must get something else which will make it possible for them to earn a living. Even more serious is the handicap that the virtues of life in the resistance during the invasion period, have now become far from virtues in a peaceful civilization. Lying, cheating, stealing and even killing was what they had to do. Now these are criminal offenses!

The whole social structure of Europe is crumbling and we might as well face the fact that leadership must come from us or it will inevitably come from Russia. The economic problem is not one we can handle with a loan to Great Britain, a loan to France, a loan to Russia. It must be looked on as a whole. When we make the loans we must be prepared to send goods. This will mean very careful allocation over here so that our people will obtain only essentials and everything else, during the next couple of years, will go where it is needed even worse.

The economic problem is tied up with the problem of food. You can not rehabilitate people and expect them to work unless they are getting an adequate diet. At present that is not possible anywhere in Europe and the Far East and shortly we are going to have a real famine in India, and Burma, I am told.

We are going to have to learn to stretch as we have never stretched before as far as food is concerned. I think we should begin an intensive campaign over the radio and in the newspapers to tell our people how to do this and to awaken in them a realization of the consequences, not perhaps this year or next, but five years hence if these people in Europe starve to death, or are not able to rehabilitate themselves and therefore are not able to buy some of our goods when our own savings have been spent. Even more serious is the threat of epidemics to world health, since starvation saps resistance to disease and there are no real boundaries today which will protect us if epidemics get started.

Second—Russia.

I do not feel that there is any mystery about Russia as Senator Vandenburg[1] in his speech, indicated. I liked his speech as a whole very much, but these unanswered questions I think, may lead to the flaming of uncertainty in this country which I think is one of the things we do not wish to do.

In a great country like the USSR where her soldiers for the first time have discovered what other people have in the way of consumer goods, it must be realized that in one way or another, all people being human beings, they are going to demand the satisfying of normal desires of people for better living. For that reason I think that intelligent people at the head of their government are anxious to establish economic conditions which will allow them to import and export without difficulty. Hence the agitation in Iran, the Dardenelles, etc. They are going to ask for political control to safeguard economic agreements but it is security in the economic situation that they seek. They must have it to secure political security at home but I do not think the political controls are their first considerations.

Along the European border of the USSR, however, she is chiefly concerned with her military security. That is why she will try to control the governments of the nations in all these areas and why she dreads seeing Germany built up as an industrial power against her. She will liquidate or allow governments under her control to liquidate any of the displaced people now outside her borders if they show signs of dissatisfaction or unrest against her control in those countries. She has not enough real security and stability to live with an opposition at home and this is difficult for us to understand. We have no political refugees in our country since the days of the Civil War. The opposition is always in our midst and frequent changes occur, but we do it through the ballot and peacefully. They do it through revolution and the use of force. This is largely a question of maturity and of course, trust in the people themselves and not such great dependence on the absolute control of the head of the government.

It will take some time for Russia to achieve this, but there is no reason why we should not explain this to her. It will have to be stressed for her that the vast majority of displaced people in Europe today who long to go back to the countries of their origin, must be able to go back in safety and have enough freedom within their countries to feel that they control their national government internally., [*sic*] and their association with the Soviets is exclusively a real protection for the future.

This holds good for what we call the Balts who are people from Estonia, Latvia, Lithuania and also for many Ukranians [*sic*] outside of Ukrane [*sic*] today.

Poland has several factions and people going back, if they are not shot by one faction or afraid of being shot by the other. I suppose this holds good and will hold good for some of the other countries. Czechoslovakia seems to have worked out under Dr. Benes,[2] a fairly satisfactory kind of government for everyone concerned. She does, [*sic*] not however, seem to feel free to differ with the Soviets judging by the way Mazarak[3] voted and that is because the Soviets haven't really been strong enough to explain that they are willing to have people do what they thought was right and they would not attribute to them any less fundamental agreement amongst them.

I think we should get a very much better understanding of the displaced persons situation but perhaps that can wait until the committee on refugees makes its report to the UNO. It might be well to prepare our people for the report, however, and also to make clear why certain things have to be said to Russia.

Third—Mr. Winant[4]

If Mr. John G. Winant could be made our permanent member on the Economic and Security Council, I think he could make the most valuable contribution of any one I know because of his long association with the Europeans on the ILO,[5] and as Ambassador to London. He is really liked and trusted. I know that there are some stories circulated about him, but I am quite sure that he is fundamentally a loyal and honest person. I should like to give him a chance to tell his side of any stories if they should be brought up as a reason for not appointing him.

Fourth—Food

I wonder if in your food program, we could not enlist the cooperation of South America and possibly increase their production by allotting to them some agricultural machinery.

Fifth—Mr. David Gray

Mr. David Gray, our Minister to Ireland, asked me to give you his regards and to tell you we were going on leading the fight to have the Irish turn over the German diplomatic people to the courts as has been requested. Ireland is a curious country and even the Catholic Church situation is different from anywhere else in the world. I hope if Mr. Gray does get permission to return for a time this spring that you will allow him an opportunity to tell you about their very peculiar politics.

Notes

1. Michigan Republican Arthur H. Vandenburg.
2. Eduard Benes.
3. Tomas G. Masaryk.
4. John Gilbert Winant, former politician from New Hampshire and chairman of the Social Security Board (1935–1937), was ambassador to Great Britain from 1941 to 1946.
5. International Labor Organization.

Eleanor Roosevelt to Henry A. Wallace
April 27, 1946

In a letter to Secretary of Commerce Wallace, Mrs. Roosevelt probed him on several matters, including the United Nations and the economic situation in Germany.

April 27, 1946

Dear Mr. Secretary:

I wonder if you have ever got the interdepartmental committee started and whether anything is being done in connection with the United Nations for the idea which I talked over with you.

I realize that not having a permanent home yet for the United Nations, it can not be done immediately and yet I think if they are considering spending two or three years in their temporary location, it could be done right there as a start. I should be very glad to know how it is proceeding. I talked with Secretary Forrestal,[1] Secretary Patterson[2] and Mr. Dean Acheson[3] as well as with you, and also with Mr. Oscar Chapman[4] when I was in Washington, but have heard nothing from any of you.

I also want to tell you that I have read through Mr. Pajus' material on the economic situation in Germany. It seems to me a very dangerous situation and my feeling about Mr. Murphy is that he will always play in with the group in Great Britain which would want to build up a strong industrial Germany and that they are more afraid of Russia's changing their economic situation than they are of Germany starting another war. People do not matter as much to this group as money, but I really think we should do something about it.

Very cordially yours,

Notes

1. James Vincent Forrestal, secretary of defense from 1947 to 1949.
2. Robert Porter Patterson, secretary of war from 1945 to 1947.
3. In 1946 Acheson was undersecretary of state.
4. Oscar Littleton Chapman of Colorado was secretary of the interior from 1950 to 1953.

Eleanor Roosevelt to Harry S Truman

June 1, 1946

During her first year of service on the United States delegation to the United Nations, Mrs. Roosevelt corresponded with President Truman expressing her regret that Edward R. Stettinius, former secretary of state, had resigned as the United States delegate on the Security Council. She inquired if the president would tell her the reasons for his departure and encouraged him and the new secretary of state, James F. Byrnes, to try to convince Stettinius to remain. Mrs. Roosevelt took this opportunity as well to express her concern about whether the Soviet Union really believed the administration would stand behind its stated policy.

June 1, 1946

Dear Mr. President:

I read in the papers this morning that Mr. Stettinius's resignation has really come in and that you and Secretary Byrnes hope he will reconsider.

I am wondering just what his reasons are, but in any case, I feel there is no one who has had his long experience, nor been as devoted to the ideal of the United Nations, and if it is possible for you and Secretary Byrnes to get him to continue, I think it will keep a great many of us from feeling that the cause is a lost cause.

I can not help feeling that we need to be firm but we haven't always been firm in the right way in our foreign policy because one can only be successfully firm, if the people one is firm with, particularly the Russians, have complete confidence in one's integrity and I am not sure that our attitude on questions like Spain and the Argentine[1] and even in Germany itself, has been conducive to creating a feeling that we would always keep our word and that we would always talk things out absolutely sincerely before we took action. We are bound to differ, of course, because we have fundamental differences, but I think these should be made clear, if at the top there is a complete sense of confidence and security and the policies at the top were really carried on at every level.

Very cordially yours,

Note

1. In April 1946 Spain received a $7.5 million Argentine loan to buy food. Later that year, Spain, under the rule of Francisco Franco, sent an economic mission to Argentina, where Juan Peron ruled as dictator. The terms of another Argentine loan were negotiated in October and announced in December.

Eleanor Roosevelt to Harry S Truman

June 30, 1946

As Truman settled into the presidency and began to deal with the many burdens of his office, he started planning for the congressional elections of 1946. A concerned Mrs. Roosevelt wrote to offer suggestions, especially with regard to the role of women in the Democratic Party. She strongly encouraged Truman to use the women effectively.

June 30, 1946

Dear Mr. President:

I have just received an item from News Week, which states that you have told your advisers to be on the lookout for women qualified to take over several top jobs in the Administration.

This item was sent to a friend of mine who forwarded it to me, by the chairman of the Women's Congressional Committee, in Washington. This group represents a rather large number of women's organizations and I think among them, there are several people who have been afraid that in the reorganization of the government, women were being eliminated from important jobs and functions, such as the Children's Bureau, which had been of particular interest to women, in being integrated with other groups, were passing out of control of the women who had headed them and might be completely changed in their aims. This item will, I think, encourage them.

I used to have to remind the gentlemen of the Party rather frequently that we Democrats did not win unless we had the liberals, labor and women largely with us. Among our best workers in all campaigns, are the women. They will do the dull detail work and fill the uninteresting speaking engagements which none of the men are willing to undertake. I hope you will impress this fact on those who are now organizing for the Congressional campaigns and in preparation for 1948.

With every good wish, I am,

Very cordially yours,

Eleanor Roosevelt to Harry S Truman
November 8, 1946

The mid-term elections resulted in the Republican Party gaining control of Congress for the first time since the Hoover administration. This was clearly a setback for Democrats, but Mrs. Roosevelt endeavored to emphasize positive aspects of the outcome when she wrote to the president. Truman responded on November 14, agreeing with her that the situation in Congress could not be much worse than it had been earlier. He thought he could get more done, or at least go on record for change with a Republican Congress. He belived he could achieve more than would have been the case "had we been responsible for a Congress which was not loyal to the party."

November 8, 1946

Dear Mr. President:

I know the election must have been a disappointment to you, as it was to me. I had expected some losses but not quite such sweeping ones.

However, I am not at all sure that you will not get as much out of a straight out Republican Congress, which now has to take the responsibility for whatever happens, as you got out of the type opposition which the coalition of reactionary Democrats and Republicans created.

With my very best wishes to you and my warm regards to Mrs. Truman and Margaret,[1] I am,

Very cordially yours,

Note

1. Margaret Truman, daughter of President Harry Truman.

Eleanor Roosevelt to Harry S Truman
April 16, 1947

As usual Mrs. Roosevelt did not hesitate to tell President Truman what she thought of world affairs. In this letter she comments on the Greek-Turkish problem. This

*related, of course, to the efforts of Communist movements to subvert the govern-
ments of Greece and Turkey in the immediate postwar period, which led to massive aid that became known as the Truman Doctrine. Mrs. Roosevelt is rather critical of Averell Harriman of New York, a man who ranked as a first-rate diplomat. She
did think Dean G. Acheson, one of Truman's foreign policy advisers who later served
as secretary of state, was too pro-British. Her strong words, like those of most everyone else in this period, underscored her anxiety about the Soviet Union, offering
her advice to that which Truman had obtained from other quarters.*

April 16, 1947

Dear Mr. President:

The enclosed wire has just come to me and I am sending it on to you because I think you should read it.

I have been very much disturbed by the whole Greek-Turkish situation. I went to see Averell Harriman and I do not feel happy after talking to him. I have known him since he was a boy and he is not a very strong person, though a very nice and well meaning one.

Between the Pepper Bill[1] and the Vandenberg Amendment[2] to the Administration Bill, there is a middle course which you could lead. Our domestic and our foreign policies are so closely tied together, and the various moves which have been made of late, are so evidently politically oriented, that I feel some very clear, far-sighted thinking is needed.

I do not believe that the Democratic party can win by going the Republican party one better in conservatism on the home front. Nor do I believe that taking over Mr. Churchill's policies in the Near East, in the name of Democracy, is the way to really create a barrier to communism or promote Democracy.

I do not think your advisors have looked far enough ahead. Admiral Leahy[3] as always, will think of this country as moving on its own power.

Both in Commerce and in Agriculture, we have not been far sighted enough to see that it was through:

1.the safe guarding of food supplies even though it might mean we had a little more than we need on hand

2- the getting of business men to work in Europe, and that includes Russia, that we can really hope to rehabilitate Europe and establish democracy.

Mr. Acheson is rather more sympathetic to the British point of view than I would be, and what with Mr. Lewis Douglas[4] who will certainly be sympathetic to Mr. Churchill's point of view, I am afraid we are apt to lose sight of the fact that if we do not wish to fight Russia, we must be both honest and firm with her. She must understand us and she must also trust us.

Please give my kind regards to Mrs. Truman and to Margaret.[5] I hope the latter is feeling encouraged about her work. So many people have spoken favorably to me after hearing her on the radio.

Very cordially yours,

Notes

1. Named for Sen. Claude D. Pepper of Florida.
2. Named for Sen. Arthur H. Vandenberg of Michigan.
3. Adm. Willian D. Leahy, chief of staff for Roosevelt and Truman during World War II.
4. Lewis W. Douglas, United States ambassador to Great Britain.
5. Margaret Truman aspired to be a professional singer but was sometimes panned by the critics.

Eleanor Roosevelt to Harry S Truman
April 17, 1947

The day after writing the previous letter, Mrs. Roosevelt forwarded another version of it. They are almost identical, but the second one was slightly longer. Which of these letters, or both, were mailed is not known.

April 17, 1947

Dear Mr. President:

I have carried on a lengthy correspondence with Secretary Acheson and I have seen a State Department representative sent by Secretary Acheson, to explain the Greek-Turkish situation to me.

I went to see Averell Harriman the other day to try to get some enlightenment from him. I know that his appointment was very favorably received. Harry Hopkins thought highly of him but that was largely because he knew he could count on Averell to carry out directions. He is rich and generous and well meaning. I have known him since he was a boy. I like him very much personally but I came away from talking to him, feeling that there was not sufficient realization of the domestic situation we are facing and its tie up with the foreign situation.

Our domestic and foreign policies are so closely tied together and the various moves made of late are so politically oriented, I feel some very clear sighted thinking is needed.

Between the Pepper Bill and the Vandenberg Amendment to the Administration Bill, there is a middle course. For that reason I am enclosing a copy of a wire which has come to me that expresses anxiety and makes some suggestions similar to those which have been made by other people. I am not sending it because it came from Aubrey Williams,[1] but because it is comprehensive enough to be a good sample of a considerable amount of thinking which seems to be going on throughout the country.

I do not believe that the Democratic party can win by going the Republican party one better in conservatism on the home front. Nor do I believe that taking over Mr. Churchill's policies in the Near East, in the name of democracy, is the way to really create a barrier to communism or promote Democracy.

I do not think your advisors have looked far enough ahead. Admiral Leahy as always, will think of this country as moving on its own power.

Both in Commerce and in Agriculture, we have not been far sighted enough to see that:

1.The safe guarding of food supplies for the world, even though it might mean keeping a little more than we need on hand was a wise policy.

2.The getting of business men to work in Europe and Russia is the only way we can hope to rehabilitate Europe and establish democracy.

Mr. Acheson is rather more sympathetic to the British point of view than I would be, and what with Mr. Lewis Douglas, who will certainly be sympathetic to Mr. Churchill's point of view, I am afraid we are apt to lose sight of the fact that if we do not wish to fight Russia, we must be both honest and firm with her. She must understand us, but she must also trust us.

Please give my kind regards to Mrs. Truman and to Margaret. I hope the latter is feeling encouraged about her work. So many people have spoken favorably to me after hearing her on the radio.

Very cordially yours,

Note

1. Aubrey W. Williams, an Alabama social worker and editor who had been a New Deal administrator.

Eleanor Roosevelt to Harry S Truman
May 16, 1947

In May 1947 Mrs. Roosevelt wrote to President Truman to urge him to do what he could to have the papers of her husband placed in the library in Hyde Park, New York. She fervently wanted to carry out her husband's wishes.

May 16, 1947

Dear Mr. President:

Because of the various things I have heard, I am sending you this note.

I know that it was my husband's wish and intention that all of his papers should eventually be in the Library at Hyde Park. He particularly did not want them left in the Archives in Washington or in the Library of Congress because he felt that concentration in one place was very unwise. He also felt that they would be more available to historians in the library at Hyde Park and I am sure they will be.

I hope you will not mind my telling you this, but I feel so strongly that in this one particular I would like to see his wishes carried out, that I am expressing what I have heard my husband say over and over again.

Very cordially yours,

[*HSTL*]

Eleanor Roosevelt to Harry S Truman
June 7, 1947

Mrs. Roosevelt kept attuned to the political situation in the United States, even if at times she miscalculated matters. This letter is a candid report on the situation in California and a conflict that existed between her son James and the party leaders of California, especially Edwin W. Pauley, an oil operator who had been treasurer of the Democratic National Committee in 1944, and Gael Sullivan, second assistant postmaster general who resigned in 1947 to become executive director of the Democratic National Committee. She expressed concern regarding Pauley's contention that a draft policy statement from California insulted Truman, but after she had read it carefully she saw no such insult. Essentially, she worried about the impact on the Democratic Party, both nationally and in California, at a time when unity was needed badly. She referred to his opposition to Helen Gahagan Douglas, a liberal member of Congress who lost the United States Senate election in 1950 to Richard M. Nixon, who attacked her as a Com-

munist. Mrs. Roosevelt also commented on Secretary of State Gen. George Marshall's speech at Harvard, where he proposed aid to the countries of Europe as a way of assisting them in their recovery and of combating the spread of Communism. This was the origin of the Marshall Plan.

June 7, 1947

Dear Mr. President:

I was deeply distressed when I got out to Los Angeles to speak at the dinner for the Southern California State Committee group to find that Mr. Pauley and my son, James, had entirely different points of view on a proposed policy plan which had been drawn up by James and the policy committee for submission to the State Committee.

I found that owing to Mr. Pauley's suggestion, this document which was to have been given to the people at the Jackson Day dinner, was not to be distributed but that James told them he would have to have it mailed to members of the State Committee for future action and when that was done, of course it would be in the papers.

Mr. Pauley took the position that he disagreed with certain things in the statement and felt that what was said on foreign policy was an insult to you. I read it through very carefully and it did not seem to me in any way insulting. It voiced simply the questions which are in many people's minds and it seemed to me that it gave to Mr. Gail Sullivan an opportunity, if he wanted to, to clear up some of these questions, and if he disapproved, to ask the State Committee to change the things he thought unwise. He could even have expressed censure of James as state chairman and I think it would have left the feeling better among the people who attended the dinner.

I, of course, had no sense that his presence or absence at the dinner was any insult to me, but I think he did do harm to the position of the Democratic Party in the eyes of one of the largest dinners that they have ever had in Los Angeles.

You know I have never seen eye to eye with Mr. Pauley. He has always fought Mrs. Helen Gahagen Douglas and I have always believed in the things she has stood for. He did a very good job of raising money for the national committee. He often disagreed with my husband.

As I think back upon the many things which were said about my husband by southern Democrats and others within the Party, I can not see that the language in which this proposed statement is couched, is in any way insulting to you. I think a clever national chairman with a wiser national committeeman could have handled the situation and left the party in better condition instead of in a worse condition.

I understand that Mr. Pauley was much annoyed because in a press conference, I said that I felt ways had to be found to get on with Russia. That does not mean we have to appease Russia. I do not believe the Russians want to go to war. Neither do we but I think the ingenuity to find ways to get what we want rests with us.

I thought General Marshall's speech at Harvard was the beginning of a constructive suggestion, but it seems to me some thing has to happen very soon and some people in the industrial world in this country have got to be brought to the realization that the thing which will strengthen Russia above everything else, is a depression in this country. She is waiting and longing for that and the effect on the rest of the world will be disastrous. I do not attribute high-mindedness to the Politbureau. I think undoubtedly they hope that the peoples of the world will turn to communism. There is only one way of answering that and that is by proving to the peoples of the world that Democracy meets their needs better. This isn't a question of Greece and Turkey alone. This is a question of many things which have to be worked simultaneously on a world scale.

There is too much to be done in the world to allow for resentments. The real honest questioning such as was contained in the California State Committee document might much better have met with real answers which many people are confronting and on which they seek wider understanding of government policies.

I hope you will forgive my speaking so frankly, but I have your interests and the interests of the Party at heart.

Very sincerely yours,

Eleanor Roosevelt to Jonathan Daniels

June 18, 1947

Within two years after the death of Franklin Roosevelt, members of the Roosevelt family decided to donate the "Little White House" in Warm Springs, Georgia, to the state of Georgia. Mrs. Roosevelt wrote to Jonathan Daniels, son of Josephus Daniels, an important figure in the Woodrow Wilson era as secretary of the navy, who was to take her place at the transfer and dedication ceremonies.

June 18, 1947

Dear Mr. Ambassador:

I am very happy that you are taking my place at these ceremonies when the little house in Warm Springs, in which my husband spent so many happy hours, is to be turned over to the State of Georgia.

It means a great deal to me that Miss Laura Delano, my husband's cousin, who was with him in Warm Springs when he died, will represent our family at these ceremonies since none of the near family could be present.

I hope the "Little White House" in Georgia will give pleasure and interest to many visitors who may come to Warm Springs and to the patients there. I hope it will serve as a reminder of what a gallant spirit can accomplish in spite of physical handicaps.

With many thanks for your constant and warm friendship, I am,

Affectionately yours,

Eleanor Roosevelt to George C. Marshall
Draft, n.d. [June 1947?]

Eleanor Roosevelt was very concerned about the loyalty oaths President Truman had instituted and the fact that the State Department had dismissed a number of people who had not been proven guilty of anything. As a delegate to the United Nations, she felt constrained in speaking out on this matter, but she planned to write about it in her column after the current session of the U.N. General Assembly was over. To that end, she drafted a letter to George Marshall, Secretary of State.

[June 1947?]

Dear Mr. Secretary:

I had hoped to see you or talk with you over the telephone before you left for Europe, however, I am afraid now you will be off before I have the chance to do so. I wish you well on your trip! It looks to me as though the Russians had reached the point where they wanted to come to terms. I certainly hope so.

There is one thing which has troubled me very greatly. Being on the delegation, I have felt that I could not write about it in my column but I shall do so as soon as the Assembly comes to an end, and before doing so I want to tell you what my feeling is. From every side, from all my Liberal, Democratic & Republican friends, I am getting protests on the State Department's attitude towards the people which it has dismissed. I know it was not a policy initiated by you, but evidently Mr. Lovett[1] felt that he had to go along with it and you felt that you had to back him up. The story in the Herald Tribune has made a deep impression on a lot of people.

I understand you had to dismiss these people because Mr. Tabor[2] [*sic*] published a list and refused any further appropriations unless you did. I know what pressure Congress can bring to bear. I do not know whether this story is true or not but it seems to me that even Congress would have to recognize that in peacetime, things which might be condoned in wartime, take on a different aspect. People are entitled to a hearing or else resigning without prejudice. The situation will soon be that a person who leaves the State Department unless he is offered a job before leaving, is going to find it hard to get another job as people will think there is something against him. I am not very happy about the President's Loyalty test because any communist would sign to it and the rest of us feel a little besmirched as we sign, and not quite sure that our country is a strong enough Democracy not to fear Communism.

I have written the President a letter and I enclose a copy of it. As I go to the Human Rights Commission meetings I am not quite sure that I think our country is preserving its freedoms as carefully as I would like.

I hope to leave for home on the 18th of Dec. I hope that you too will be coming home at this time.

Sincerely yours,

Notes

1. Robert Abercrombie Lovett of New York served as secretary of defense from 1951 to 1953.

2. John Taber, Republican chairman of House of Representative Committee on Appropriations.

Eleanor Roosevelt to Jonathan Daniels

June 20, 1947

In 1947 Jonathan Daniels sent Mrs. Roosevelt clippings of an article and an editorial regarding the relationship between James A. Farley and Franklin Roosevelt. Farley had been Roosevelt's campaign director and was later postmaster general. He wrote an article for Collier's *magazine in which he outlined the five reasons that he broke with Roosevelt in 1940. According to the newspaper article, Farley quoted Mrs. Roosevelt as saying, "Franklin finds it hard to relax with people who aren't his social equals. I took this remark to explain my being out of the infield." Mrs. Roosevelt wrote to Daniels to thank him for the clippings and to explain some things about the relationship between her husband and Farley.*

June 20, 1947

Dear Mr. Ambassador:

Thank you very much for sending me your article on Jim Farley. I never have made such a statement and I am afraid he must have misunderstood what I said. I probably said that Franklin might not easily relax with people who did not have the same types of interest and that I did not think he had as good a time. His friendship with Churchill, with whom he sometimes disagreed, was real and they had a good time talking nonsense rhymes and talking of things of a variety of interest.

I always felt that with Al Smith he admired him for his statesmanship, his ability in government and his great development in many ways, from a meager background to a prominent position. As people they had few mutual interests, so they did not have that flow of natural intercourse, when you don't talk business or politics or things of mutual interest.

I never realized he was so sensitive and felt so insecure and could be so easily hurt by little things or I would have thought more about him. He just didn't seem like that sort of person. Sometime I am going to go see him and try to straighten out some of these things but not while these articles are going on.

Affectionately,

Eleanor Roosevelt to Harry S Truman
July 26, 1947

While vacationing at Campobello in Canada, Mrs. Roosevelt heard from a friend that President Truman planned to nominate her again for the United States delegation to the United Nations. This was a note of thanks.

Campobello Island
New Brunswick, Canada
July 26, 1947

Dear Mr. President:

Hershel Johnson[1] told me that you were sending my name to the Senate again as a member of the United States Delegation to the United Nations General Assembly.

I am very grateful to you for this further opportunity to work with the United Nations and only hope that we will accomplish something worth while and justify your confidence in us.

I hope the summer is proving a little restful for you and your family.

Very cordially yours,

[*HSTL*]

Note

1. Herschel V. Johnson, a foreign service officer who was a United States representative on the United Nations Security Council.

Eleanor Roosevelt to Harry S Truman
August 9, [1947]

On July 26, 1947, President Truman's mother, Martha Ellen Young Truman, died at age ninety-four in Grandview, Missouri. Because she knew how close he had been to his mother and because of his sorrow, Mrs. Roosevelt sent Truman a handwritten note of condolence on his loss.

August 9, [1947]

Dear Mr. President:

I have waited to write you because after sending off one wire I realized what an avalanche of messages that you would receive. Nevertheless I want to send my deep sympathy for I know so well how much you will miss your mother. As long as the older generation is with us we feel a certain protection. When they go we become the frontier ourselves & it is a lonesome feeling.

The fact that your Mother was ill was a preparation for the final blow but when you have thought daily about someone their passing is an added ache. She must have been a wonderful person & her pride in you must give you happiness.

I hope your trip will bring you some diversion & I just wanted you to know that our thoughts were with you & your family in the sad days just passed—

Cordially yours,
Eleanor Roosevelt

P.S. Please do not answer.
[*HSTL*]

Eleanor Roosevelt to Henry A. Wallace

September 25, 1947

*Disturbed by a speech that Wallace, now editor of the New Republic, had deliv-
ered before the electrical workers in Boston, Mrs. Roosevelt quickly defended
those individuals within the electrical workers union who had been fighting the
Communist groups. She particularly praised the work of James B. Carey, who
was national secretary of the Congress of Industrial Organizations (CIO), a
supporter of President Roosevelt's policies, and a former member of the Production Planning Board of the Office of Production Management.*

September 25, 1947

Dear Mr. Wallace:

Your speech before the electrical workers in Boston has just been brought
to my attention.

By implication you seem to be condemning the little group within the
electrical workers union which has fought the communist group. Perhaps
you do not remember that Jim Carey was ousted by the communist group
and was one of a small group which continued to agitate for the things for
which he stood, and that group, under his leadership has been trying to regain control.

I wondered if you knew this and realized that what you said was thought
by many people to be an attack on Jim Carey and his group.

Very sincerely yours,

Eleanor Roosevelt to Dwight D. Eisenhower

October 24, 1947

*Because of his hero status from World War II, Gen. Dwight D. Eisenhower was
sought after as a speaker. Mrs. Roosevelt was no exception in her interest in him
and the publicity his presence could bring to groups. This letter was another
invitation from her to speak at a ceremony honoring a British woman whom
Eisenhower had known during the war.*

October 24, 1947

Dear General Eisenhower:

On February 9th, 1948, the National Achievement Award which is sponsored by Chi Omega, will give its annual award to Lady Reading. This is con-

fidential because the name of the person to receive the medal is not announced until the evening of the presentation.

This award is given to women in various fields as an encouragement and inspiration to young women in colleges and in various fields of art, science and business. It has always been given in the past to an American woman. Dr. Alice Hamilton,[1] Frances Perkins, Katharine Cornell[2] are some of the American women who have received this award.

The committee of which I am a member felt that this year we wanted to name Lady Reading in recognition of the magnificent job she did with the women of Great Britain during the war and the democratic way in which it was done. She could not come to the United States this fall, so we are postponing the ceremony until next February.

Because of your association with Lady Reading we would be very happy to have you attend the dinner at Pierre's at 7:00 p.m. on February 9th. There will be a larger meeting in the same hotel at 8:45 p.m. The details of when we would like to have you speak are not yet worked out, but if you are able to be with us the full details will be sent you very soon.

Very cordially yours,

[*DDEL*]

Notes

1. A pioneer in industrial toxicology and a social reformer.
2. Katherine Cornell, an actress and producer.

Eleanor Roosevelt to Harry S Truman
November 13, 1947

In a draft letter, Mrs. Roosevelt expressed serious reservations about loyalty tests and other activities to discover communists in the bureaucracy inaugurated by the Truman administration. Truman responded by assuring her that numerous safeguards had been provided to protect the civil rights of government employees. Mrs. Roosevelt felt sorry that she would not be able to see him before departing for the Human Rights Commission meeting in Geneva, Switzerland. The strikeouts were parts of the draft that she deleted and the underlined words are those that she inserted.

11/13/47

Dear Mr. President:

I have wanted to write you for a long time as I have been getting from all of my friends, Republicans and Democrats alike, such vi (?) reactions to the Loyalty Tests. And now, after the dismissal of the 10 people from the State Department and the article in the Herald Tribune, I feel I must write you.

I particularly do not feel that ~~Mrs.~~ Meta Glass[1] should be ~~the head of~~ only on the Committee for Review as she is not a strong enough person. I feel another woman should be appointed. Perhaps Mrs. Lewis Thompson[2] of Red Bank who is a strong Republican but also a liberal, together ~~with other women who might want to be on the committee, if it is possible to put any more people on it at the present time.~~ might help interpret the work of the committee to the public. Certain things ~~which have been done should~~ need to be interpreted to the public. My own reaction is anything but happy. I feel we have capitulated to our fear of Communism, and instead of fighting to improve Democracy, we are doing what the Soviets would do in trying to repress anything ~~else~~ which we are afraid might not command public support, in order to insure success of our own way.

I am sorry that I cannot see you before I go to Geneva ~~on~~ to the Human Rights Commission meeting and since this session of the General Assembly is drawing to an end, I want to thank you for your kindness in appointing me. It has been interesting work and I hope that I have been helpful. When I return from Geneva and the holidays are over, I will try to come to Washington in order to see you again.

With best wishes to Mrs. Truman and Margaret and congratulations to her on her successes, and wishing you all a Happy Thanksgiving and Christmas season, I am,

Very sincerely yours,

Notes

1. Dr. Meta Glass, former president of Sweet Briar College.
2. Geraldine Thompson, longtime correspondent with ER who was involved in prisons, reformatories, and mental institutions in Massachusetts and New Jersey.

Eleanor Roosevelt to George C. Marshall
[November 13, 1947?]

In November 1947 Eleanor Roosevelt contacted Secretary of State Marshall about her concern that the civil liberties of some people were being threatened by the government's policy regarding security risks. She mentioned the Dies Committee, headed by Democratic congressman Martin Dies Jr., the 1930s predecessor

of the House Un-American Activities Committee (HUAC). Mrs. Roosevelt dis-
cussed the infamous FBI list of subversive organizations and noted that Franklin
Roosevelt's mother was on the list as a contributor to one of the organizations
and thus of questionable loyalty. Robert Lovett, Under Secretary of State, an-
swered her letter on behalf of Secretary of State Marshall, who was out of town
at the time.

Draft, not typed n.d.   [November 13, 1947?]

I read in the press of the action taken by the Dept. & I was very glad. I am
grateful to you for your letter & for the sense of security it gives me to know
that you are watching out for the preservation of certain fundamental democratic procedures.

One of the other rumors that has come to me is that the accusation primarily urged against one of the people under suspicion was that he was an
active member of the PCA.[1] It happens that I have given up any activities
with PCA because I am convinced that there are people in the top level in
that organization that still are closely connected with the Communist party
in this country or who are too chicken hearted & afraid of being called red-
baiters. Therefore, they serve the purposes of the party. Nevertheless, I do
know a great many people who are active in PCA who are just straight liberal &
are sincerely troubled by the hysteria on communism which is sweeping the
country at the present time as well as by certain gov't actions which rightly or
wrongly they feel tend to create an atmosphere which may bring about war. I
do not think that any man can just be condemned because he is a member of
PCA unless one found something on which to question his loyalty.

Of course I am so familiar with rumors I sometimes discount too much.
Therefore I had not thought about this very seriously but when 2 or 3 people
spoke to me about it I decided it was worth mentioning it.

I do not doubt that some of these people have questionable things in
their record, but I remember when my husband & I heard about a list the FBI
had of organizations that were considered subversive & anyone who had contributed to those organizations was automatically considered by the Dies Com
to be questionable. My husband told me I could ask to see it & we spent an
evening going through it & believe it or not, my husband's mother was one
of the first people named because she contributed to a Chinese relief organ &
both Secy Stimson[2] & Secy Knox[3] were listed as having contributed to several
organizations. Of course it is evident that they could stand up under those
accusations but little people would be condemned for as flimsy a reason.

Forgive me for writing a long letter again but I have been troubled by what looks like a real chance that some of the methods of the Russians might be coming our way.

V. Cord yrs,

Notes

    1. Progressive Citizens of America.
    2. Secretary of War Henry Stimson.
    3. Secretary of the Navy Frank Knox.

Eleanor Roosevelt to Harry S Truman
November 25, 1947

As Mrs. Roosevelt prepared to travel to Geneva, Switzerland, for the Human Rights Commission meeting, she wrote a note to President Truman to congratulate him on his courage and to inform him that the former Greek premier, succeeded by Themistocles Sophoulis, had expressed the profound gratitude of his country for the support Truman had provided when the president in March 1947 asked Congress for funds to help Greece and Turkey resist Soviet pressures. Congress authorized the expenditure of $400 million to implement the Truman Doctrine, aimed against totalitarianism in Europe.

November 25, 1947

Dear Mr. President:

I read your message to Congress and I want to tell you that I thought it very courageous and very good in every way. I am sure you have had many favorable comments.

The old Greek Prime Minister[1] came to see me and asked for me to tell you how grateful they are for what has been done for Greece. They hope you will back some form of a middle-of-the-road government and try to draw the two extremes together.

I leave on Friday for the Human Rights Commission meeting in Geneva, and I am sorry not to have had the opportunity of seeing you before I go. I hope I shall be able to get to Washington around the 12th of January, and that you will be free to see me. If I may, I shall ask for an appointment when I know just when I will be in Washington.

With my every good wish to you and Mrs. Truman and Margaret, I am,

Very cordially yours,

Note

    1. Constantin Tsaldaris.

Eleanor Roosevelt to Harry S Truman
December 23, 1947

Shortly after she returned from the Human Rights Commission meeting in Geneva, Switzerland, Mrs. Roosevelt sent President Truman a letter to praise him for several things. She supported the civil rights report and mentioned with some glee that the Republican attitude over the Marshall Plan, the European Recovery Program for aiding nations in economic restoration after World War II, would hurt the GOP in the long run. Mrs. Roosevelt asked for an appointment with him so that she could report on her sojourn in Europe.

December 23, 1947

Dear Mr. President:

This is just to tell you that I read your committee's report on Civil Rights and thought it very good.

While I am writing about this, I want to tell you how very courageous I thought your message was on the Marshall Plan. The Republicans are playing into our hands with their voluntary anti-inflation measures but we will have to act immediately to make the best of it. If they do a lot of arguing over the Marshall Plan I think they will find themselves in hot water there too.

I am coming to Washington on the 12th of January and hope very much you will have some free time on the 13th, as I should like to report to you on the Human Rights Commission session.

With every good wish to you and Mrs. Truman and Margaret for the New Year, I am,

Very cordially yours,

Eleanor Roosevelt to Harry S Truman
[draft 1948?]

Apparently in early 1948, Mrs. Roosevelt expressed concern about the world situation to President Truman. She worried about the rising conservative trend and the related possibility of Republican victories. Her views on the Middle East and the importance of its oil seemed almost premonitory in light of later events. Her opinion as to the results of a possible Republican victory is surprising.

[draft 1948?]

Dear President:

I have been meaning to write you for the last few days but because the letter is not too pleasant, I have been putting it off.

It is hard for the people around a President to tell him they are troubled and of course, there are many people who tell him only what they think will their serve their own interests or what they think he will want to hear.

I spoke to you when I was in Washington of the feelings that I sense that people are worried over the increasing military influence in the government. Now since the photo came out of the Marines going to the Pacific,[1] every young marine I know has told me that the men went with battle gear and they ask me are we landing in Greece, what are we doing any way, are we getting ready for war?

There is an increasing anxiety everywhere. There is also a fear of the conservative influence that is being exerted on the economic side and I am afraid that this deposition of Mr. Eccles[2] which the New York Times takes as a triumph of "orthoxody and conservatism in fiscal policy as represented by John W. Snyder, Secretary of the Treasury" is going to emphasize this feeling considerably.

Believe me, Sir, it is going to be impossible to elect a Democrat if it is going to be done by appealing to conservatives. The Republicans are better conservatives than we are. If the people are going to vote conservative, it is going to be Taft[3] or Dewey[4] and we might just as well make up our minds to it.

In addition we are going to need Jewish and Negro votes and something must be done about it from that point of view. The present embargo on arms to Palestine and the situation in the UN on that question are very serious. It seems to me that we should be preparing to tell the UN that we, at their request, are removing the embargo on arms and will help them to recruit a police force. It could be done on a voluntary basis but if we do not do it, I am very fearful that the Russians will do it which will move them into that part of the world and make them heroes in the UN.

Now I know very well that the defense people and probably the oil people are saying we must not offend the Arabs, that we need the oil and we will need it particularly if we are going to have trouble with Russia. I feel it absolutely essential that we do not have trouble with Russia but we can prevent it by being cleverer than Russia and keeping her out from the places where we do not wish her to be without offending her. That means we move first and we have a definite policy.

Great Britain has been arming the Arabs and has cooked up much of the trouble in that area for the very simple reason that Gr. Britain knows that only two people will buy Arab oil—the US and the United Kingdom. Russia will walk in and take it when she is ready. We have to out-think Gr. Britain as well as Russia and I am very much afraid that some people in the State Dept. and some people in the defense group are not thinking very far ahead and if the UN becomes a second League and disintegrates as it well may if it gets no support in this situation, then another war is inevitable. On top of that a Republican election is inevitable.

I hate to say these disagreeable things, but I would not feel that I was doing my job if I refrained from telling you what I believe at the present time.

I do not know Secy. Forrestal well enough to write him unsolicited but I am quite willing that you should tell him what I feel. There are two things that I wish to avoid above all else, one, war, two, a republican victory which would I think lead us in time to communism,

With deep humility and anxiety, I am,

Very sincerely yours,

Notes

1. In 1945 and 1946 several photographs appeared in American periodicals, such as *Time* and *U.S. News & World Report*, regarding the role of the United States Marines in China and the factors that led to Truman's decision to keep United States forces in dangerous areas.

2. Marriner Stoddard Eccles, chairman of the Federal Reserve Board from 1936 to 1948.

3. Robert A. Taft, Republican senator from Ohio.

4. Thomas E. Dewey, Republican governor of New York.

Eleanor Roosevelt to Harry S Truman

January 16, 1948

Anna Rosenberg, a Hungarian-born woman active in the Roosevelt administration in the National Recovery Administration, was sent on wartime missions to Europe by both Presidents Roosevelt and Truman. Truman later appointed her assistant secretary of defense, in which capacity she served from 1950 to 1953. Whether Mrs. Roosevelt's endorsement of her in this letter contributed to the appointment is not known. Mrs. Roosevelt seized upon this opportunity, however, to encourage the president regarding the social programs he had outlined and to warn about Henry A. Wallace, former vice president and probable presidential candidate in 1948, and how he could cut into the liberal cause.

January 16, 1948

Dear Mr. President:

I happened to see Mrs. Anna Rosenberg last evening and I find she is not doing very much in the public field at present and would like to be useful. I do not think she could give full time, but could give several days a week. She is a wonderful organizer and I thought perhaps you would like to consider her as head of your consumer food group.

She would not be interested unless it is really planned this time to do a truly educational job and an honest one all down the line.

I hope that you are going to make a real fight for every one of the social things that you mentioned in your message. Our party people in Congress should truly back you on those. With a little help from the liberal Republicans we ought to get some of them through.

The great trouble is that Mr. Wallace will cut in on us because he can say we have given lip service to these things by having produced very little in the last few years.

Very cordially yours,

[*HSTL*]

Eleanor Roosevelt to Walter White

January 20, 1948

In 1948 Eleanor Roosevelt was serving on the United Nations under the appointment of President Truman. Since she was so busy, she tried to resign as a member of the board of the National Association for the Advancement of Colored People (NAACP). Executive Secretary Walter White wrote her expressing the strong opinion of the board, who did not want her to resign. White said, "Your name means a great deal to us, particularly during this time of reaction when the bigots are trying to undo what you and your late husband fought for so valiantly." Mrs. Roosevelt bowed to the wishes of the board, and she commented on some UN activities in her letter to White.

January 20, 1948

Dear Mr. White:

I wrote to the UN about Mr. McClane[1] but I will write again.

I am very much flattered that the Board should want me to remain and of course, I will come to meetings when I can but I am afraid I am going to be a very unsatisfactory member this winter and spring.

I want to tell you that I doubt if you quite understood what happened in the Committee on Minorities and Discrimination in Geneva and in the Human Rights Commission. Jonathan Daniels moved to accept all petitions which would have included accepting the NAACP petition though nothing as yet be done about it. The Russians refused to include all and promptly suggested that only the NAACP and the International Democratic Women's group, which is communist dominated, should be received because they represented the most people. Naturally it could not consent to that and when it came up in the Human Rights Commission I took the same stand, namely, that we must accept all or none as we could not let the Soviet get away with attacking the United States and not recognize their own shortcomings. I think, however, we did one useful thing which was to recommend to the Economic and Social Council a review of the whole question of petitions and a request that they suggest ways of dealing with the petitions since the present institution is most unsatisfactory.

Very sincerely yours,

Note

1. G. Warren McClane, recommended by Walter White to fill the vacancy in the Radio Liaison Division of the U.N.

Eleanor Roosevelt to Harry S Truman

January 29, 1948

The future of Palestine, in light of the British decision to withdraw from that area, was of vital importance to Mrs. Roosevelt—as it was to the president and other American leaders. She took every opportunity to remind Truman of the role of the United Nations and of the United States in this area.

January 29, 1948

Dear Mr. President:

I read Mr. Reston's[1] article in the New York Times the other day and I feel I want to write you on the question of Palestine and the United Nations.

It seems to me that if the UN does not put through and enforce the partition and protection of people in general in Palestine, we are facing a very serious situation in which its position for the future is at stake.

Since we led in the support of the UN and since we feel that the existence of the UN is essential to the preservation of peace, I think we should support a move on their part to create an international police force, perhaps from among the smaller nations, we should stand ready at the request of the UN to remove our embargo on arms and to provide such things which are essential to the control of the Arabs, namely, modern implements of war such as tanks, airplanes, etc.

If we do not take some stand to strengthen the organization at the present time, I shall not be surprised if Russia does which will put us in a difficult position to say the least.

Great Britain's role, of course, is not only to placate the Arabs, but probably to arm them because she knows very well that only the United States and Great Britain are going to buy Arab oil and she wants to be sure to hold her full share.

If the UN is going to be the instrument for peace, now is the crucial time to strengthen it.

With the deepest concern, I am,

Very sincerely yours,

Note

1. James Reston, writer for the *New York Times*.

Eleanor Roosevelt to Lyndon B. Johnson
[January 1948]

In January 1948 Lyndon Johnson, at the time a congressman from Texas, inserted in the Congressional Record a letter written by Fleetwood Richards, one of Johnson's constituents, on April 13, 1945, the day after President Roosevelt's death. It was a glowing tribute to Franklin Roosevelt. Mrs. Roosevelt wrote Johnson to thank him for his thoughtfulness. This is a draft written by Mrs. Roosevelt's secretary.

[handwritten draft; no date except January 1948]

Dear Mr. Johnson—

Grace Tully[1] sent me a copy of the remarks you inserted in the Congressional Record on my husband's birthday. The letter from Mr. Richards is a beautiful letter. I shall write him a note of gratitude.

I sincerely appreciate your tribute to my husband's memory & I shall always be grateful that my husband had your loyalty & support.

Note

1. One of FDR's secretaries.

Eleanor Roosevelt to Fleetwood Richards

[January 1948]

After Congressman Lyndon Johnson of Texas inserted in the Congressional Record a letter from a constituent praising Franklin D. Roosevelt in January 1948, Mrs. Roosevelt wrote to Mr. Fleetwood Richards, the author of the letter, to show her appreciation for his thoughts. This is a draft written by Mrs. Roosevelt's secretary.

[handwritten draft; no date except January 1948]

Richards

I have just read your letter which Repr Lyndon Johnson inserted in the Cong Record on my husband's birthday & I am deeply touched by it.

It was because of such friendship & loyalty as yours that my husband was able to accomplish what he did accomplish.

With my sincere gratitude, I am

Eleanor Roosevelt to Harry S Truman

February 20, 1948

In 1948 a serious question arose over whether Democrats could win in that year's election. President Truman appeared to be especially vulnerable. Mrs. Roosevelt worried about the appeal of Henry A. Wallace, the former secretary of agriculture, secretary of commerce, and vice president, who had become estranged from Truman and seemed to be a potential opponent in the presidential election that year. Mrs. Roosevelt wrote to advise Truman on the situation, especially in urban areas where people tended to be more radical, using the opportunity to comment upon the issue of an international peace force.

February 20, 1948

Dear Mr. President:

I was interested in your comment on the defeat of Ed. Flynn's[1] candidate in Bronx County. I think Ed. Flynn has proved the point which he has been trying to make for a long time, namely, that in large urban areas there are great groups of people who are extremely radical and very much opposed to what they feel is Military and Wall Street domination in our present Administration.

The people in the Bronx followed my husband because they felt he understood their needs and they were getting, domestically, protection which they had never had before. There has always been a strong element of communism in this section of the Bronx. I can remember it specifically among the youth groups back in 1933 and 1934. I noticed the night I spoke that every time Mr. Wallace's name was mentioned, it was cheered.

I was not very much surprised by the results of the vote because in the big, urban centers, even those who are Democrats just do not come out to vote because they are still radical enough to be unhappy about what they feel are certain tendencies they observe in our Administration.

Ed. Flynn has told you this, I think, on a number of occasions. It is important because if the Democrats are going to win in a State like New York, they have to carry by a great majority, the big urban centers. I am sure you are well aware of this, but I feel it my duty to re-enforce what [has] already been said, disagreeable as it is.

I never thought this district was a good one to hail as a pilot light of what would happen in the national election, but naturally it would be one which Mr. Wallace and the American Labor Party would pick to make much of, since they were almost sure of success.

Ed. Flynn, I think, felt that his organization would do much better than it did, but he did not count on the fact that even Democrats in areas such as this are unenthusiastic at the moment.

I wrote in my column the other day, as a result of the indications I find in my mail, that the two things bothering the average man most at present are inflation and the fear of another war. Congress is doing all it can to help us, I think, because certainly they are showing a complete disregard for the high cost of living as it affects the average human being, but you never know how many people realize this.

I know that in order to obtain what we need in the way of Military strength for defense, it would seem almost essential to whip up fear of communism and to do certain things which hurt us with the very element which we need in the election. How can we be firm and strong and yet friendly in our attitude toward Russia, and obtain from Congress what we need to keep us strong, is one our most difficult problems. I have often thought if you could explain the whole situation over the radio in a series of talks to the people of our country, it might clear up some of our difficulties, because I find great confusion in the minds of the average citizens.

Very sincerely yours,

P.S. James told me of Mr. Forrestal's feeling that no American should be allowed to volunteer in an International Police Force. I think Mr. Forrestal is entirely wrong. I was shocked at the suggestion that any American volunteering to fight in Palestine could lose his citizenship, and I could not understand why that was not invoked when Americans went to Canada and enlisted in the Canadian forces before we were in the war. It seems to me that if the UN calls for an International Police Force, it might very well say that the quotas should be equal from all nations, big and little, and then we should call for volunteers within our nation. To say that just because Russia might have some soldiers in Palestine on an equal basis with us and all the other nations involved, we would have to mobilize fifty percent for war, seems to me complete nonsense and I think it would seem so to most of the people of the United States.

Note

1. Edward Joseph Flynn, New York City Democratic boss.

Eleanor Roosevelt to George C. Marshall
Draft, not typed; first page only [February 1948?]

During the postwar era, Eleanor Roosevelt expressed concern about the situation in the Middle East, especially as the state of Israel was about to be recognized by the United States. She wrote George Marshall on more than one occasion. He answered her on February 16, 1948, emphasizing his concern about violence in the Palestinian area and stating that the United States wanted to approach the problem through the U.N. rather than unilaterally. Mrs. Roosevelt answered the letter, but only the first page of her response has survived.

Dear Mr. Secretary:

Thank you for your letter of Feb. 16th.

I am, of course, entirely in accord that we should approach the matter through the UN and not unilaterily, but in placing an embargo on arms we seem not to have interfered with the Arab's ability to get arms and the Jews seem to be getting them sub-rosa, so to speak, which isn't such a good thing. That is why the embargo seems to me unwise at the present time.

I would be in complete accord that we should do whatever the UN asks of us but I am seriously worried that Mr. Forrestal advises the President that even if the UN suggests a UN police force in which all nations have an equal quota, he would feel should Russia go in with the rest of us that he had to mobilize the US fifty percent for war at once. That seems to me utter nonsense and I do not understand it very well. It is an explosive situation and I think everyone should try to be as calm about it as they can. This last Jerusalem episode was certainly bad . . .

Eleanor Roosevelt to Harry S Truman
March 4, 1948

Concerned in 1948 with the deteriorating relationship between the United States and the Soviet Union, Mrs. Roosevelt wrote this letter to President Truman to bolster his courage against both those who would sell out to the Russians (former vice president Henry A. Wallace, perhaps) and the southern politicians such as Democratic senator Harry F. Byrd of Virginia and Democratic representative Edward E. Cox of Georgia, who took a narrow view of the world situation.

March 4, 1948

Dear Mr. President:

I was very much interested in your letter of February 27th, and I am glad you are not going to line up with those who want to sell us out to the Russian government, or with the Byrds and the Eugene Coxes!

These Southern statesmen seem to be very short-sighted and you are right when you say that the leadership in the Democratic Party is tired. Perhaps the people are too. Unfortunately, this is a bad time to be tired.

Thank you for your good wishes on my trip to Europe. I shall try to observe conditions and I shall try to find out from the Secretary of State before I go whether he has any particular points that he wishes stressed and any he wishes me to avoid in any speeches which I may make. I am going to London as you know, and to Brussels and to Holland. If you have any suggestions I shall be grateful to you if you will send them to me.

I hope your trip to Florida was enjoyable and of great benefit.

Very cordially yours,

[HST]

Eleanor Roosevelt to George C. Marshall
March 13, 1948

Mrs. Roosevelt was extremely worried about the Cold War and the possibility that we were on the verge of World War III. She wrote Secretary of State Marshall her concerns in some detail on the same day she sent a similar letter to President Truman.

March 13, 1948

Dear Mr. Secretary:

You will forgive me, I hope, if I write to you at this time, but I am becoming more and more worried. The situation abroad seems to me to be deteriorating rapidly as regards Russia and ourselves.

I think it has almost reached a point where it is essential that you and the President, with a picked group of two industrialists, two labor leaders, two people representing the general public, should really demand that Great Britain, Russia and ourselves, sit down around a table before we actually get to a point where we are in a war.

You say the situation is serious and any one can see that we can not let the USSR go on pulling coups in one country after another. It looks as though Sweden and Norway were pretty worried as to whether they will not be treated to the same kind of "invitation" that Finland has had, and certainly it will not be very difficult to pull a coup off in Italy.

Congress should be told in no unmistakable terms that its slowness and lack of imagination have caused much of the difficulty but they can not remedy that.

I am sure that we have not been blameless and probably the Russians think we have done some things against them. I am sure they believe we are trying to build up Germany again into an industrial state. I some times wonder if behind our backs, that isn't one of the things that our big business people would like to see happen in spite of two World Wars started by Germany.

If war comes and this final effort has not been made, I am afraid the people of this country are not going to feel that we have done all that we should have done to try to find a solution to the deteriorating situation between ourselves and the USSR.

I do not think that Ambassador Austin's[1] speeches on the Palestine question have given much impression that we really know what our policy is and that we are clear and decisive and ready to lead. The result is that I think the Arabs are taking advantage of us and of the situation as a whole.

I think the general public's feelings about the UN is one of increasing fear that it will not get the support from us which will make it a going concern.

Perhaps I am being a pessimist and I pray that I am, but the things that you and the President have been saying, plus the things that have been happening in the world the last few days, give me a sense that we need to do something drastic.

With apologies for troubling an overburdened man and assuring you that I do not want you to answer this, as I am really saying this so that I will have a clear conscience, I am,

Very sincerely yours,

Note

1. Warren Austin, a Republican internationalist from Vermont, served in the United States Senate from 1931 to 1946 and as United States representative to the United Nations from 1946 to 1953.

Eleanor Roosevelt to Harry S Truman
March 13, 1948

Worried about the Cold War and the possibility of World War III, Mrs. Roosevelt outlined her concerns in the letter to Secretary of State George C. Marshall above.

March 13, 1948

Dear Mr. President:

I am enclosing to you this copy of a letter which I have just sent to the Secretary of State.

I do not think I have been an alarmist before but I have become very worried and since we always have to sit down together when war comes to an end, I think before we have a third World War, we should sit down together.

You and the Secretary must feel the rest of us are a nuisance. Nevertheless, as a citizen I would not have a clear conscience if I did not tell you how I feel at the present time.

Very cordially yours,

[*HSTL*]

Eleanor Roosevelt to Harry S Truman
March 22, 1948

In the spring of 1948 Mrs. Roosevelt became so disillusioned with the policies of the Truman administration toward the United Nations that she offered her resignation as a representative to the UN from the United States. In this letter she vents her opinions frankly.

March 22, 1948

Dear Mr. President:

The events of the last few days since my last letter to you, have been so increasingly disquieting that I feel I must write you a very frank and unpleasant letter.

I feel that even though the Secretary of State[1] takes the responsibility for the Administration's attitude on Palestine, you cannot escape the results of that attitude. I have written the Secretary a letter, a copy of which I enclose, which will explain my feelings on this particular subject.

On Trieste[2] I feel we have also let the UN down. We are evidently discarding the UN and acting unilaterally, or setting up a balance of power by backing the European democracies and preparing for an ultimate war between the two political philosophies. I am opposed to this attitude because I feel that it would be possible, with force and friendliness, to make some arrangements with the Russians, using our economic power as a bribe to obstruct their political advance.

I can not believe that war is the best solution. No one won the last war, and no one will win the next war. While I am in accord that we need force and I am in accord that we need this force to preserve the peace, I do not think that complete preparation for war is the proper approach as yet.

Politically, I know you have acted as you thought was right, regardless of political consequences. Unfortunately, it seems to me that one has to keep one's objectives in view and use timing and circumstances wisely to achieve those objectives.

I am afraid that the Democratic Party is, for the moment, in a very weak position, with the Southern revolt and the big cities and many liberals appalled by our latest moves. The combination of Wall Street objectives and military fears seem so intertwined in our present policies that it is difficult to quite understand what we are really trying to do.

I realize that I am an entirely unimportant cog in the wheel of our work with the United Nations, but I have offered my resignation to the Secretary since I can quite understand the difficulty of having some one so far down the line openly criticize the Administration's policies.

I deeply regret that I must write this letter.

Very sincerely yours,

Notes

1. George C. Marshall.
2. A city in northeastern Italy taken over by the United Nations in 1946 and divided into two military zones.

Eleanor Roosevelt to George C. Marshall
March 22, 1948

When Mrs. Roosevelt wrote President Truman on March 22, 1948, she disclosed that she had expressed her views to Secretary of State George Marshall and decided to enclose a copy to Truman. This is the copy of the letter she sent to Marshall the same day. It states the same ideas she revealed to Truman, but the language is even more forceful. Although uncomfortable that she found herself is a strong position of opposition to the administration, Mrs. Roosevelt concluded that she had no other alternative, given her commitment to the United Nations.

March 22, 1948

Dear Mr. Secretary:

Yesterday I read your statement on Palestine twice with great care. I have a deep respect for you, but I feel that what you state is not satisfying from the point of view of achieving the desired results.

You say that we are seeking a peaceful solution of the Palestinian problem and you suggest that the new Mandate be set up. The new Mandate will have to enforce peace in just the way that the United Nations Commission would have had to enforce peace. If we have entered into some arrangement by which Great Britain's soldiers remain in Palestine, I do not think we will have peace and certainly if we try to set up a Mandate giving it to several nations and leaving the USSR out, we will offend the USSR deeply and create more tensions between us.

I had heard that Secretary Forrestal was so worried about the possibility that the UN might ask for a force in Palestine to which both the USSR and ourselves would have to contribute, that he felt we would never get the USSR out of Palestine and he would therefore feel that he had to mobilize this country fifty percent for war immediately. I wrote to the President some time ago that this seemed to me ridiculous and that we had to face the fact that joint forces, sometimes of equal strength, were the ultimate objective of the United Nations.

My feeling at the present moment is that in every possible way, the United States is acting to hurt the United Nations and to act on a unilateral basis. Our action on Trieste seems to bear this out and while I am conscious of the fact that we must defend ourselves against the Russians and we must be strong, I think it is unfortunate to do things which bring us legitimate criticism, and in this case, it looks as though the USSR were the only government that was upholding the United Nations Assembly decision.

I can not blame Senator Austin because he never was in agreement with the decision, but since it was taken largely to strengthen the United States and since I can not see that we have changed by our present action the possibility of having to use military force, I am deeply unhappy.

As you know, I feel we have a moral obligation, due to our acceptance of the Balfour Declaration[1] and our tacit agreement in the forming of a Jewish homeland by allowing capital to be spent and people to settle in the Palestine area. This new Mandate would have all of the problems such as immigration, and we have added to the Arabs' determination.

My greatest concern is for the UN even though I also have concern for upholding what I think is a moral obligation. I feel at the present time that we have more or less buried the UN. I can hardly see how it can recover and have the slightest influence, since we were the only ones who could give it any force and we now have been the ones to take it away.

I shall have to state my feelings publicly because I have been asked how I feel on this subject, and I do not feel it honest not to say what I believe.

If you wish me to resign from the Human Rights Commission I will, of course, be glad to do so, since I realize it is extremely difficult for you to have some one serve under you who openly criticizes the attitude of the Administration.

Very sincerely yours,

Note

1. A British government document, issued in 1917 by British Foreign Secretary Arthur J. Balfour, that dealt with the establishment of a Jewish homeland in Palestine.

Eleanor Roosevelt to Harry S Truman
March 26, 1948

On March 25, 1948, President Truman answered Mrs. Roosevelt's letter of March 22 and indicated that he had read the copy of the letter she sent to Secretary of State George C. Marshall. Marshall promised to dispatch Charles E. Bohlen, one of his assistants and an expert on Russian affairs, to confer with Mrs. Roosevelt, explain American policies, and answer her concerns. Truman reiterated as strongly as possible his support of the United Nations, being especially adamant that Mrs. Roosevelt not resign from the Human Rights Commission. Emphasizing that her resignation would be "calamitous" and was "unthinkable," he stated that there was "no one who could, at this time, exercise the influence which you can exert on the side of peace." This is Mrs. Roosevelt's response to Truman.

March 26, 1948

Dear Mr. President:

Your letter has reached me on the eve of my departure. It is a very fine letter and I am grateful to you.

I had a talk with Mr. Bohlen this afternoon and though I haven't heard from the Secretary he brought me some messages from him. I must say that talking with Mr. Bohlen did not give me a feeling of any great decisions on various questions, though he did make me feel that there was deep concern, and I understand some of the difficulties and intentions better than I did before.

However, I can not say that even now the temporary measures that we have suggested for Palestine really makes anything simpler or safer than it was before, but perhaps it will prove to be a solution and I certainly pray it will.

At the end of his visit Mr. Bohlen asked me about a statement which Franklin, junior had made and I want to tell you that while Franklin told me he intended to make this statement, he did not ask me for my opinion.

There is without any question among the younger Democrats a feeling that the party as at present constituted is going down to serious defeat and may not be able to survive as the liberal party. Whether they are right or wrong, I do not know. I made up my mind long ago that working in the United Nations meant, as far as possible, putting aside partisan political activity and I would not presume to dictate to my children or to any one else what their actions should be. I have not and I do not intend to have any part in pre-convention activities.

Very sincerely yours,

Eleanor Roosevelt to George C. Marshall
March 27, 1948

Secretary of State George Marshall had promised on March 13 that he would send Charles E. Bohlen, special assistant to the secretary of state, to brief Mrs. Roosevelt on the State Department's thinking on various foreign policy issues. On March 26, 1948, Bohlen visited her, but she was not convinced that the policies would work. She mentioned the E.R.P. (European Recovery Program), better known as the Marshall Plan, and she was still worried about the situation in Palestine.

March 27, 1948

Dear Mr. Secretary:

I am very grateful to you for sending Mr. Bohlen to see me yesterday. I, of course, understand your problems. I am not quite sure that I think we can rest until six months from now when E.R.P. is rolling even with the move which Mr. Bohlen outlined to me.

On the Palestine question, I still do not see that we are any better off with the present move or have any fewer problems than we had before.

As to the last thing which Mr. Bohlen said to me about the statement which Franklin, junior made, I told him that I never tried in any way to interfere with my children once they were grown. I haven't taken part in partisan politics and I do not intend to as long as I am on the United Nations, but the children must do whatever they think is right. Mr. Bohlen told me that you felt this move would so jeopardize President Truman's standing that it would hurt the position of our foreign policy in the world. I hardly think that is really true. In an election year all countries know that the man who is at the head of the government may not win. I happen to be a Democrat and to believe that it should be the liberal party of the country and I would be distressed to see liberalism in this country such [suffer] such a tremendous defeat that it could never be resusicated.

I know as you do that Senator Vandenberg is the best educated person on foreign affairs on the Republican side, but we are not sure of his nomination by the Republicans any more than we are of Mr. Truman's or anybody else, by the Democrats.

It is unfortunate that we have to have an election at a crucial time in the nation's history just as it was in 1940 and 1944, but we managed to have elections in both of those years when the rest of the countries gave up holding elections temporarily. I rather think we will weather holding an election this year. The rest or the world, including Russia, is quite conscious of public opinion and feeling that there [is] a movement for any other candidate growing in the country will not I think, be harmful as long as it is clearly understood that the foreign policy which the Administration and you are advocating, has the support of such people as may suggest other individuals for various reasons as possible candidates.

I understand your anxiety not to have anything rock the boat at the present time, but I doubt if the injection of any new Democratic or Republican candidate is going to have any great effect on the actions of the rest of the world.

Very sincerely yours,

Eleanor Roosevelt to Adlai Stevenson
April 28, 1948

In 1948 Adlai Stevenson was unknown nationally, but he was well acquainted with Eleanor Roosevelt from his earlier work in the New Deal. In 1948, despite his desire to run for the U.S. Senate, he agreed to his party's request to be the Democratic candidate for governor of Illinois. In response to an apparent request for help in the campaign, Mrs. Roosevelt demurred, mostly because of her position at the United Nations.

April 28, 1949

Dear Mr. Stevenson:

I would love to come out to help you but I am in a rather difficult position. I do not know whether I will be renominated for the General Assembly. If I am, I do not know when I would have to leave, but I would probably go a little before the opening as there are two or three things which if I go to Europe, I would like to do.

In any case, in view of the fact that I have disagreed with the policy of the Administration on the Palestine issue and was told by them that they would like to at least, to stay on the Human Rights Commission in spite of my feelings on the Palestine question, I think I had better not take any part in partisan politics as long as I am on the UN. It is a funny, mixed-up world, but for the moment I think the most important thing is to work on the UN as long as I can. I am very unhappy about going back on the Assembly decision on Palestine and I feel the handling of it up to this time, has brought about much of the Arab arrogance and violence. Certainly our proposal for a change does not seem, from my point of view, to have put us in any better position. Some body will have to implement a truce and somebody will have to implement a trusteeship. Some time the issue of serving on an equal basis with Russia under the UN will have to be faced.

Because I have said all this so firmly to both the President and the Secretary of State, I think it would be unwise for me to take an active part in partisan politics.

With every good wish for the success of your state ticket, I am,

Very cordially yours,

Eleanor Roosevelt and Gov. Adlai Stevenson. (Courtesy of the Franklin D. Roosevelt Library)

Eleanor Roosevelt to May Craig
May 11, 1948

May Craig, a longtime journalist from Maine who represented several newspapers and radio stations in the state, was a friend of Mrs. Roosevelt's. In 1948 she wrote Mrs. Roosevelt about the political situation—who was leading for the Republican nomination and details about President Truman running again. Mrs. Craig told the former first lady that her statement about not getting involved in partisan politics while serving the United Nations was being interpreted as her refusal to support President Truman for renomination and reelection. The matter concerned a number of people. Mrs. Roosevelt's answer was a bit evasive.

May 11, 1948

Dear May,

The affection expressed abroad for my husband is easy to understand because there are no politics involved. He was a friend who helped and encouraged them in time of crisis.

It seemed bad taste to me to ask me whether or not I would support the President as I came out of a meeting with him which was a business meeting on the Human Rights Commission, which neither he nor I could avoid. Even if I meant to oppose him, it would not be the appropriate moment to say so.

If I stay in the United Nations and go abroad to the General Assembly, I can't be active in the campaign. If I am not renominated, and do not go to Paris, then I'll decide. I was sure reporters would deduce much as you outline it but I haven't made up my mind.

This is for your confidential information.

I have no plans which include Washington but if I come and I have any free time, of course I'll let you know.

Affectionately,

Eleanor Roosevelt to George C. Marshall
May 11, 1948

Mrs. Roosevelt wrote this letter to the Secretary of State regarding the status of the Jewish state and sent a copy of it to President Truman with a similar letter. She explained how she believed the administration policy on the Jewish state should be made public, while taking the opportunity to discuss some of the problems with the draft Declaration of Human Rights of the United Nations.

May 11, 1948

Dear Mr. Secretary:

Thank you for sending me Ambassador Douglas's[1] letter. I am very happy that he told you what I said and that he felt the visit to Great Britain was helpful and created good feeling. I hope the visits to Holland, Belgium did the same.

I have just heard from some of the Jewish organizations that they have heard that Russia will recognize the Jewish State as soon as it is declared which will be midnight on Friday, I imagine. The people who spoke to me are afraid that we will lag behind and again follow instead of lead.

I have no idea what the policy of the Administration and the State Department is going to be on this, and I am only just telling you what you probably already know about the Russian position. I have no feeling that they have any principles or convictions in what they are doing, but wherever they can put us in a hole they certainly are going to do it.

The attitude of the International Law Committee of the Association of the Bar of the City of New York on the draft declaration of Human Rights and the Convention, of course, is going to coincide with the British Government's attitude as expressed by Lord Jowitt[2] in Parliament the other day. Neither country, apparently, is anxious to do anything at the present time. I feel that the Human Rights Commission has an obligation to present the best draft it can to the Economic and Social Council, but if they wish to recommend to the General Assembly that the Assembly consider the present documents and then refer them to governments for further comment, that is up to the Economic and Social Council or even to the Assembly itself.

It would please the Russians to begin all over again as they have suggested in this meeting, and try to find points on which we can all agree and base a Declaration on such points. I doubt very much if they at any time would consider a Convention.

I doubt very much also if the very restricted Convention suggested by the Bar Association will satisfy the European countries or the smaller countries on the Human Rights Commission, but I think we may have to state quite openly that we want a document which the larger number of governments can adhere to, that we hope there will be future conventions and that perhaps even we, ourselves, in view of the fact that Congress would have to ratify such treaties, can not agree to wording which goes beyond our own Constitution. It is an acknowledgement, of course, of the fact that we have discrimination within our own country. As that is well known, I do not see why we should not acknowledge it and bring out the fact that the Supreme

Court has just taken a step forward and we feel we are moving forward, but that in international documents it would be a deception to agree to go beyond what we could obtain ratification for in Congress.

I am sorry I did not see you when I was in Washington and I shall be delighted to have a chance to talk with you whenever it is possible. Just now my presence at the UN daily seems to be the most important thing for me.

Very cordially yours,

P.S. I failed to say that personally I believe there is right back of the establishment of a Jewish State.

[*HSTL*]

Notes

1. Lewis W. Douglas, U.S. ambassador to Great Britain.
2. Lord William A. Jowitt, Labour Party lord chancellor and presiding officer of the House of Lords.

Eleanor Roosevelt to Harry S Truman

May 11, 1948

In 1948 the future of the Jews in the Middle East assumed major proportions. The creation of a Jewish state—Israel—was on the minds of many. Mrs. Roosevelt wrote President Truman to express her belief that the American position needed to be made clear as soon as possible. She believed that United States relations with the Soviet Union and the Arabs would have been better if the American position were better. Enclosing a letter to Secretary of State George C. Marshall on this matter, she added in a handwritten postscript that she believed in a Jewish state.

May 11, 1948

Dear Mr. President:

I have just sent a letter to the Secretary of State, a copy of which I enclose for your information.

As I have said, I have no idea what the attitude of the Administration on the recognition of the Jewish State is going to be. If we are going to recognize it, I think we should make our position known as quickly as possible and the reasons for whatever position we take.

This action, as far as I am concerned, is interesting to me only from ethical and humanitarian points of view, but of course, it has political implications which I am sure your advisers will take into consideration. I am quite hopeful that whatever our policy is, it will be clear and consistent for I am more convinced every day that had the Arabs been convinced of what we really meant to do, they might have accepted the UN decision and not put us in the rather difficult position which the Security Council, minus any force, finds itself in today. I have heard it said that we were afraid of a UN force which included the Russians because of the difficulties we have had with them in Germany and Korea. Some day or other we have to be willing, if we are going to work out some peaceful solutions, to serve in some kind of a joint force and to agree we will all leave whatever country we may be in when the UN tells us to leave.

I was much encouraged by the report on the conversations between Ambassador Smith[1] and Mr. Molotov[2] as it came over the radio this morning. I think that kind of straight forward statement of fact is helpful and leaves the way open for peaceful negotiations in the future.

With my warm regards to Mrs. Truman and Margaret, I am,

Very cordially yours,

I failed to say that I personally believe in the Jewish State.

[*HSTL*]

Notes

1. Ambassador Walter B. Smith, U.S. ambassador to the Soviet Union.
2. Soviet commissar of foreign affairs.

Eleanor Roosevelt to Harry S Truman

May 13, 1948

Frequently, various groups approached Mrs. Roosevelt because of her influence with various public agencies and officials. This is a plea she received dealing with conscientious objectors from World War II who had not been pardoned in the action taken in 1947 by President Truman. She sent the statement along to Truman with her endorsement of a full pardon.

May 13, 1948

Dear Mr. President:

A group of people came to see me the other day about conscientious objection as related to human rights. At the same time they spoke to me about the conscientious objectors of the last war.

The following is an excerpt from their statement to me:

"The second matter has to do with the amnesty or pardon, for conscientious objectors in the United States in World War II. As you undoubtedly know, the commission headed by former Justice Roberts[1] reported to the President in December and on December 23, 1947, the President issued pardons to the persons listed by the Robert's Commission.

"However only about 1500 of the 15,000 Selective Service violators were included in the pardon. Of the approximately 1100 recognized as conscientious objectors by the Department of Justice only about 150 received pardons. Of the 3,000 or more Jehovah's Witnesses only a couple of hundred were included.

"In a very real sense those who were not included in the Commission's recommendation are now worse off than they were before, since the Department of Justice is taking the position that these persons have all been considered and is therefore declining to consider applications for individual pardons.

"Another extremely serious aspect of the matter is that the Roberts Commission applied a very narrow conception of 'religious relief' in determining which conscientious objectors were entitled to pardon. This appears to open the way for retrogression in dealing with conscientious objectors under any future military training or service act.

"The American Friends Service Committee, the Federal Council of Churches, and the American Civil Liberties Union, as well as the Committee for Amnesty, which is composed mainly of non-pacifist sponsors, have protested and urged a full amnesty, that is restoration of civil rights, for all conscientious objectors and Jehovah's Witnesses. However, at present there appears to be no progress."

I am sending this to you to ask if now full pardon should not be given?

Very cordially yours,

[*HSTL*]

Note

1. Former United States Supreme Court Justice Owen J. Roberts.

Eleanor Roosevelt to George C. Marshall

May 16, 1948

Mrs. Roosevelt never hesitated to inform government officials of her views on various matters. As an American delegate to the United Nations, she seemed especially vulnerable to criticism of American foreign policy. She was especially bothered by the manner in which the United States recognized the new state of Israel and what she perceived to be a lack of communication between the higher levels of the Truman administration and those at lower levels, such as the United Nations. The next day she sent a copy of the letter to President Truman.

May 16, 1948

Dear Mr. Secretary:

Having written you before what I had heard on the subject of the recognition of Palestine, I feel I should write you again.

The way in which the recognition of Palestine came about has created complete consternation in the United Nations.

As you know, I never wanted us to change our original stand. When I wrote to the President and to you the other day what I had heard, I thought, of course, that you would weigh it against the reports which you were getting from the United Nations. Much as I wanted the Palestine State recognized, I would not have wanted it done without the knowledge of our representatives in the United Nations who had been fighting for our changed position. I would have felt that they had to know the reason and I would also have felt that there had to be a very clear understanding beforehand with such nations as we expected would follow our lead.

Several of the representatives of other governments have been to talk to me since, and have stated quite frankly that they do not see how they could ever follow the United States' lead because the United States changed so often without any consultation. There seems to be no sense of interlocking information between the United States delegate and the State Department on the policy making level. This is serious because our acts which should strengthen the United Nations only result in weakening our influence within the United Nations and in weakening the United Nations itself.

More and more the other delegates seem to believe that our whole policy is based on antagonism to Russia and that we think in terms of going it alone rather than in terms of building up a leadership within the United Nations.

This seems to me a very serious defect and I do not see how we can expect to have any real leadership if,

1. We do not consult our people in the United Nations on what we are going to do, and

2. If we do not line up our following before we do the things, rather than trusting to influencing them afterwards.

I can not imagine that major considerations on policies such as this are taken at such short notice that there is not time to think through every consequence and inform all those who should be informed. I have seldom seen a more bitter, puzzled, discouraged group of people than some of those whom I saw on Saturday. Some of them I know are favorable to the rights of the Jews in Palestine, but they are just nonplused by the way in which we do things.

I thought I had to tell you this because I had written you before and as you know, I believe that it is the Administration's desire to strengthen the United Nations, but we do not always achieve it because, apparently, there is a lack of contact on the higher levels.

With deep concern, I am,

Very sincerely yours,

Eleanor Roosevelt to Harry S Truman

May 17, 1948

This letter to President Truman was primarily to explain the attached letter to Secretary of State George C. Marshall that Mrs. Roosevelt had mailed the previous day. She apologized for bothering him but believed she should address matters of concern to her.

May 17, 1948

Dear Mr. President:

I am enclosing a copy of a letter which I just sent to the Secretary of State.

You will begin to find me such a nuisance you will wish I would go home and stay there! However this question of having the foreign policy integrated with the work of the United Nations seems to me of paramount importance.

Very sincerely yours,

Eleanor Roosevelt to Dwight D. Eisenhower

June 8, 1948

Eleanor Roosevelt often wrote letters of introduction and tried to get prominent people to listen to ideas for which they might not always be receptive. This was such a letter.

June 8, 1949

Dear General Eisenhower:

Mr. George Catlin[1] whom I have known for some time, is over here and very much interested in doing something which I think might be of value at the present time and interesting to any one of us regardless of party politics.

Mr. Vincent Massey[2] wrote me about this some time ago and I saw Mr. Catlin in London. He is now lecturing at Ohio State[3] and is in New York only occasionally. He is anxious to have a chance to tell you of his ideas and I am sure you will find them interesting and worth while.

I wish so much that I had not been so busy on the Human Rights Commission as I want to see you and Mrs. Eisenhower just as soon as we finish, and I hope you and she will motor up to Hyde Park some day and lunch with me or spend the night.

With warm regards,

Very cordially yours,

Notes

1. Edward Gordon Catlin, an English political scientist and educator.
2. A Canadian diplomat.
3. Ohio State University.

Eleanor Roosevelt to Madame Chiang Kai-shek
[1948]

By 1948 the Nationalist government of China led by Chiang Kai-shek was facing increasing pressure from the Communist movement led by Mao Zedong. Mrs. Roosevelt had sent some gifts to Madame Chiang, including a book of Franklin Roosevelt's boyhood letters. Madame Chiang wrote her a thank-you note and mentioned she had heard that Mrs. Roosevelt had not been well. She noted the hot and humid summer in China and the floods in many parts of the country, but added she hoped for a better harvest in the fall. This is a handwritten draft written by Mrs. Roosevelt's secretary.

[No date except answering a letter of 8/7/48]

Dear Mme Chiang

It was a pleasure to receive your letter. I am so glad you find my husband's letters interesting. My son, Elliott, is working on a 2nd & third volume which I think will be more interesting.

Two young friends of mine are going to China for the State Dept.—Mr. & Mrs. Robert Aylward & I have taken the liberty of giving them a note of introduction to you. I think you will find them interesting.

We have had a wonderful summer & are slowly getting the farm here on a business basis.

With every good wish—

Affec

Eleanor Roosevelt to Harry S Truman

September 12, 1948

As she was leaving for a conference in London, Mrs. Roosevelt forwarded a letter to President Truman to express once again her concern about the actions of the Soviet Union in the Middle East and the vulnerability of the new state of Israel. She did not believe that the Jewish people in Israel were particularly susceptible to Communist ideas, but if they felt abandoned they might look toward the Soviet way of life.

September 12, 1948

Dear Mr. President:

On the eve of leaving for the conference in Paris, I have tried to make my column useful for the Democratic cause. I have to leave several to cover the days on the ship when I can not file.

I will remember what you asked me to do while I am in Paris.

There is just one thing that I want to mention to you, namely, I am hearing from various sources that the Russians are again making a great many friendly advances to the State of Isreal. I do not think because there are a good many Jews who came, or whose parents came from Russia, in the days when Russia oppressed the Jews, that there is any real desire to turn to communism, but just as in some of the other countries it is not a question of what you desire, but a question of what you must have to have in order to live. The Balkan States can not turn any where but to Russia and it may come to a point where it looks that way to Isreal. They have fought battles so far very unprepared with British equipped Arabs.

In shaping your policy as to recognition of Isreal and the lifting of the embargo and the granting of the loan, I hope the angle of where Isreal is going to turn will be taken into consideration. If the new State is our friend we have a very strategic position in the Near East, which could command in the long run great influence on all the other countries.

These decisions seem to me to be highly important in the United Nations because if we stick to what we say, we will have a following. We shocked those following very badly by our vacillation on Palestine and we must not this time take any steps which we do not mean to carry through on.

I hope that we will have a firm attitude on Russia but I also hope we will not make it an antagonizing one. We are big enough to offer Russia what we think she deserves and to make it easy for her to come our way. I am totally opposed to appeasement but I think we should be just and drive a hard bargain but a firm one with all the little pin pricks of irritation carefully avoided.

I say this now because I think I may be rather alone in feeling this way on the delegation and I would not like you not to know exactly what my position is.

With all good wishes, I am,

Very cordially yours,

Eleanor Roosevelt to Frances Perkins

October 4, 1948

In October 1948 President Harry Truman was running a desperate battle for reelection, and most observers believed he was going down to a massive defeat. Frances Perkins, secretary of labor in the Roosevelt administration, wrote Mrs. Roosevelt a letter questioning why she had not made a public endorsement of Truman for reelection. As the most prominent Democrat other than the president, her silence was ominous. Mrs. Roosevelt wrote Perkins in early October as to why she had been silent.

Hotel Crillon
Paris
October 4, 1948

Dear Frances:

I haven't actually endorsed Mr. Truman because he has been such a weak and vacillating person and made such poor appointments in his Cabinet and entourage, such as Snyder[1] and Vaughan,[2] that unless we are successful in electing a very strong group of liberals in Congress, in spite of my feelings about the Republican Party and Governor Dewey,[3] I can not have much enthusiasm for Mr. Truman. Though there are many people in the government that I would hate to feel would not be allowed to continue their work, I still find it very difficult to give any good reasons for being for Mr. Truman.

That is why I told him the last time I saw him, that I was keeping completely inactive in partisan politics, though I would say in my column that I am a Democrat and voting the Democratic ticket, and I would write what I could that would help the Democratic Party.

Nevertheless, since you asked me to send you the enclosed letter, I am doing so because you are quite right, if we are going down to defeat, we probably should go down having done what we could for the candidate and we should try for a good vote. I have addressed my letter to the President as being the most effective way.

Affectionately,

Notes

1. John Wesley Snyder of Missouri, a St. Louis banker, served in Truman's Cabinet as secretary of the treasury from 1946 to 1953.

2. Harry Hawkins Vaughan, a native of Missouri, was the military aide to Truman from 1944 to 1953. He was considered by Mrs. Roosevelt and others as part of the "Missouri Gang" of cronies Truman had installed in the White House.

3. Gov. Thomas E. Dewey of New York, Republican candidate for president.

Eleanor Roosevelt to Bernard Baruch
October 4, 1948

Mrs. Roosevelt continued her relationship with Bernard Baruch and often corresponded warmly with him about various world issues, as in this case in October 1948 when she was in Paris. The relationship between Baruch and Truman was chilly despite all that Mrs. Roosevelt could do. This was a wide-ranging letter.

Hotel Crillon
Paris
October 4, 1948

Dear Mr. Baruch:

I have been meaning to write to you ever since I got here.

In my Committee #3, I notice a slight change in the attitude of the Russians. They are less vituperative and in the first item on our own agenda which was the control of the new narcotic drugs not covered by previous conventions, they presented their arguments against the Colonial Clause always insisted upon by the British, accepted defeat and accepted the convention and informed the secretariat that when the convention was open for signature, Russia would sign immediately.

This was a great surprise to me and I spoke of it to Mr. Spaak[1] of Belgium and he told me he had noticed exactly the same thing in Committee #1. He feels it might indicate a change of policy in the Kremlin.

Of course, the proposals made by Mr. Vishinsky[2] on atomic energy and arms reduction are utterly and completely dishonest but if people as a whole can be made to see what they really mean so that the Russians are defeated and we can carry better resolutions, I have a feeling they may possibly go along.

For this reason I am going to try to be rather polite to my Russian colleagues. I have also decided that we haven't been wise in not associating more with the Latin Americans. We have tried very hard to impress them with the fact that we did not intend to dictate to them, but they are murmuring among themselves that supposedly we should be leaders and we indicate in no way what we think should be done. Therefore I had six of them lunch with me last Saturday to discuss the points coming up. I shall continue to do this type of thing with the members of my committee. I have seen General Romulo[3] of the Philippines who has considerable influence with them.

It was fun having John Golden[4] here for a few days but I work such long hours it is very difficult for me to see much of any one outside of the range of one's work.

I often wish that you were here to consult with, but I am glad I have had the opportunities to talk with you fairly often. I think our lines of thought are frequently parallel.

I am enclosing to you a copy of a letter which I sent to the President today. I am sending it to Frances Perkins because she telephoned me last night pointing out that Drew Pearson[5] was saying that I had never come out for the President as the Democratic candidate and was supposedly in favor of Governor Dewey. That, of course, is untrue and I do agree with Frances Perkins that we should try to get as good a Democratic vote as possible. I told her there was no chance of a Democratic victory except that we might keep some of our liberal Democrats in Congress and even increase the number if we acted wisely. I hope you will approve of this letter even though I was, as you know, loathe [sic] to do more than state in general my support of the Democratic Party and its policies.

I hope you are keeping well and are not working too hard. I wish you would do some work in putting pressure on Secretary Marshall so that he will consider his approval of the Bernadotte Plan[6] was not tantamount to complete acceptance of all the recommendations contained in it, but only as being a good basis for negotiation.

It seems highly unfair to me to turn the whole of the Negeb over to the Arabs. The portion of Galilee given to the Jews is not fertile and I do not think it fair compensation because in Jewish hands the Negeb would be developed and may turn out to be the only place where they can receive immigration. I have expressed these thoughts in the delegation meetings but I do not think I carry much weight. I have only one real backer and that is Ben Cohen.[7] Neither of us was consulted before the Secretary made his announcement to the press of the acceptance of the Bernadotte report. We were simply handed a statement to read in the session after he had given it out to the press.

Affectionately always,

Notes

1. Paul-Henri Spaak, a politician and statesman from Belgium.
2. Andrei Vishinsky, Soviet vice commissar of foreign affairs.
3. Carolos Romulo of the Philippines, a diplomat and first Asian president of the UN General Assembly.
4. A film producer.
5. A nationally syndicated columnist.
6. Count Folke Bernadotte, a Swedish diplomat, drafted a plan in 1948 to see peace in the Arab-Jewish conflict in Palestine.
7. Benjamim V. Cohen, counselor to the State Department.

Eleanor Roosevelt to Harry S Truman

October 4, 1948

On the same day that Eleanor Roosevelt explained to Frances Perkins (former secretary of labor) the reasons she had not endorsed President Truman for reelection, she contacted the president to confirm her advocacy of his candidacy, but her support seemed lukewarm, and she tended to emphasize the election of liberal Democrats to Congress more than his own reelection, which at the time seemed hopeless.

Hotel Crillon
Paris
October 4, 1948

Dear Mr. President:

I understand that there is some comment in the newspapers in the United

States that I have not come out for you as the Democratic candidate and prefer the election of the Republican candidate. I have stated my position clearly in my column. I am unqualifiedly for you as the Democratic candidate for the Presidency.

This year I hope every Democrat and independent voter is concentrating on the election of as many liberal Democrats to Congress as possible. I hope for this particularly from the labor and farm groups who have perhaps the greatest stake in the preservation of liberal leadership.

Liberal policies during these next few years are of vast importance on domestic issues. A Democratic administration backed by a liberal Democratic Congress, could really achieve the policies for which you have stood.

As delegate to the United Nations I have become very much aware of the fact that stability in our own government and in its policies is essential to help the Democracies on their road to rehabilitation.

With every good wish, I am,

Very cordially yours,

Eleanor Roosevelt to Dwight D. Eisenhower

December 3, 1948

In addition to her newspaper column, Mrs. Roosevelt regularly appeared on radio and television programs on topics of public interest. She was always seeking prominent guests, and General Eisenhower was one of the most popular men in America.

Hotel Crillon
Paris
December 3, 1948

Dear General Eisenhower:

My daughter, Anna, and I are doing three radio broadcasts a week which go over 260 stations in the United States.

This is to ask you if you would be willing to be a guest on one of our programs after I return to the United States which I hope will be around the 13th of this month. I think a program on academic freedom would be very important at this time and I know you feel strongly on this subject. It will be short, about five or six minutes and you can ad lib if you wish, or I can send some one to see you who will write a script for you and make all the arrangements so you will have to give as little time as possible.

If you will send your reply to me at 29 Washington Square I shall appreciate it very much.

Very sincerely yours,

[*DDEL*]

Eleanor Roosevelt to Harry S Truman
December 28, 1948

In late 1948 Mrs. Roosevelt attended a postwar conference in Paris. Just before Christmas President Truman wrote the former first lady, agreeing to see her in January and asking her to submit a memorandum in advance so that they would have a basis for discussion. He praised her patience in dealing with the "maddening technique of the Russians." Truman pointed out that they not only had been deliberately uncooperative, but "they have conducted themselves with a boorishness worthy of stable boys." He noted with delight how Mrs. Roosevelt had dealt with them, stating, "I have observed with great satisfaction that you have put them in their place more than once." Mrs. Roosevelt, shortly after Christmas, sent an extensive report to Truman.

MEMO FOR THE PRESIDENT   December 28, 1948

First of all I want to tell you, Mr. President what [*sic*] when the news of your election reached Europe, there was general rejoicing. It gave to many statesmen and even to the people on the street who felt there might have been a change in our foreign policy, a sense of security that that which is now being done would be continued.

Next, I think I should say that generally there is a feeling that Mr. Harriman has done a very good job and a devoted one. As you know, I have not always felt that he had a broad enough point of view and grasp of the world situation, but he struck me as having greatly broadened and having been capable of growing with the opportunity[1] which you have given him, which after all, is the greatest thing that one can ask of any one. He has chosen a good staff and everywhere I heard good things said of these people. People wrote me about the representatives they considered particularly good in a number of cases. I heard also that Mr. Harriman had handled labor very well.

France, as he undoubtedly told you, is the greatest headache of all still. I think he understands what some of the greatest difficulties are. Many of the young men who fought in the resistance movement, or who were taken to camps and forced labor out of the country, returned or finished their period of the war, depleted physically and mentally. The food has not been sufficient in energy giving qualities. You can not, for instance even today, unless you are willing and able to buy in the black market, get butter and sugar and only small children can get milk. Until one comes back physically, one can not come back mentally and spiritually. Also the constant change of governments, due in large part to a very complicated situation which I will be glad to explain if you are interested, has made life for the working people in the cities very difficult and creates a lack of confidence in the government.

The hardships are real and the Soviets through their communist party in France have offered both rural and city people certain benefits which they could not well resist. The French are not naturally communists but they find it hard to be staunch in the sense that the British are and so they have accepted many communist things. This does not frighten me for the future but it creates great difficulties for the present.

This question of economic well-being is exploited by the USSR in all nations and they promise much until they gain complete control, then people are worse off than they were before, but up to that time they have hopes of being better off and this is what creates one of the dangers for us. Since we are really fighting ideas as well as economic conditions and the Russians do a better propaganda job than we do, because it is easier to say that your government is a government of workers for the benefit of workers than it is to say that a democratic government which is capitalistic benefits the workers more in the end. The only way to prove that to them, I think, is gradually to have more of them see conditions in our country, under supervision of course, and with every arrangement made for them to return to their own country, but the USSR is as loathe [*sic*] to let them come over as we have been to allow them to enter which makes this solution very difficult.

Great Britain is going to pull through because it has stood up under incredible drabness of living, and I think will know how to use the aid coming to good account. Our relations with the British must, I think, be put on a different basis. We are without question, the leading democracy in the world today, but so far Great Britain still takes the attitude that she makes the policies on all world questions and we accept them. That has got to be remedied. We have got to make the policies and they have got to accept them. Mr. Bevin[2] has been unwise in many ways but I will not put on paper what I would be willing to tell you.

I hope very much that the situation between ourselves and the USSR can change in the coming year and that we can accomplish final peace settlements. Germany can not return to any kind of normality until this is done, for at present the heap of ruins and disillusioned people in the center of Europe makes it difficult for all around to recover.

I have a feeling that your attitude on Palestine did a great deal to straighten out our own delegation and help the situation from the world point of view. The Arabs have to be handled with strength. One of the troubles has been that we have been so impressed with the feeling that we must have a united front in Europe that it has affected our stand in the Near East. I personally feel that it is more important for the French and for the British to be united with us than for us to be united with them, and therefore when we make up our minds that something has to be done, we should be the ones to do what we think is right and we should not go through so many anxieties on the subject.

There are all kinds of hidden reasons why nations and their statesmen desire certain things which are not the reasons they usually give. The most truthful of the statesmen that I talked to while in Paris was Robert Schuman of France,[3] but it does require some knowledge of the past and much background to be always on your guard and figure out what are the reasons for certain stands that are taken.

I have great admiration for the Secretary of State[4] and for many of the people in our State Department, but sometimes I think we are a little bit too trusting and forget the past. In giving me as an adviser, Mr. Durward Sandifer, a lawyer of great experience and assistant to Mr. Dean Rusk[5] in the Department, I could not have been better served but I still feel it is hard for the Department to accept policies, without certain individuals trying to inject their own points of view and I do not think all of them have the knowledge and experience to take a world point of view instead of a local one, and by local I mean the point of view which is affected by the particular area in which they have special knowledge and experience.

I should like to say a word to you when we meet on the subject of the bipartisan policy and the representatives of the other party.

I also learned that the Philippine representatives were very much affected by the Equal Benefits Bill which is in Congress and I think if this goes through we will have a remarkable rise in their loyalty.

The thing above all others which I would like to bring to your attention is that we are now engaged in a situation which is as complicated as fighting a war. During the war my husband had a map room and there were experts who daily briefed him on what was happening in every part of the world. It seems to me now we are engaged in the war for peace in which there enter questions of world economy, food, religion, education, health and social conditions, as well as military and power conditions. I have a feeling that it would be helpful if you could build a small group of very eminent non-political experts in all these fields whose duty it would be to watch the world scene and keep you briefed day by day in a map room. No one man can watch this whole world picture or have the background and knowledge to cover it accurately. It must be achieved by wise choice of people in the various fields to do it well and understandingly.

I have a feeling that our situation in Europe will be solved in the next year without too much difficulty. Our real battlefield today is Asia and our real battle is the one between democracy and communism. We can not ruin America and achieve the results that have to be achieved in the world, so whatever we do must be done with the most extraordinary wisdom and foresight in the economic field. At the same time we have to prove to the world and particularly to down trodden areas of the world which are the natural prey to the principle of communist economy, that democracy really brings about happier and better conditions for the people as a whole. Never was there an era in history in which the responsibilities were greater for the United States, and never was a President called upon to meet such extraordinary responsibilities for civilization as a whole.

I think you are entitled to the best brains and the best knowledge available in the world today. Congress must understand this picture but it can not be expected to follow it in the way it has to be followed for the knowledge must come from a group which you set up and from you to them. You need something far greater than political advice, though that is also an essential to the picture at home as well as abroad. The search should be for wise men of great knowledge and devoted to mankind, for mankind is at the cross roads. It can destroy itself or it can enter into a new era of happiness and security. It seems to me that you are the instrument chosen as a guide in this terribly serious situation and if there is anything which any of us can do to help you, you have a right to call upon us all.

Notes

1. Mrs. Roosevelt is referring to the fact that Harriman, secretary of commerce from 1947 to 1948, was appointed to the Economic Cooperation Administration in 1948 after Congress approved the appropriation for the Marshall Plan.

2. Ernest Bevin, Labour Party leader and government official.

3. Statesman and economist who founded the European Coal and Steel Community.

4. George C. Marshall.

5. Later secretary of state from 1961 to 1969.

Eleanor Roosevelt to Madame Chiang Kai-shek

January 9, 1949

As the Nationalist government in China was falling to the onslaught of the Communist movement of Mao Zedong, Mrs. Roosevelt wrote to Madame Chiang to express her concern for her safety. Her confidence in the Nationalists holding on to Formosa (Taiwan) was weak, since she saw nothing they could do that they were unable to do when Gen. George Marshall was there earlier representing United States interests and providing American aid.

January 9, 1949

Dear Madame Chiang:

I was very sorry to read in the papers that you are actually leaving in a few days. I shall feel very anxious about you and frankly I would be happier if your husband were to join you here.

It does not seem to me possible for the Nationalists at the present time to do what they were not able to do in the days when General Marshall was in China. The people of China seem to have made their decision and I doubt if Formosa can stand out against it.

I understand your feelings and they are courageous but sometimes the things that courage can lead one into that serve no real good and certainly there is very little that you can now do in Formosa. I should think you would add to the burden of the men besides giving your friends and family considerable anxiety, I am sure.

With affection and good wishes, I am

Very cordially yours,

Eleanor Roosevelt to Chester Bowles

May 10, 1949

Chester Bowles was a New Dealer who had also worked in the Truman administration. In 1948 he despaired of Truman's reelection, and he joined several prominent Democrats who tried to entice Dwight D. Eisenhower to become a Democratic candidate for president. During the same year, Bowles ran and was elected governor of his home state of Connecticut. Early in his new term, Mrs. Roosevelt wrote him expressing her views on issues facing him, especially racial discrimination and the housing crisis. These were special issues for Mrs. Roosevelt, as well.

May 10, 1949

Dear Governor Bowles:

Your reasonable presentation of your program should, I think, be persuasive with your Republican legislators. When the measures come before them in concrete form, I hope this view of mine will not be found to be too optimistic.

Most of the measures with which the two pamphlets deal are subjects of especial concern to me. I am glad you added to the recommendation in your inaugural message a request for legislative action to abolish the discrimination against Negro citizens that still exists in the Connecticut National Guard. In my view you show great wisdom in stressing at this time measures that should have an appeal not limited by party sympathy—the need of a comprehensive budget, the need of more and better schools, a concrete and aggressive housing program.

In looking over your special message on the housing program I am particularly interested in your willingness to consider a modification of the principles contained in your original housing recommendations. It seems to me that you meet very well the three major objections made to your original housing proposals: (1) the objection on principle to direct governmental subsidies; (2) the objection to making the tenant's income the determining factor, with the result that tenants would pay unequally for comparable dwellings; (3) the failure to provide for those that want to buy, rather than to rent.

I confess that I shy away from the principle of direct government subsidy except in emergencies not soluble by other means. The present housing situation is, of course, an emergency; but I envisage a state housing program (under whatever emergency it may be begun) as a measure that should incorporate a valid and permanent policy. For this reason I am particularly interested in the methods of financing you suggest as one who was around this problem, in answer to some to some of the criticisms. I am not a financial expert and I cannot concretely evaluate the financial methods suggested; but I certainly salute the direction of your suggested practical ways of taking care of the housing emergency involved in your original proposal.

My hope is that you will be reelected and thus assured of opportunity to carry out your overall intention to achieve an economical reorganization of the state government, a reorganization that will make it possible to provide for the continuance and development of the measures you are now urging as to schools, housing, budgetary competence.

Very sincerely yours,

Eleanor Roosevelt to Frances Perkins

May 16, 1949

Frances Perkins, secretary of labor for Franklin D. Roosevelt and the first woman cabinet member, remained active during the Truman administration. Mrs. Roosevelt, concerned about the rights of individuals, spoke out when she saw injustice. In this letter, she complained to Perkins about the functions of the Civil Service Commission being taken over by a committee of the American Bar Association. She asked Perkins to use her influence to convince President Truman to restore the commission to its proper function.

May 16, 1949

Dear Frances:

I am very much troubled by the rumor which I hear of the committee of the American Bar Association which has taken over some of the most important functions of the Civil Service Commission.

It seems to me that it is vitally important that the committee be done away with. Just reinstating people whom they have screened out will not really get to the root of the trouble.

I am glad that Tom Stokes[1] has started to publish the first of the stories of what they have done to the ICC[2] and I think before long a story should be written on what they have done—not only removing present incumbents but on their refusal to appoint any liberals from the new lists.

I hope that you will urge the President to take every possible means to restore the commission's proper functions. It seems to me astonishing that the American Bar Association has had the nerve to set up such a committee.

Are you coming up for the lunch to Rose on the second of June? I was sorry not to see you at the press club dinner as I had hoped to have a chance to speak to you about the above.

Affectionately always,

Notes

1. Thomas L. Stokes, United Features Syndicate columnist.
2. Interstate Commerce Commission.

Eleanor Roosevelt to Frances Perkins

May 20, 1949

This was a follow-up letter to Frances Perkins regarding Mrs. Roosevelt's con-

cerns about recent actions of the Civil Service Commission. She was especially bothered by the way the Board of Examiners could fire a government employee without appeal to the commission. Mrs. Roosevelt sent this statement to Perkins asking for her reaction and ideas.

May 20, 1949

Dear Frances:

Supplementing my letter to you of May 15th,[1] I am sending you the following:

"The Civil Service Commission apparently has sublime faith in the Board of Examiners, even to the extent of giving it supreme power, without appeal to the Commission, on the part of those unjustly treated.

"This Board has broader powers than any I ever heard of connected with a Government agency. It has complete and unchecked power to fire or demote trial examiners and administrative judiciary in twelve Federal agencies, without the usual procedures for discovering fitness for the job. Indeed, its chief objective seems to be to get rid of competent and courageous men.

"Through the registrar for trial examiners which it has established, the Board screens appointees and builds a favored list of men subservient to its views of what NLRA[2] should mean.

"The partisan nature of the Board is evidenced by the choice of Carl McFarland,[3] counsel for the many corporations, and now counsel for the NAM,[4] as the Board's chairman. Mr. McFarland, like Joseph W. Henderson,[5] another Board member, has appeared before the NLRB[6] and in NLRB court cases in behalf of corporations.

"The papers sent me show that the Board has been particularly vindictive in getting rid of Jews, regardless of their length of service or competence. A Negro, of course, would have no chance of appointment.

"The fact that the Board has fired so many experienced, competent men, who have conscientiously tried to carry out the intent of the NLRB, is evidence that it represents a special interest group and is determined to weed out all liberals or progressive men.

"Labor's interest and the public's interest is without protection at the hands of this Board.

"The most important step is obviously to wipe this Board out of existence. Whatever agency of this type might be set up, there should be representation of other interests at stake. The very existence of a body of this sort is a threat to fairness and democracy."

I shall be anxious to get your side of the story on this.

Affectionately,

Notes

1. She probably meant May 16.
2. National Labor Relations Act.
3. Attorney, educator, and government official.
4. National Association of Manufacturers.
5. A Pennsylvania lawyer.
6. National Labor Relations Board.

Eleanor Roosevelt to Harry S Truman

June 21, 1949

In 1949 Mrs. Roosevelt served on the Human Rights Commission of the United Nations. In the summer she composed a short report to President Truman on her meetings with that group. She made similar comments about the Russians after most meetings, but her remarks about the uncooperative attitude of the British appeared uncommon. As usual, she gave him her opinions of the various policies available for his consideration.

June 21, 1949

Dear Mr. President:

I want first to thank you for the opportunities you have given me in working on the Human Rights Commission. The session closed last night.

Realizing that you probably do not want to be bothered by a personal report at the present time, I am writing this, though, of course, if you want me to come to Washington I shall do so.

The result of our work is only the first draft of the Covenant. We discussed only political and civil rights. The document which will go to the governments, however, will be accompanied by different plans for ways of enforcing the rights that are accepted in the final Covenant.

Our only plan is a joint plan with the United Kingdom and it will go forward with the others. This is the only thing on which we were able to agree with the United Kingdom. I have never known them to be so uncooperative as they were in this session. That may be due to the fact that the young Foreign Office adviser on the delegation staff accepted all the directions that came from the Foreign Office as being final and therefore was not able to negotiate on any changes of any kind in words. It was unfortunate especially because in previous sessions we have been able to get together with the United Kingdom on many situations.

Needless to say we practically never agreed with the USSR and they felt that the document was a very poor one because the economic and social rights were not really discussed and are going to the governments simply as additional articles for comment by governments.

One of the things we shall have to decide before the next meeting is whether in this Covenant we shall include any of these rights. Many of our people in this country lean toward the belief that civil and political rights without some measure of economic and social rights, have comparatively little value but these are new rights to many governments. Whether we wish to deal with economic and social rights in a second Covenant to follow the first one, or whether we wish to include them in separate protocols which nations can ratify one by one as they find the atmosphere of their countries favorable, are the questions. These must be decided as far as our attitude is concerned before the next meeting.

The state dept. will be working on these questions. I have written Secy Acheson and I will, of course, come down at any time.

I shall be in Hyde Park all summer and I am looking forward to rest and leisure which however will be conditioned on the behavior of a large number of children who are going to be on the place! I hope you and Mrs. Truman and Margaret will have a pleasant and happy summer and that Congress will give you some of the things that you want so that you may have the satisfaction of feeling that your hard work has achieved good results. Franklin, junior enjoyed having an opportunity of seeing you. I hope he will be a good democratic congressman.

With many thanks again and my best wishes, I am,

very cordially yours,

Eleanor Roosevelt to Herbert Lehman
July 11, 1949

Herbert H. Lehman, a leading New York politician, served as governor of New York from 1933 to 1942 and contemplated seeking a seat in the United States Senate. The Catholic church, led especially by Cardinal Francis J. Spellman of New York, was taking a more aggressive stand in public affairs at the time. Mrs. Roosevelt wrote Lehman in July 1949 to encourage him to run for the Senate, suggesting that the cardinal did not necessarily speak for all Catholics in New York state.

July 11, 1949

Dear Herbert:

Some one has just told me that Cardinal Spellman has been foolish enough to say that because you went on the committee to prevent The Nation from being banned from public schools, he is going to ask the Catholics of the State to oppose you.

I do not know that this is true but it seems too stupid to be true, but the Cardinal has been doing stupid things of late. For that reason I want to write you a line to say if you would be willing to run for the Senate and can do so, I personally feel that the State of New York should be deeply grateful for your willingness to serve.

If there is anything that I can do that is not incompatible with my work on the United Nations which must come first, I will certainly be happy to do it at any time. You know you can count on my whole-hearted support.

In thinking over this threat of Catholic opposition, I can not take it very seriously because they have had the experience of your Governorship and no one has ever been fairer to all races and creeds. They certainly could expect nothing better from any one, and they are certainly heading into deep waters if they are going to oppose as a candidate, a person as well fitted as you are for the Senate.

With every good wish, I am,

Very cordially yours,

Eleanor Roosevelt to Harry S Truman
July 31, 1949

When Mrs. Roosevelt learned that she would be nominated for the American delegation to the next General Assembly of the United Nations, she wrote President Truman to state that she would not be offended if he chose to remove her name from consideration. The controversy between her and Cardinal of New York Francis J. Spellman of the Catholic church had intensified to the point that she feared it would prove embarrassing to Truman.

July 31, 1949

Dear Mr. President:

I have heard unofficially that my name is on the State Department list to be presented to you for the next General Assembly of the United Nations.

Because of this strange campaign that Cardinal Spellman has started against Mr. Lehman and against me in public fashion, I am wondering if it will not embarrass you to send my name to the Senate. I want you to know that if your decision should be to leave me off I will quite understand and will not be in any way upset.

With every good wish, I am,

Very cordially yours,

Eleanor Roosevelt to Agnes E. Meyer
August 8, 1949

Mrs. Roosevelt's relations with the Catholic church, especially with Cardinal Spellman, were quite strained in 1949, mostly over the issue of federal aid to education. Mrs. Eugene Meyer, wife of the publisher of the Washington Post, was a friend of Mrs. Roosevelt's who never hesitated to advise her on certain matters. She wrote Mrs. Roosevelt that efforts were under way to bring the former first lady together with Cardinal Francis J. Spellman so that they could discuss their differences. Agnes Meyer told Mrs. Roosevelt that the Catholic church would endorse federal aid only if parochial schools were supported equal to public schools. Quite unhappy with the church's stand on education and wanting Mrs. Roosevelt to understand her position, Mrs. Meyer told the former first lady that her experiences had been bitter and disappointing, and she wanted "to do anything I can to help you establish the fact that you are not hostile to the religion but to the material ambitions of the Church in our country." Mrs. Roosevelt's answer to Mrs. Meyer revealed her attitudes.

August 8, 1949

Dear Mrs. Meyer:

Thank you for your letter of August 4th. It was Ed. Flynn[1] and not Mayor O'Dwyer[2] who finally made the Cardinal telephone me.

However, after a long conversation with the Cardinal's secretary, a very comfortable looking Monseigneur whose name I never did discover, I am more convinced than ever that they will never help us to get federal aid for education unless they think they are going to get it too for parochial schools.

I told him I was to begin almost immediately discussing in my column what I think should go into a federal aid bill and he said that he quite understood that. I also asked him if the Cardinal would be anxious to see child health taken entirely out of the schools and placed under hospitals or clinics and would back a child health bill which was entirely separate from the schools, but which would require that every child be taken for yearly examinations and recommendations actually carried out. He assured me the Cardinal would back such a bill.

It is still difficult for me to understand what made the Cardinal so willing to take a conciliatory attitude and let me state that he had called me, and agree to my last paragraph in my statement. Perhaps when I have worked with them as long as you have I may have a little better understanding. At the present moment I confess to being highly suspicious and to having more than ever a feeling that they are not interested in improving education, but interested in getting as much federal money as possible so they can slide out from under any expenses which might be carried by the federal government.

Hoping that I will see you again before long so we can talk about these various problems, I am,

Very cordially yours,

Notes

1. New York politician Edward J. Flynn.
2. William O'Dwyer.

Eleanor Roosevelt to Joan Carol King
July/August ?, 1949

Mrs. Roosevelt often received letters from people she did not know asking her opinion or seeking her support for some cause. In 1949 a student at Stephens College, a women's college in Missouri, wrote her about the definition of both citizenship and world citizenship. The young woman was president of the World Citizenship Organization on her campus. Mrs. Roosevelt was brief but definite in her response. This is a draft written by Mrs. Roosevelt's secretary.

[Handwritten draft; no date except answering a letter of 7/25/49]
King

There is no such thing as "world citizenship" so I would not be able to define it.

One can be a good citizen of one's own country but accepting a responsibility of what occurs & by working especially in a democracy to constantly improve & strengthen democracy. In that way & by taking an interest in what is happening in the world, one contributes eventually to a better world.

Eleanor Roosevelt to Harry S Truman

October 6, 1949

In addition to her other numerous activities, Mrs. Roosevelt continued to remain active and interested in politics in New York City and New York state. In 1949 she wrote to President Truman expressing her concern for the two leading Democratic candidates and urging his intervention to overcome some of the opposition the candidates were receiving. The continuing controversy between Mrs. Roosevelt and the Catholic church surfaced here once again.

October 6, 1949

Dear Mr. President:

From what I hear I am getting rather anxious about the way the campaign is going here for both Governor Lehman and Mayor O'Dwyer.

It is quite evident that the Catholic Church is showing no great backing for Governor Lehman and with Mr. Dubinsky[1] anxious to stress the Liberal Party and not anxious to stress the Mayor, I feel that perhaps it would be very advisable if you could combine a big meeting, sponsored by the other labor groups, in Madison Square Garden, for both the Governor and the Mayor.

My chief concern is the good of the Party in the future. If in this state, it is evident that there has been defection in the Catholic vote where Governor Lehman is concerned, I am afraid it will mean a desertion from the Democratic Party by a great many of the Jews, some Protestants and some liberals—all of whom will join the Liberal Party which will weaken the Democratic Party.

This kind of thing is bad for our democratic system which should if possible, primarily remain a two-party system.

I feel a little responsible for the situation here because undoubtedly Governor Lehman's statement against the Cardinal's[2] letter to me is one of the things influencing the Catholic hierarchy and there are always some Catholics who can be influenced by a word passed down to the priests.

I do not know whether you are being urged to make other speeches here for the two candidates or not, but I do not feel the campaign is going any too well and upstate the Republicans are making a vigorous Senatorial fight, which will help the Fusion candidate in New York City. Apparently the Republicans by their holy crusade against the communists are making a direct appeal for the Catholic vote and will be so recognized by them. It has nothing of course to do with the actual issues of the campaign or the value of either candidate, but like so many campaign tricks, it may succeed in swinging the votes.

You will know better than I do whether politically any of this is important enough for you to think about, but I felt I should tell you what my feelings are at the present moment.

Very cordially yours,

Notes

1. David Dubinsky, Labor union official.
2. Francis Joseph Spellman.

Eleanor Roosevelt to Walter White

December 15, 1949

Eleanor Roosevelt in 1948 attempted to resign from the board of the National Association for the Advancement of Colored People (NAACP) but was persuaded by Executive Secretary Walter White to remain on the board. In late 1949 she again asked not to be reelected to the board because of the press of duties, especially on the United Nations. The Harlem newspaper, Amsterdam News, criticized her and suggested that the motivation for her resignation was her longtime friendship with Walter White, who was under attack within the NAACP. White wrote to apologize for the attack and to plead with her again to stay on the NAACP board.

December 15, 1949

Dear Walter:

In answer to your letter, it really makes very little difference to me what the Amsterdam News says.

I haven't been able to go to a board meeting of the NAACP for months and I am not going to be able to go for some time. I can tell in advance because my schedule is too crowded and while my plans are a bit vague I know I am going to be in Hyde Park or on trips most of the time.

I do not think it fair to stay on the Board particularly because I do not think Mr. Wilkins[1] is in the least interested in consulting with me or would agree with my point of view on many things.

My resignation, of course, has nothing to do with my being a friend of yours and the fact that the Amsterdam News wishes to misinterpret what I do is just something we will have to stand. I have stood a good many misinterpretations and they do not bother me much.

I am glad your trip was so successful and I shall look forward to seeing you before long.

Very sincerely yours,

Note

1. Roy Wilkins, editor of *The Crisis*, the magazine of the National Association for the Advancement of Colored People (NAACP) from 1934 to 1949 and executive secretary of the NAACP from 1955 to 1977.

Eleanor Roosevelt to Henry A. Wallace

December 21, 1949

After conferring with President Truman on December 20, 1949, Mrs. Roosevelt reported to Wallace on the nature of their conversation, stating that the president would notify Democratic members of the House Un-American Activities Committee that Wallace should have a full and complete hearing to present his case on questions that had been raised previously.

December 21, 1949

Dear Henry:

I saw the President yesterday. He realizes full well the importance to the party of these accusations and said that he would pass the word along to the Democratic members of the Un-American Activities Committee that he felt you should have a full and complete hearing. He does not, however, feel, and I agree with him, that he should take a hand in naming an impartial board. He did agree that if you did not get a full hearing that the Senate should appoint a committee to go to the bottom of the question.

He seemed to understand quite well the underlying causes of all this and I hope you will find it possible to get a hearing and a complete chance to present your case.

Very cordially yours,

Eleanor Roosevelt to Winston Churchill

[1950]

Mrs. Roosevelt was often called on for public statements and other public appearances because of her prestige. Through the years she often appeared on radio and television, often as the host, to discuss current issues. In 1950 she contacted Win-

*ston Churchill, then out of power in England, to see if he would be willing to agree
to an interview that would be broadcast on American radio and television.*

[Telegram, undated except 1950]

WINSTON CHURCHILL
IN VIEW OF YOUR PLEA FOR A RESUMPTION OF BIG THREE MEET-
INGS AND YOUR EXPRESSED BELIEF THAT ONLY THROUGH MEET-
INGS THROUGH THE HEADS OF STATE OF ENGLAND, THE SOVIET
UNION, AND THE UNITED STATES, CAN A POSSIBLE SOLUTION BE
FOUND TO THE TRAGIC DRIFT TOWARD ALL OUT ATOMIC AND HY-
DROGEN BOMB WAR, I HAVE BEEN ASKED BY THE NATIONAL
BROADCASTING COMPANY TO CONTACT YOU AND FIND OUT
WHETHER YOU WOULD AGREE TO AN INTERVIEW ON THIS SUB-
JECT FOR THE AMERICAN RADIO AND TELEVISION PUBLIC VIA THE
TRANSATLANTIC TELEPHONE. YOUR APPEARANCE ON THE TELE-
VISION WOULD BE TELEVISED ON FILM BY THE BRITISH BROAD-
CASTING COMPANY AND FLOWN OVER HERE FOR BROADCAST TO
THE AMERICAN PUBLIC AND THE RADIO PORTION WOULD BE RE-
CORDED AND BROADCAST SIMULTANEOUSLY WITH THE FILM
OVER THE COMPLETE FACILITIES OF THE NATIONAL BROADCAST-
ING COMPANY TO AMERICA. I WOULD APPRECIATE IT IF YOU
WOULD SEND ME A REPLY BY CABLE COLLECT TO THE PARK
SHERATON HOTEL, NEW YORK CITY, IF YOU AGREE THAT SUCH A
BROADCAST AND TELEVISION INTERVIEW IS OF SUFFICIENT VALUE
TO UNDERSCORE AND EMPHASIZE YOUR VIEWS TO THE PEOPLE
OF THE WORLD. I WOULD APPRECIATE IT IF YOU WOULD ADVISE
ME HOW SOON YOU WOULD WANT TO MAKE THIS BROADCAST.
WITH EVERY BEST WISH TO MRS CHURCHILL AND YOURSELF.
MRS FRANKLIN D ROOSEVELT

Eleanor Roosevelt to Dwight D. Eisenhower
January 6, 1950

*In 1950 Gen. Dwight D. Eisenhower was president of Columbia University, yet
some people showed interest in the possibility that he might become a candidate
for president of the United States either as a Democrat or Republican. Mrs.
Roosevelt hoped to take advantage of his celebrity to bring attention to a television and radio program that she was initiating. In this letter of invitation, she*

brings her persuasive powers to bear, especially in flattering him and promising to discuss issues about which he cared deeply.

January 6, 1950

My dear General Eisenhower:

In association with the National Broadcasting Company, I am initiating a program in February which it is planned will be broadcast over the facilities of their television and radio networks. It will be a public service program and will bring together outstanding national leaders, with somewhat varying points of view, on selected issues in order to give the public fuller information on these issues.

A fateful question of our century, as you have recognized, relates to the activities which should be the responsibility of a central government and which should be left to local and individual enterprise. Most of the political debates of our times seem to revolve around the differing answers that are given to this question.

There has been the keenest interest in the viewpoint which you have expressed on these matters and I should like to extend an invitation to you on behalf of the National Broadcasting Company and myself to discuss informally with us this very problem of government versus individual and local responsibility in such areas as health, education and social security.

I suggest these specific areas because of your interest in them. Naturally, we will be free to discuss the relationship of these problems to the wider ones of democratic government and individual freedom.

The program will be a half-hour one and I should like to have you join me on the first one which will take place Sunday evening, February 5th at either six or seven P.M.

If you concur in the educational usefulness of this program and can join us, the form of the program can then be discussed in greater detail. My function will be to serve as moderator rather than as advocate and I hope that we can have someone like the Vice President[1] also taking part. While the program will be unrehearsed, the topics to be covered as the specific questions that might come up will be in your hands long before the day of the program.

May I again express my belief in the profound importance of a full discussion of these matters and the pleasure and instruction it would afford me and the people of the United States to have you with us on the first program. I very much hope that Mrs. Eisenhower[2] will be able to attend the broadcast and join me for supper afterwards.

With every good wish, I am

Very cordially yours,

[*DDEL*]

Notes

1. Alben W. Barkley of Kentucky.
2. Mamie Doud Eisenhower.

Eleanor Roosevelt to Burt Drummond
February ?, 1950

Burt Drummond of Buffalo, New York, wrote Mrs. Roosevelt from time to time. He clearly disagreed with many of her opinions, and he hoped to influence her thinking on several matters. In this instance, he was "shocked and revolted" by her comments concerning the Alger Hiss incident, the infamous case during the Cold War. Hiss, an important member of the New Deal in several positions, was accused in 1948 by Whittaker Chambers of being a Communist during the 1930s. Mrs. Roosevelt, concise in her response, clearly offered her views.

[Handwritten draft; no date except answering a letter of 2/7/50]
I have read your letter & the copy of your letter to the N.Y. Times. You are very sure of your opinions. I am not sure of mine but circumstantial evidence has convicted innocent people in the past & juries are made up of human beings. That is all that I think we must bear in mind.

Eleanor Roosevelt to Burt Drummond
February ?, 1950

Not satisfied with Mrs. Roosevelt's answer to his letter of February 7, 1950, regarding the verdict in the Hiss case, Burt Drummond forwarded a two-page letter in which he chastised her for weakening the jury system by her criticism of the verdict in the Hiss case and for her wish for a verdict of acquittal of Hiss. Again, Mrs. Roosevelt was succinct but clear in her response. He asked her to be big and courageous by commenting in her column that her statements were not intended as a reflection upon the sanctity of trial by jury. This is a draft written by Mrs. Roosevelt's secretary.

[Handwritten draft; no date except answering a letter of 2/18/50]
In ans to your letter, I made no denunciations whatsoever. I did not even state what is true that we are at present as a nation swayed by certain hysterical & often accuse people who only differ with us of being subversive.

I did not hope for an acquittal. I would have simply felt the evidence was insufficient either to convict or acquit.

It would, I consider, neither be big or courageous to do something you do not believe in.

Eleanor Roosevelt to Robert L. Humphrey
March 4, 1950

In February 1950 a Mr. Robert Humphrey, a leader of Methodist youth, wrote Mrs. Roosevelt seeking her support for a Constitutional amendment to promote the teaching of religion. Like so many other people, Humphrey believed that Mrs. Roosevelt agreed with him, even if there were no evidence to support such an assumption. Mrs. Roosevelt did not hesitate to explain her views, even though she was incorrect in saying that two-thirds of the states are necessary to ratify a Constitutional amendment; the number is actually three-fourths of the states.

March 4, 1950

Dear Mr. Humphrey:

I have your letter and your enclosure.

To offer a Constitutional amendment is a very serious thing. You have to be prepared to go to work to have it ratified by two-thirds of the states of the Union.

As a matter of fact there is no reason why young people should grow up Godless just because they do not study during their public school years, some particular version of the Bible. The Bible should be read as literature and if you give it to young people as a religious document which they are forced to study, you may be asking some youngsters to do something which is against their bringing up.

Why isn't it much better to allow them to look to their homes and churches for religious training and to teach ethics and conduct in the public schools.

I would not, therefore, support a Constitutional amendment of this kind.

Very sincerely yours,

Eleanor Roosevelt to Walter White

March 29, 1950

Eleanor Roosevelt's membership on the board of the National Association for the Advancement of Colored People (NAACP) continued to be a matter of concern. She thought she had received a letter from Roy Wilkins, acting secretary of the NAACP, that said Walter White's marriage to a white woman had caused trouble for the NAACP and that Mrs. Roosevelt should "take a stand." White wrote Mrs. Roosevelt to say that Wilkins denied vigorously that he had written such a letter and asked if she could find out who had written the letter. Her response did not help resolve the question.

March 29, 1950

Dear Walter:

I am sorry if I did Mr. Wilkins an injustice. I distinctly remember having a letter and I thought it was from the acting secretary, the name I would not particularly notice. It certainly mentioned the fact that your marriage created a problem for the organization, and that was one of the reasons I felt I should resign.

However, it might well be some one connected with the Amsterdam News or some other organization, or some one else on the Board. That is why I was urged to attend a board meeting and why I tried to go to the next one after deciding to recall my resignation.

I realize in talking to you I should not have pinned it on any particular person when I did not have the letter in hand. My files are not in very good shape and I can not trace the letter, and the letter is not in the NAACP file which makes me think it was some one else.

Very sincerely yours,

Eleanor Roosevelt to John Gunther

June 2, 1950

In May 1950 John Gunther, the noted travel author, sent Mrs. Roosevelt a copy of a book he had just written on Franklin Roosevelt. He expressed his hope that she would not disagree with too much of what he said. Some parts of the book had been published in magazines, but he said they did not give the whole story. He told Mrs. Roosevelt that he had received "all manner of abuse in letters" and some called him "perverted" because he admired Franklin Roosevelt so much. He had even been accused of being in the pay of the Roosevelt family. Mrs.

Roosevelt answered his letter, but before it was mailed someone (perhaps her secretary) read it and wrote her a brief note that her letter sounded mysterious and as if she possibly had something to hide. The note said, "Gunther may be reliable but the letter might get into some one else's hands." At the bottom of the note Mrs. Roosevelt wrote, "Have I made it clearer?" On the copy of her letter, she penciled the changes, shown here in brackets.

June 2, 1950

Dear Mr. Gunther:

I waited so long to write you because it seemed to me that in the articles you had made some mistakes in your deductions. I am now half way through the book and how you achieved, with so little personal knowledge of my husband, as much understanding is extraordinary.

I know you wrote with admiration and a desire to be completely fair. There are certain things you did not entirely understand and of course, certain things that neither you nor anyone else knows anything about outside of the few people concerned. Whether it is essential they should ever know is still something on which I have [not] made up my mind. [since they are personal & do not touch on public service.]

Of course, I am sorry that you incurred the kind of criticism which I am afraid will always come to those who try to be fair to this controversial family.

I hope you and your wife will have a wonderful trip to Japan and I shall look forward to hearing your impressions. When you get back let me know and if I am not back on the General Assembly of the United Nations, do come with your wife for a week end.

Very cordially yours,

Eleanor Roosevelt to Joan H. Pera

July 21, 1950

Eleanor Roosevelt continued to write her newspaper column, "My Day," long after she was no longer first lady. She often received letters from readers either agreeing or disagreeing with her comments. Usually she did not respond individually to readers, but occasionally she did. One instance was the letter to Joan H. Pera of San Francisco in 1950. She may have responded to this letter for two reasons: because Mrs. Pera wrote a long and thoughtful letter and because Mrs. Pera asked her if she wrote only one paragraph for her column each day. Mrs. Pera wrote about peace, democracy, the Korean War, the Communist threat in America, the proposed anti-Communist Mundt-Ferguson Bill, and the Fair

Employment Practices Commission (FEPC). In her reply, Mrs. Roosevelt dealt with each of the issues Mrs. Pera had covered.

July 21, 1950

Dear Mrs. Pera:

In answer to your letter I never write one paragraph. I am limited to 450 words in my column but very frequently the newspapers cut for lack of space and frequently also they cut because they do not like what I write.

I think by now you probably listened or read the President's speech on Wednesday night in which he gave the history of the whole Korean situation. If you haven't I would suggest you get a copy of a news paper that carried it in full because it will give you the explanation of the Korean situation and the reason why the United Nations declared it a case of aggression and the President's feeling that our hope for peace lay in showing that the United Nations would be upheld by those of us who believe in peace and justice.

I agree with you, of course, that the more fully we live democracy in our own country and the more we continue to improve it, the better it will be an answer to communism. I am firmly convinced, however, that Russia has not yet reached the level where she really believes that other people want peace and it may take them some time to do so. I believe the Russian people want peace but with a totalitarian government you can command your people and also you can fool them. I do not feel at all hopeless but I do feel we may have some uncertainty in the world for some time and it will require great strength on the part of our people to live through this period of uncertainty when what they want is security and peace.

I am against the Mundt-Ferguson Bill just as you are. I approve the FEPC and have voted for that and similar legislation and similar rights. I hope there will be no all-out war with Russia and I do not think she will attempt it but I think she will try to nag us first in one place and then in another just as she is doing in Korea because she still believes that some day she will bring about a world revolution. Stupid people like Senator McCarthy create the idea that our government is filled with communists and the Russians use that in their propaganda abroad saying that if they just wait we will join them as a communist nation.

We will probably until Russia accepts the fact that she is not going to bring about a world revolution, have to keep a mobile military force. I hope we can keep our economy from getting out of balance and our people from losing their heads and beginning to hoard which will push prices up and force us on a real war basis of rationing and restrictions, which I do not think at all necessary at the present time.

I have three sons all in the Reserves of the different services. They are all busy with their lives and deeply interested in what they are doing and they do not want to go to war any more than any other citizen, so I understand well how you and your husband feel. The issue of a free world is before us now and has to be fought out, point by point, wherever we meet aggression whether instigated by Russia or not.

I do not feel that comforting is condescending. It seems to me that Mrs. Luce[1] used it in the sense that there are times when I could do with a considerable amount of comforting but I think I can remain fearless and that I can be honest.

Very sincerely yours,

Note

    1. Clare Booth Luce, a noted playwright, served in the U.S. House of Representatives from 1943 to 1947 and as U.S. ambassador to Italy from 1953 to 1956. She was one of the first women to serve in a major diplomatic post.

Eleanor Roosevelt to W. Averell Harriman

July 31, 1950

Averell Harriman, an old friend of Eleanor Roosevelt's who administered the European operations of the Marshall Plan in 1950, was someone Mrs. Roosevelt could contact on many matters. In 1950, at the height of the Cold War, she wrote him regarding the status of Countess Alexandra L. Tolstoy, the youngest daughter of the famous Russian writer, who founded the Tolstoy Foundation in New York City to direct resettlement programs for refugees or escapees from Communist countries. The tone of her letter reflects something of the tension of the period concerning international relations.

July 31, 1950

Dear Averell,

    Countess Alexandra Tolstoy came to see me this morning. She is running out of money and she has talked to George Kennan[1] and many other people about this situation. They feel she has done valuable work in bringing other Russians, who are not communists, into the country and they promised to try and help but as far as I can find out, they have not been able to do anything and by the first of September she will be without funds.

Eleanor Roosevelt and Gov. Averell Harriman. (Courtesy of the Franklin D. Roosevelt Library)

She is very anxious to talk to you because she says the pamphlets now being done for use among the Russian people are pretty bad. She has an amazing amount of material in her office which could be helpful and she would like to help in getting good material over the radio and in written form. She says what is now going out over the Voice of America would be meaningless to the majority of Russian people and I must agree with her on that.

Above everything else she wants to see you and I think it might be useful to see her and get some of her ideas. She does not speak with the voice of the aristocracy, being Tolstoy's daughter, and she has been in prison with Stalin and others in the Politburo, so she knows a good deal about them. She has been here a number of years and is a pretty good American and she has worked hard for the Russian refugees. Her address is Tolstoy Foundation, 289 Fourth Avenue, New York City.

I only bother you because these are really troublesome times and we have to get across the difference between the people themselves and their government.

Very cordially yours,

Note

1. American diplomat credited with the development of the Containment Policy against Soviet expansion.

Eleanor Roosevelt to W. Averell Harriman

1950

In August 1950 Averell Harriman, from his office in the White House, wrote Eleanor Roosevelt concerning a note she had sent him regarding his statement about President Roosevelt's ideas at the Yalta Conference as to Manchuria. He mentioned that the Soviets had broken the agreement. Harriman asked her to keep this letter personal, adding that he had had breakfast recently with her son James.

[Handwritten, no date except 1950]

Dear Averell:

Of course I will consider anything you write as personal & please do the same with my letters.

I am quite sure the Russians have broken a great many agreements but I sometimes wonder if they understand what they agree to when they make agreements. I have come to think them actually stupid in actually taking in what we mean.

Jimmy told me he had a delightful time with you.

Affec

Eleanor Roosevelt to Dwight D. Eisenhower

September 22, 1950

Always a strong defender of the United Nations, Mrs. Roosevelt welcomed prominent people who advocated it as well. Gen. Dwight D. Eisenhower, the hero of World War II in Europe, was president of Columbia University in 1950. He served on the National Committee for a Free Europe, an organization that Mrs. Roosevelt endorsed, but she feared its stated purpose to support the UN was not clear. In this letter, she asked Eisenhower to clarify the organization's approval of the UN. Gen. Lucius Clay was the American commander in Germany.

September 22, 1950

My dear General Eisenhower:

I should like to congratulate you and your associates on the National Committee for a Free Europe for the effective nationwide Freedom Crusade that was launched by your speech on Labor Day. There is certainly a great need for people throughout the United States to understand the nature of the struggle in which we are engaged, and there is every indication that your committee will be able to carry its message to the average citizen.

However, there is one aspect of your campaign which concerns those of us who have been working with national organizations and communities to develop appropriate observances of United Nations Day throughout the country. The Freedom Crusade will be terminated with the ringing of the bell in Berlin on United Nations Day. However, there is no indication in the literature of your committee, nor in the Freedom Pledge which people will be asked to sign, nor in the publicity which is being given to your campaign on the radio and in the newspapers, that the Freedom Crusade is identified in any way with the United Nations. Indeed, some people have assumed that the Freedom Crusade is opposed to the United Nations and therefore does not support its present efforts to achieve peace with freedom and justice for all.

This has led to confusion in many communities where the various groups have been asked by both the Freedom Crusade Committee and by the local United Nations Day Committee to put on a store display or to conduct a religious program based upon the ringing of bells or to arrange an appropriate school program during the period of United Nations Week, October 16 to 24th. Since it would be impossible for these various groups to put on duplicate programs, the question is naturally being raised whether the two might not be combined.

It seems to me that the two programs—that of the Freedom Crusade and of the National Citizens' Committee for the United Nations Day—can go hand in hand. There is no conflict in the aims, since the programs are promoting the two arms of United States foreign policy today, and consequently can mutually support each other.

I am sure that we are in agreement in this, and I feel, as I hope you do, that we should answer the many requests coming in from all over the country by explaining that there is no conflict between the two programs and there is no reason why the local programs cannot be tied in with each other.

I am sending a copy of this letter to General Lucius Clay.

Very sincerely,

[DDEL]

Eleanor Roosevelt to Mrs. Hugh N. Marshall
December 11, 1950

A few months after the United States entered the Korean War to prevent South Korea from becoming Communist, Mrs. Roosevelt in New York received an angry letter from Mrs. Hugh N. Marshall, who lived in a rural area outside Dayton, Oregon. Incensed over what she interpreted as an American sellout to the Soviet Union and seeing Communists everywhere in government and Communist sympathizers in positions of prominence, Mrs. Marshall demanded to know where Mrs. Roosevelt stood on Communism during the height of the Cold War and on Communist conspiracy theories, hoping that the former first lady would clarify the confusion. Refusing to ignore Mrs. Marshall's disrespectful outburst, Mrs. Roosevelt retorted superbly. It was classic and vintage ER at her best.

December 11, 1950

Dear Mrs. Marshall:

I am very glad to try to answer your questions.

You ask "where do you stand on communism" and then you go on to say something about my husband's recognition of Russia[1] which opened the door to the trouble we find ourselves in today.

There is absolutely no connection since whether we had recognized or not recognized Russia we would have had difficulties with her as soon as she became strong enough to think she could bring about a world revolution.

Now to answer your question about myself. I am not a communist and I do not believe in any kind of communism but I do know the difference between intellectual Marxist communists and the present day Moscow communists.

I think very few mistakes have been made "in favor of Uncle Joe."[2] I do not happen to have ever referred to him in that way. My husband believed always that if you expected good from people they frequently lived up to this expectation. He, however, watched carefully.

I have no recollection that my husband ever had anything to do with Gerhart Eisler. My own connection with him was very slight. I simply forwarded information on to him and requested an investigation, as was the common practice about people who wished to come into the country. He was probably more of a fascist than a communist, but then the two have many things in common.

I do not happen to have been a close friend of Hallie Flanagan,[3] but I do believe that she did a magnificent job in the W.P.A.[4] theatre movement.

As to my young friend, Joseph Lash,[5] he has never been a protégé of mine. He organized the Students' Union years ago and was put out by the communist group.

I can see no reason for not backing Helen Gahagan Douglas.[6] She has no leaning toward Moscow and she has probably done more to fight communism because she has tried to help improve conditions in our own country. Communism thrives where people are not content with their home conditions.

Melvyn Douglas[7] is not a communist and has never been.

As to your last assertion about the Secretary of State,[8] you must have misunderstood a Christian remark. He simply did not cast another stone. Alger Hiss[9] was not convicted as a communist. He was convicted of perjury. I do not know, since the evidence is circumstantial and based on information from an ex-communist, whether even now I understand what lies back of the whole case, but I have never questioned the decision of the court.

Naturally no one approves of key positions in the government being held by communists or communist sympathizers.

It seems to me that your last question is a disloyal question. You can not believe that your government is selling you out to the communists anywhere. A suggestion such as yours makes me tremble for your good sense. Does it mean that you are primarily motivated by partisan feelings or that the type of newspaper and radio that you read and listen to, is so one-sided that you have no way of realizing that the great preponderance of truth lies not in people like Fulton Lewis[10] or in Westbrook Pegler[11] and John O'Donnell,[12] but with some of the decent people who believe in their government and in the decency of their public officials?

Very sincerely yours,

Notes

1. The United States formally extended de jure diplomatic recognition to the Soviet Union in 1933.

2. Premier Joseph Stalin was the Soviet dictator and general secretary of the Communist Party from 1922 to 1953.

3. Flanagan, a friend of Harry Hopkins, FDR's friend and former head of the Federal Emergency Relief Administration (FERA), was director of Vassar College's Experimental Theatre. In 1935, despite her radical vision and controversial beliefs, she became director of the Federal Theatre Project under the Works Progress Administration.

4. Works Progress Administration.

5. Joseph P. Lash was editor of the *Student Outlook*. In 1935 he led a new American Student Union to fight against fascism, wars, and racial bigotry.

6. Helen Gahagan Douglas, an actress, opera singer, and Democratic National Com-

mitteewoman for California, served in the United States House of Representatives from 1945 to 1951. She was unsuccessful in her endeavor to win a seat in the United States Senate in 1950.

7. The husband of Helen Gahagan Douglas, Melvyn Douglas enjoyed a long career as a distinguished American dramatic actor from Broadway to Hollywood. In 1930 he played opposite Helen Gahagan in David Belasco's last production, *Tonight or Never*.

8. Dean G. Acheson was secretary of state in President Harry S Truman's cabinet from 1949 to 1953.

9. Alger Hiss, who served in the Department of State from 1935 to 1947, surfaced in the late 1940s as the center of a national controversy over Communist infiltration in the United States government. In 1950 a jury found him guilty of perjury. After the collapse of the Soviet Union in 1991, a Russian general in charge of intelligence declared that Hiss had never been a spy for the Soviets.

10. Fulton Lewis Jr., a national affairs radio commentator for the Mutual Broadcasting Company, was a consistent right-winger who adamantly attacked President Roosevelt's New Deal and President Truman's Fair Deal. He supported the actions of Sen. Joe McCarthy of Wisconsin to investigate Communist infiltration in the government.

11. James Westbrook Pegler, an ultraconservative newspaper columnist who won the Pulitzer Prize in 1941 for his exposès on labor union racketeering, wielded his scathing, malevolent style like a weapon against liberal Democrats. His widely syndicated columns appeared in the *New York World-Telegram* and *Sun* and for the King Features Syndicate throughout the 1930s, 1940s, and 1950s. In the early 1960s, he wrote for the John Birch Society's *American Opinion*.

12. A Republican publisher and editor, John O'Donnell put forth a strong and forthright editorial policy from his base in Pennsylvania. In 1929 he moved to Oil City, Pennsylvania, where he was general manager of the Derrick Publishing Company and editor of the *Oil City Derrick*. He remained unrelenting in his fierce opposition to the Roosevelts.

Eleanor Roosevelt to Harry S Truman

December 14, 1950

Usually Mrs. Roosevelt wrote President Truman each time she returned from a meeting of the United Nations or one of its committees. In this report, made after the Korean War had begun, she expressed concern about the lack of friendship and support the United States had received from the smaller nations of the world. She seemed bothered that the United States was often grouped in their minds as a colonial power, along with Great Britain and other European countries.

December 14, 1950

Dear Mr. President:

The General Assembly has come to an end for all intents and purposes, though I understand it will probably only recess and that the delegates may be on call.

In any case, I want to thank you for giving me the opportunity of serving in this General Assembly and to tell you that I have been somewhat disturbed by the atmosphere which I found prevalent toward the United States.

Committee #3, not being a political committee as you know, the members of the various delegations act with a good deal of freedom and less direction from the top than they would in a political committee where the results of their actions would have more immediate political repercussions. Therefore, I think one sees what might be called honest-to-goodness trends of feeling.

It certainly is a trend of dislike of the domination of big nations and a feeling that small nations should have more to say.

The race question has become a very vital one since much of the feeling is that of the colored races against the white race. We are classed with the Colonial Powers as having exploited them because our business men in the past have exploited them, so we have no better standing than the United Kingdom or any other Colonial Power. I think we have to reckon with this in our whole world outlook because we will need friends badly and it is surprising how few we have in spite of all we have done for other peoples in the past.

I realize I sound like Cassandra,[1] but I think this situation should be better understood by our people as a whole and we should be bending every effort to correcting it as soon as possible.

Very sincerely yours,

Note

1. From classical mythology, now referring to a person who prophesies doom or disaster.

Eleanor Roosevelt to Henry A. Wallace
December 16, 1950

On December 12, 1950, Wallace wrote to Mrs. Roosevelt at her New York Park Sheraton Hotel residence complaining about the treatment he had endured regarding an ambiguous invitation he had received to appear on her Sunday afternoon television program on NBC. Mrs. Roosevelt apologized for the misunderstanding, claiming she had not known he had been asked to make an appearance and that she had issued her staff strict orders that in the future she wanted to be consulted before anyone was invited to come on the television program.

December 16, 1950

Dear Mr. Wallace:

I had no idea that you had been asked to go on my program. I would never have given you an excuse that was not a real one, had I known.

The people who run my program had an idea that it would be a good thing to have a program with all the people who had changed their minds about Russia since Korea. You were asked before I was told about the program and I refused to have such a program not knowing that you had been asked.

I am very sorry you were treated in this discourteous manner, and I am much annoyed with my own people for doing so. I have given strict orders that no one is to be asked to come on the program without consulting me first. I apologize to you.

However, I do not think it would have been good to have that kind of a program just now. Perhaps in the future it may seem wiser.

Very sincerely yours,

Eleanor Roosevelt to Winston Churchill

March 12, 1951

Mrs. Roosevelt often called on Winston Churchill to appear on television and radio programs with her. In 1951 she was planning to be in Geneva and then was to go to London to film a broadcast. She wanted Churchill to appear with her.

March 12, 1951

Dear Mr. Churchill:

While I am in Geneva during the month of April for the Human Rights Commission of the United Nations, I am planning to come to London to make a television program.

The BBC has agreed to make their facilities available on the evening of Sunday, April 22nd, for a half hour broadcast at eight-fifteen.

I should be very much honored if you would agree to do this program with me. It would simply be an informal discussion during which you will present matters which you believe to be of particular significance at this critical time in our history.

It is planned that this broadcast will be seen in Great Britain and simultaneously filmed for rebroadcast over the NBC network in the United States.

If for any reason you think it would be undesirable to broadcast the program in Great Britain, the BBC is quite willing to make the film which would then appear in the United States only.

Because of the great host of your admirers in the United States who wish to see and hear from you, I have been emboldened to impose on you to make this program which, I believe, will be a real contribution to British-United States understanding and good will.

If you are able to accept our invitation, Mr. Henry Morgenthau III[1] who assists me in making arrangements for my television programs will fly to London at the end of this month to work out all details with your office and the BBC in advance.

I hope to hear from you at your earliest possible convenience, and I shall look forward in any event to calling on you and Mrs. Churchill during my visit.

With affectionate regards,

Note

1. Henry Morgenthau III was the elder son of Henry Morgenthau Jr., FDR's secretary of the treasury. He produced ER's television program, *Prospects of Mankind,* in 1960–61.

Eleanor Roosevelt to Dwight D. Eisenhower
March 13, 1951

During her later career Mrs. Roosevelt made a number of television programs promoting causes in which she believed. While serving on the Human Rights Commission of the United Nations, she was planning to film a program in Paris to be broadcast later in the United States. She hoped to get Eisenhower to appear on the program, since his hero status from World War II would attract viewers. The former first lady was even willing to allow him to pick the topic of discussion for the program. Appointed president of Columbia University in 1948, Eisenhower had been granted an indefinite leave of absence in 1950 to serve as commander of NATO forces in Europe.

March 13, 1951

Dear General Eisenhower:

While I am attending the United Nations Human Rights Commission meeting in Geneva during the month of April, I plan to make a weekend visit to Paris in order to film a television program for subsequent broadcast in the United States by the NBC network as a public service. Film facilities for this purpose are being made available by the French National Broadcasting System on Saturday, April 21st.

I should be most highly honored if you would agree to appear on this program for an informal discussion of any matters of your choice. Of course, I should also be delighted if you would care to have any members of your staff appear on the program with you.

I feel most deeply that the continuing awareness of developments in Europe by our fellow citizens in the United States is a matter of primary importance. I was again impressed with this fact by the clear and simple eloquence of your words spoken during your last visit here. As you said, "the preservation of free America requires our participation in the defense of Western Europe. . . . . Success is attainable. Given unity in spirit and action, the job can be done."

I believe that a television program for the American people once again emphasizing the importance of this "unity in spirit and action," would have real significance at this time. I, therefore, hope that you will see fit to crowd it into your very heavy schedule.

Very sincerely yours,

Eleanor Roosevelt to J. Edgar Hoover
April 12, 1951

In 1951 Republican senator Joseph R. McCarthy of Wisconsin was vigorously pursuing his anti-Communist activities. J. Edgar Hoover, head of the Federal Bureau of Investigation (FBI), apparently wrote Mrs. Roosevelt a letter in which he raised several issues that concerned her. In her reply to him, she was critical of congressional investigating committees, although she did not specifically refer to McCarthy's activities, and revealed support for the role of the FBI in protecting American liberties.

April 12, 1951

Dear Mr. Hoover:

I have been trying very hard to get across the idea that the FBI should supersede all these Senate investigating committees. I know very well there are other groups that have responsibility for other than the particular federal offenses that fall under the FBI. I have felt for a long time that because of the rules under which the FBI operates, we would guard our freedoms much better if we operated primarily through them than through the other rather irresponsible channels of some of the investigating committees.

I think the second comments on the subject of investigating by the Kefauver Committee[1] were simply trying to suggest the idea that the FBI was capable of bringing people to the bar of justice, though I realize quite well in this particular instance it is really the local and state officials would have to be on their toes and of unquestioned integrity. The Kefauver Committee did perhaps a good piece of work in bringing it home to people that because of political influence these enforcement agents were not always effective.

Now as to the first remark you quote. I did not remember that it was on a broadcast but I have written it many times in my column, namely, that I would rather see more money go to the FBI and less to the congressional committee, and more money paid to the highest type people that can be obtained. I did say that I had heard of investigators whom I did not feel were the highest type. I can not give you any names of people who have told me of interviews but I think I can give you some instances. For instance I know of some one who is a great reader and has always read on every side of all questions. He takes as a regular thing a number of controversial magazines and papers, not because he is in any way in favor of what they say, but because he wants to know what they say. Some one from the FBI visited him and picked up one publication and said "this is a dangerous thing to have around" and proceeded to take it for granted that this man was in sympathy with such thinking.

It seems to me that the investigator would find out before hand the type of person he was visiting and not make such a mistake.

I also have been told of questions asked about people who were being checked up on when people whom they had given as reference were visited and I can not say that these things always seemed to show either great intelligence or great care in preparation.

If you will look in your files you may find the letter I wrote to you when the FBI checked up on Mrs. Helm.[2] That is the type of thing that should be eliminated if possible.

Very sincerely yours,

Notes

1. Headed by Tennessee senator Estes Kefauver.
2. Edith Helm, Mrs. Roosevelt's White House social secretary.

Eleanor Roosevelt to Harry S Truman
April 24, 1951

During her visits around the world, Mrs. Roosevelt usually reported to President Truman about her impressions. In this letter she comments that the "unanimous feeling over here" is favorable to Truman's dismissal of Gen. Douglas MacArthur during the Korean War. That certainly was not the opinion in the United States. Clearly, her first priority during these years was the Human Rights Commission of the United Nations. Her comments on French television are interesting.

April 24, 1951

Dear Mr. President:

I have just sent Mr. Hickerson[1] a copy of the enclosed statement which is the gist of a conversation I had in London, after dinner when I was there last Sunday.

Colonel Arthur Murray, who is now Lord Elibank, is an old friend of my husband's. He has had a long experience in military and diplomatic life. I also enclose a copy of a letter which he wrote to the London Times. If these have no interest, just destroy them but I thought it might be a slant on British thinking that might be helpful.

There is a unanimous feeling over here that your action on General MacArthur has brought new hope into the international situation. If only we can keep China from an all-out offensive which will mean more casualties in Korea, and perhaps set-backs which will tend to make it necessary to carry out the plans which the General has advocated and which we all pray we will not have to carry out. That is the only reason that I thought this conversation might have some value.

We move slowly on the Human Rights Commission but I hope by next week the votes will have been taken and the discussion ended on some of the toughest questions. Ratification by the Senate of whatever is agreed upon is a distant hope, I fear but one never knows what may happen.

We are taking pretty big gambles these days in so much that we do in different parts of the world that I think it is wonderful that any of the people who carry the responsibility can sleep at night. What a headache the Near East has become!

I saw Ambassador Jessup[2] for a few minutes in Paris where I was last

Saturday doing a television program on film with Mr. Schumann and Mr. Monnet[3] which will be flown back to the United States. They certainly are far behind us in television equipment and of all of the silly things, they have two different television companies and put out two different television sets and you can not get the programs of the rival companies on the same set. I think it will take some time to develop television in France.

With my very best wishes to you, I am

Very cordially yours,

Notes

1. John D. Hickerson, assistant secretary of state.

2. Philip C. Jessup, Hamilton Fish professor of international law and diplomacy from 1946 to 1961 at Columbia University, who also held various other positions such as United States representative to the United Nations General Assembly (1948–1952), United States ambassador-at-large (1949–1953), legal counsel to Dean Acheson, and member of the International Court of Justice. In 1938 he published a two-volume biography of Elihu Root, a New York Republican who served in the cabinets of Presidents William McKinley and Theodore Roosevelt.

3. Jean O.M.G. Monnet, father of the European Economic Community.

Eleanor Roosevelt to George C. Marshall
April 27, 1951

After the Korean War began, President Truman, unhappy with his secretary of defense, recalled Gen. George Marshall from retirement to take a second appointment in his cabinet. In April 1951 Mrs. Roosevelt wrote Secretary Marshall to update him on conversations she had with the head of the International Red Cross. She was especially concerned about developments in mainland China.

April 27, 1951

Dear General Marshall:

The other night at dinner, I had a talk with the head of the International Red Cross, Dr. Ruegger.[1] He said many fine things about his devotion to you. The Consulate[2] here has had some difficulties in getting any answers from him as regards prisoners of war in Korea. He murmured to me, when I asked him about these difficulties that there was no difficulty on top levels between the United States and the International Red Cross and you and he had always been friends. He said he had sent many inquiries but had been unable to get any answers and I imagine he was irritated at being asked when he could not get any answers, so perhaps this little difficulty will soon blow over.

I did want to tell you that I asked him about the trip from which he has just returned. He went to Peking with his wife. He says that Madame Sun Yat Sen is active in the government, that he saw some other people who were working and had a long talk with Chou-en-lai. He says he does not think he is a communist, certainly not a communist in the Russian sense. Dr. Ruegger seems to think that the reforms are genuine and that they were actually trying to get a clean government, free of graft. Chou said nothing which Western Europe could resent and I thought he felt that with proper handling something might be done to straighten out the present difficulties between China and the outside world.

I am enclosing to you a report of a conversation which I had in London and which might give you a side light on a certain type of British thinking. My conversation with Dr. Ruegger coming on top of it seems to confirm some of the things said and make it advisable for us, by hook or by crook to find out whether a United Nations advance would get any consideration in Peking.

Dr. Ruegger said he had just had a letter from the Chinese Ambassador whom he had seen over there. He thinks that is the only link with the outside world and that link should not be broken. He also felt he was feeling his importance somewhat.

He has admiration for Nehru,[3] but he felt Nehru has not stood on the right side very often of late and I think it is because Nehru was appalled at the thought of having China as an enemy.

I know we can not appease and I am not suggesting any action, because I do not know enough but I felt these two observations might be of some help to you and to the efforts made by the United Nations if there is a chance that there may be Chinese officials who are not communists. Some of the efforts being made for peace might have a hearing.

Very sincerely yours,

Notes

1. Paul J. Ruegger.
2. The Consulate of Switzerland.
3. Prime Minister Jawahralal Nehru of India.

Eleanor Roosevelt to Chester Bowles

June 1, 1951

Chester Bowles, governor of Connecticut and a former official in the New Deal, was interested in preserving the papers of Franklin Roosevelt and making them available for research. He agreed to help Averell Harriman develop a private foundation to raise money to be used for putting the papers, currently located in Hyde Park, in shape for use. Mrs. Roosevelt's letter to Bowles shows her interest and, incidentally, her attitude about the firing of Gen. Douglas MacArthur by President Harry Truman.

June 1, 1951

Dear Mr. Bowles:

I am so glad that you have agreed to help Averell Harriman and I do hope the Foundation gets under way. I will be glad to see you at any time. Perhaps you and Mrs. Bowles will come to Hyde Park for a night. I will be away from the 17th to about the 26th, but otherwise I expect to be here fairly steadily.

Now to answer your questions.

I feel that one of the first things the Foundation should do is to try to help the government to make available the papers dealing with this period of history which are now in the library at Hyde Park. It will be years before the government will get them in shape for use unless some help is given to it. I think the Foundation should take an interest in this memorial here and help develop it to make it of maximum value.

In addition I think probably the development of international understanding is one of the most important things we can lend our efforts to at the present time. Anything that could be done to develop that in the people as a whole would, from my point of view, be both a memorial to my husband and a real service to the world as well as a safe-guard to the US.

I do not know whom we could get as a paid executive director. I wish I did.

I think the fund raising should be done on two levels. One—asking for a few people who might want to contribute sizeable sums of money and through them, getting money which could carry the administrative part of the fund. Two—asking people to contribute small sums so they will feel it is their fund and take more interest in the work.

I was abroad during the MacArthur episode, but I was appalled by the reaction. I am relieved that it is dying out. I do not think it will really harm the Administration, but it shows in the people a lack of understanding of the international situation.

Very cordially yours,

Eleanor Roosevelt to Leon E. Johnson
July 20, 1951

In June 1951 Leon E. Johnson of Hobart, Oklahoma, associated with a construction company, wrote Mrs. Roosevelt about a plan he had to build a new "colored" municipality between Denison and Sherman, Texas. He described the location, adding that he had submitted a proposal to the Federal Housing Administration. This was to be a complete community that would include a shopping center, churches, schools, playgrounds, and a cemetery with a chapel. He indicated the black residents of the area supported the concept, since it offered a much better life. Johnson was also attempting to entice a company to move to the town where it would have cheap, docile labor. There is no indication if Johnson was black himself. His letter to Mrs. Roosevelt sought her "blessing and permission" to help stimulate interest in the community. Mrs. Roosevelt sent the idea to Walter White of the NAACP for his reaction. On July 16 he wrote her that he agreed that it was a poor idea. Then Mrs. Roosevelt answered Johnson, telling him clearly what she thought of the proposal.

July 20, 1951

Dear Mr. Johnson:

I thought over your letter very carefully and I think I should tell you that while in Texas and Oklahoma this may be a good plan, in the over-all picture I do not think it will be looked upon with favor by the leaders of the colored race. They feel segregation must be on the way out and if something is done which is for their good but which is exactly for them, they feel it is in the segregation pattern. In the long run they feel equality of opportunity and treatment is the only way their race can move forward.

Very sincerely yours,

Eleanor Roosevelt to Aubrey Williams
[1951]

In 1951 Aubrey Williams, a former New Dealer under Harry Hopkins in the Works Progress Administration (WPA) who had returned to his native Ala-

bama and to journalism, wrote a brief birthday note to Mrs. Roosevelt. He said he missed seeing her and having an occasional talk, adding that he hoped she was "not too unhappy over the state of the world. It must perforce get better, for ye gods—it can hardly get worse!" Despite her anxieties in the previous few years, she seemed more optimistic at this time.

[Handwritten draft, in reply to letter 10/9/51]

Dear Aubrey,

I am very appreciative of your birthday greetings.

In Dec I go to Paris for the G.A.[1] of the UN. I may go to India, Palestine, Israel & other countries to which I have been invited. All of which means I may not be back in the US until the middle of April.

I am not too unhappy with the state of the world. We have lived through dangerous times. I am hopeful that even the USSR realizes that no one wins a war especially an atomic war.

With many thanks & all good wishes,

Note

1. General Assembly.

Eleanor Roosevelt to Harry S Truman
December 21, 1951

In December 1951 Mrs. Roosevelt reassured President Truman that the United States was being represented well in the United Nations. She stated that she would be available to see him at his convenience. Mrs. Roosevelt showed concern that her travels might delay a meeting with him, but what she had to tell him could wait.

December 21, 1951

Dear Mr. President:

I imagine as I am only going to be home from the morning of the 22nd until the after the 31st, that you will be in Independence[1] and not anxious to see me. You know, of course, that if you want to see me I could arrange to come to Washington, Friday afternoon the 28th. I can be reached on the telephone at Hyde Park where I will be from the 23rd or early morning on the 24th until the late afternoon of the 28th. My telephone in Hyde Park, is Poughkeepsie 959, and in New York City it is Circle 7-7272. Then I will be in Hyde Park until the morning of the 31st when I leave for Paris.

I am very conscious of the responsibility which has fallen on my shoulders but I can assure you it is not really very heavy, for the representatives of the State Department—Dr. Jessup,[2] Mr. Sandifer,[3] Ambassador Gross[4] of the US Mission and other members of the delegation with their staffs are doing the really important work. We are deprived of Ambassador Austin's[5] friendships with the heads of delegations here who come from the permanent groups in New York and I am sorry that I do not feel that I can make up for that constant contact which he had, but I am doing my best and I hope when the final report is in you will feel satisfied.

It is still my belief that we should do as Mr. Cohen and I suggested in trying to have General Eisenhower in civilian clothes, state the purpose of NATO but we have had no answer to the telegram so I do not know what your thought on this really is.

There is much of interest to tell you but if I go straight from Paris to Pakistan and India as the State Department asked me to do, I am afraid it will be spring before I get back to report to you. However, much of what I have to say will keep. It is long range stuff and the others will tell you what the thought is on the immediate subjects better than I can.

With every good wish to you and the family for Christmas and the New Year, I am

Very cordially yours,

Notes

1. Independence, Missouri, Truman's hometown.

2. Philip C. Jessup was Hamilton Fish professor of International Law and Diplomacy from 1946 to 1961 at Columbia University. He also held various other positions such as United States representative to the United Nations General Assembly (1948–1952), United States ambassador-at-large (1949–1953), legal counsel to Dean Acheson, and member of the International Court of Justice. In 1938 he published a two-volume biography of Elihu Root, a New York Republican who served in the cabinets of Presidents William McKinley and Theodore Roosevelt.

3. Durwood Sandifer, an assistant to Dean Rusk.

4. Ernest Gross, special ambassador to the United Nations.

5. Warren R. Austin.

Draft of Report from Eleanor Roosevelt to Harry S Truman
Attached to letter dated December 21, 1952

This is a report that Mrs. Roosevelt sent to President Truman about her assess-

ment of the world situation. It is attached to a letter to the president dated December 21, 1952; therefore, it probably was enclosed in that letter. Again, Mrs. Roosevelt is quite candid in her opinions of leaders around the world, and she does not hesitate to inform the president of them. Her opinion of Winston Churchill, who had recently returned to power in Great Britain, is telling, while her comments on France and her colonial problems, especially Vietnam, are somewhat prescient. As usual her grasp of world affairs is deep and insightful.

[Only a handwritten note, "Report to the Pres,"
attached to a letter of 12/21/52]

I did not have the pleasure of seeing Mr. Churchill but I watched the actions of the British representatives and listened to some of the conversations. I got a very clear impression that after six years of not having to deal in a close manner with the Russians or with foreign affairs in the United Nations, they are not accustomed to the procedures. Mr. Eden[1] was shocked by Mr. Vishinsky's[2] way of speaking and while I think his speech was a very good complement to our Secretary of State's[3] speech, by itself it would have seemed much too mild.

Mr. Churchill has brought to the Foreign Office Mr. Lloyd[4] who is their representative on the disarmament conference. I understand he had had no experience in this area before. He preferred to go into the financial end of the government, and was quite upset when Mr. Churchill offered him the foreign office and told him he was doing so at Mr. Eden's request. This was rather doubted by some people who felt that Mr. Churchill had not wanted him in the financial end.

I think Mr. Churchill sees himself as the conciliator and is trying to create the picture in Europe that he is the wise and temperate and balanced person while we are the intemperate, rash and not-to-be-trusted-youngsters. To be sure, we will have to furnish the cash and materials and a good-deal of man power if anything goes wrong, but where diplomacy is concerned, the English and particularly the conservatives headed by Mr. Churchill, have had a longer experience than we have had and have a right to expect us to follow their leading.

The British controlled France in the Security Council vote and many other countries had to wait for their say-so. I rather imagine that Mr. Churchill has no more love and trust in Russia than he ever had, but his margin of vote was so small in the last election that he has calculated this is a way to raise his popularity.

He is quite as cognizant as we are of the fact that whereas we think with relief that in two years from now we will have enough military strength to stand up to the Russians, our allies think when you have that in two years from now what will you do. Will this preparation bring war upon us? We will be the battle ground and we do not want to be.

It is true that the men actually in the armies probably have better morale than they had before. General Eisenhower is particularly fitted for the job he is doing now. For the first time the men have modern weapons and good equipment where it has reached them. They say that in Vietnam the morale is good. Heaven knows it might be poor there because Mr. Monet told me last year that if he had his way he would give up Vietnam because without that drain they could afford to carry a rearmament of France.

This isn't the real truth because the coal situation is the key to the real economic burdens but there is some truth in it. When I suggested to him that he was accepting for that distant spot the wave of nationalism that was sweeping everywhere in that area and asked how he would feel about Morocco, his answer was that they had been in Morocco too many years and it was too close to France for any such thing to be considered, but that was a year ago. Their feeling on Vietnam is still the same and we know very well that what keeps them there is the fact that we want our flank protected and they know that because of that fact they can make us do certain things that might otherwise not be acceptable to us.

France is not the only country that is questioning what will happen two years from now and has some fear of the United States. They are not blind to the fact that our bases are not within Europe; that they ring the borders and they see their countries the battle ground with help coming only from outside. They understand that we would eventually liberate them but they do not know whether to be liberated isn't too costly and to a great many people anything is more acceptable than war.

Since France and Italy are the two capitalist nations, it is important to us that their economies prove that they can be on a sound basis. I am quite sure that Mr. Harriman will agree that this is not so as yet. Granted that the output of coal from the Ruhr, Great Britain and France should be increased their economies would be immediately stabilized but this hasn't as yet been done.

I can only describe my conclusions in the little study I was able to make on economic and social conditions in France as an historically interesting one. Most of the large industrialists and financial leaders talk in the way our people did in the 1930s. We have a few of them left today, but they still believe that you can exploit people and expect them to fight for conditions which can hardly be called decent existence. I will not bore you with a description of the social security system in France, but it has an effect on both the political and economic situations and the tax system while it may bring in a fair amount of revenue, is about as dishonest as it can be. The peasants are gaining in power and have more representation than before. Strangely enough they are either conservative or communist. Thirty-eight percent of the vote is labor, but twenty-four percent is communist. Most of the unions are poorly organized and have no financial stability. The communist unions fortunately are not much better organized but they are able to get whatever money they need from the USSR.

I believe that the USSR does not want an all-out war but is going to foment trouble wherever possible.

We were hurt is so many little ways. For instance, the presentation of a pamphlet: "WE CHARGE GENOCIDE". While it had very little effect in the United Nations before the recess, and had not been used by the USSR because I think they felt there were enough of us to answer it, it can however now be brought back to this country with added status because of its being presented to the United Nations and will carry a great deal of weight with our American Negroes and that is exactly what the USSR would plan.

We need something dramatic to prove to our allies that we are not planning war when we have attained equal strength with the Russians or what we feel is equal power, but we must show that we are going to use NATO to bring about peace.

I think it can easily be proved that nothing can be done with the Russians except that when we have power but with SHAPE[5] doing a military organization job something dramatic must emphasize what our ultimate objectives are.

What I pointed out as what had happened in Committee #3 last year, the line up of the have-nots against the haves, has been accentuated in action in Committees #2, #4, #5. Iran and Suez have led to a tightening up of the Moslem world. Our vote on Morocco, while I recognized the over-all reason which obliged us to do what we did, gave an opportunity to the communists and the Arab world to point out that we had no real interest in the things we claimed to be interested in, that we were really just like any other colonial power, and when we needed bases, the bases mattered and not the conditions of the people of the country. We had not even taken the trouble to ask the resident Frenchman to transmit a letter of request to the Sultan as regards our bases which he took as an insult and which would have cost us very little though he had no legal standing and there was no real reason why we should make the gesture.

Sir Zufrulla Khan of Pakistan made a most violent attack on the United States because of our Moroccan position and because he, himself, was overwrought. Nevertheless what he said represented the feelings of many of those countries and if the USSR were not so violent we might find more votes in their favor than we do at present. You have more countries taking as their thesis that the underdeveloped countries have through greater communication, discovered that you do not have to live in misery and disease and that you have a right to expect the developed countries will change the situation. They want the change but through the United Nations and not by bilateral action because in the United Nations they have an equal vote with any of us and they are going to do the kind of thing they have in committee #2, because this is the field in which they can get enough Latin American votes with them to carry a majority against us. You can not argue with the Latin Americans on a purely reasonable ground so the problem is a very real one and one that requires careful study on our part.

In closing I was asked to dine between planes with the manager of the KLM Airlines.[6] He took the opportunity to give me a plan which he had presented to his Prime Minister and Queen Juliana and for which he has their support. It is an economic plan on the international level. I do not think as it is that it would be completely workable or feasible, but I think it has a germ of something which might be the economic bait, after we have military strength, which I suggested before that we might find essential, so I would like to have it looked into and really given careful consideration for possible basic use and eventual integration with the United Nations. For instance, it could become a specialized agency and we might get the USSR to come in on it when she makes up her mind she has to live in the same world and make some kind of gesture of cooperation.

Notes

1. Anthony Eden.
2. Andrei Vishinsky, the Soviet vice commissar of foreign affairs.
3. Dean Acheson.
4. Selwyn Lloyd, minister of state at the Foreign Office.
5. Supreme Headquarters, Allied Powers Europe (NATO).
6. Royal Dutch Airlines.

Eleanor Roosevelt Political Statement

n.d. [1952?]

During the presidential campaign of 1952, Eleanor Roosevelt actively endorsed Gov. Adlai Stevenson, the Democratic standard bearer. This is a statement she wrote endorsing his candidacy, but if it were published, that information is not available.

I think we will all agree that the next President of the United States, as far as world affairs are concerned, should be a man with a global point of view.

One candidate has been a glamorous General and diplomat in one area of the world. Many people do not know that Governor Stevenson, our Democratic candidate, was responsible for all the preparatory work done in London prior to the first meeting of the General Assembly of the United Nations in 1946. Before most of the rest of us had an opportunity to meet representatives from nations from every part of the world he had already made his contacts and knew them well. Since then he has kept in close touch with the United Nations and served on the United States Delegation several times. As a result I suppose he has a better world understanding than almost any other man in this country, and more important, he actually knows men who have been in their governments in practically every country in the world. This is a great asset and it seems to me that thoughtful people will be glad to have a candidate with such background and preparation.

Eleanor Roosevelt's Statement for Students for Stevenson
n.d. [1952?]

During the 1952 presidential campaign, Eleanor Roosevelt did what she could for Gov. Adlai E. Stevenson. She even prepared a statement for student organizations for Stevenson. The cause for misspelling of Stevenson's name is not known, but one might assume that it was the work of a stenographer not familiar with Stevenson. Mrs. Roosevelt was trying to stem the growing tide for Dwight Eisenhower.

STATEMENT FOR STUDENTS FOR STEPHENSON [*sic*]
Eleanor Roosevelt

It seems to me that young people have a great stake in the present election. The next four years are crucial years for the future. Either we embark on a permanent military preparedness program or we will find, at least, the first steps taken with which we move toward greater confidence in each other throughout the world.

Only a man who is fully aware of the dangers of the situation, but who also has imagination and faith in the future will bring us through this period safely. It seems to me that Governor Stevenson has demonstrated in the way he has conducted his campaign so far that he is able to think clearly, to control his emotions, and with great knowledge of the world and its people. I think this would be valuable in meeting the next four years' problems. In domestic affairs he certainly will be sympathetic to youth's interests because he has sons of his own.

I hope that the young people of the nation will listen to his speeches with care as they will undoubtedly listen to General Eisenhower's speeches and on the basis of which man seems to them to offer the greatest promise of meeting the world's problems, they should cast their votes on Election Day.

Eleanor Roosevelt to Harry S Truman

January 29, 1952

Concerned about the possible appointment of an American ambassador to the Vatican, the spiritual and governmental center of the Roman Catholic church headed by the Pope, Mrs. Roosevelt wrote President Truman to break her silence on this matter and express her feelings, especially since she wanted him to hear her views before she made a public statement. The United States restored formal relations with the Vatican in 1984 under President Ronald Reagan after Congress repealed an 1867 ban on diplomatic connections with the Italian city.

Hotel Crillon, Paris
January 29, 1952

Dear Mr. President:

I have not written you anything before but I am afraid I must now break my silence about the appointment of an ambassador to the Vatican. I am getting letters on every side as I am sure you are too and I feel that perhaps I should tell you it seems to me since we are a Protestant country, we should heed the very evident feeling so many Protestants have against having an ambassador at the Vatican. I understand that an ambassador can be appointed only when you have signed the Concordat, but it is not possible for a state which is not a Catholic state to sign. Automatically, if the Vatican has an ambassador in a Catholic state he takes precedence over the entire diplomatic corps. This, in a non-Catholic state would make a very embarrassing situation. In the case of Great Britain, they have a minister at the Vatican for this very reason because then a minister sent by the Vatican has the same standing as the papal delegate and it does not bring the conflict that having an ambassador does. For the purpose of the U.S., I have always felt that a special representative of the President gave all the advantages and avoided the pitfalls which the appointment of an ambassador or minister brings about.

It is easy to understand this present objection. The recognition of any church as a temporal power puts that church in a different position from any of the other churches and while we are now only hearing from the Protestant groups the Moslems may one day wake up to this and make an equal howl. For us who take a firm stand on the separation of church and state, the recognition of a temporal power seems inconsistent.

I write these random thoughts because I am sure someday someone is going to ask my opinion and I do not want to say that I think it not a good idea without having expressed myself to you beforehand.

I will write you a report on this session before I leave on the 8th if all is well and finished here.

Please give my good wishes to Mrs. Truman and Margaret and believe me always

Cordially yours,

[HSTL]

Eleanor Roosevelt to Dwight D. Eisenhower
February 5, 1952

Mrs. Roosevelt constantly sought support for the United Nations. While she was in Paris for a United Nations meeting, she wrote General Eisenhower, who was commanding NATO forces in Paris, asking him to send a message for the UN Association meeting.

Hotel Crillon, Paris
February 5, 1952

Dear General Eisenhower:

I have a letter from Mr. Clark [M.] Eichelberger[1] saying that you are going to be kind enough to send him a message for the UN Association meetings that are coming along in the near future. I hope you will be good enough to do this because it will mean so much in awakening interest which is difficult to do in the United States.

I am sorry not to have seen you while I have been here but I felt I was one of the few people who could not contribute to the fine work you are doing.

With kind regards to Mrs. Eisenhower and to you, I am

Very sincerely yours,

[*DDEL*]

Note

1. An author and lecturer who was national director of the American Association for the United Nations.

Eleanor Roosevelt to Harry S Truman
March 7, 1952

While on a trip to India, Mrs. Roosevelt took the opportunity to write President Truman some complimentary remarks about the American ambassador there. Chester Bowles, the former governor of Connecticut, was her longtime acquaintance and friend. She also made favorable remarks about Prime Minister Jawaharlal Nehru and the legacy of the late Mohandas K. Gandhi. Her less-than-favorable remarks about Chiang Kai-shek, the leader of Nationalist China, are interesting.

RESIDENCY GUEST HOUSE
BANGALORE
March 7, 1952

Dear Mr. President:

I want to tell to tell you now that I have been a short time in India what a really extraordinary job our Ambassador, Mr. Bowles, seems to have done. In one way I think perhaps Providence did something for us when he was defeated in the last election so that he could be available for his present post.

India seems to need very special treatment at this time and seems to be very vital to our own interests. Everywhere, without exception, and I think I have met every government official thus far, tells me what a change there has been in the feeling toward the United States since Mr. Bowles' arrival. They feel now that we understand them, that we are more understanding of their isolationism and that we are beginning to realize that they do not want to become communistic but their problems are so great they feel they cannot take sides.

I only hope that we can do the things that seem essential to them. The problem here is much the same as that of China, though in Nehru we have a leader of infinitely higher quality than Chiang. Mr. Nehru has around him a great many good men. Gandhi has left his mark and there is an unselfish service being given among young and old which might be of help even in our own democracy.

Mr. Bowles has done everything possible for me but I am afraid I can never accomplish what the Indians want as a result of my visit.

With all good wishes,

Very cordially yours,

[*HSTL*]

Eleanor Roosevelt to Chester Bowles
April 21, 1952

After Mrs. Roosevelt returned from India, she mailed a letter to Chester Bowles, the American ambassador to India. His response on April 10 caused her to respond with this letter, which answered several of the questions he had asked.

April 21, 1952

Dear Mr. Bowles:

I have been waiting to write you but your letter makes me send you this preliminary report.

Shortly after my return I met with the President and the Secretary[1] and told them much about the India part of my trip. Both seemed very interested. I got Franklin, junior, to get together some Republicans and Democrats, members of the House Foreign Relations Committee. He said they were the more important and more vocal. They asked me questions which I answered as fully as possible and he told me that the evening was really of value. I hope it was.

I am going to Washington again on the 6th of May. Franklin said he would ask Senator Lehman to call together some of the Senators so I could do the same with them.

Everybody is so immersed now in the primary campaigns that it is difficult to get their minds off domestic questions. Governor Stevenson has bowed himself out which I deeply regret and New York is making Averell Harriman its favorite son. Franklin, junior, is going to run the citizens' committee.

I could not manage the broadcast with Ed. Murrow.[2] I did not know it was one of the things you wanted but I just could not do it at the times he wanted me.

Taft[3] and Eisenhower seem to run closely together but I think Eisenhower has much more appeal. It may result in Warren[3] and I hope as you do, it will not be Stassen.[4] Kefauver[5] appeals to me less and less.

Both Jimmy and Franklin wish to be remembered to you because both of them were so anxious to hear about everything that was going on and they both have a great admiration for what you are doing and realize that Mrs. Bowles and the children are doing their part valiantly.

Esther was very much interested when I talked to her on the telephone. Unfortunately I haven't been able to see her and hope she will come into New York City soon because I am tied to the Human Rights Commission.

With my best wishes to you and Mrs. Bowles, I am

Very cordially yours,

Notes

1. Secretary of State Dean Acheson.
2. Edward R. Murrow, a radio and television newsman.
3. Sen. Robert A. Taft of Ohio.
4. California governor Earl Warren.
5. Harold E. Stassen, former Minnesota governor.
6. Tennessee senator Estes Kefauver.

Draft Reply to Two Telegrams
April 1952

In April 1952 Mrs. Roosevelt received two telegrams, one from the editor of an African American newspaper and the other from a board member of Bethune-Cookman College, asking Mrs. Roosevelt to comment out on the treatment of the founder of the college, Mary McLeod Bethune, who had been denied the opportunity to speak at a school in New Jersey. As Carl Murphy, the editor, said of Mrs. Bethune, she "is not a communist, never has been one, would not be one, and because of her social, economic and Christian practices would not be acceptable to the communists themselves." This is a handwritten draft response to the two telegrams. Mrs. Roosevelt mentions a "statement" by Mrs. Bethune, but it is not available.

Handwritten reply to two telegrams dated April 1952

I think the enclosed copy of Mrs. Bethune's "Statement" is the best I can give you.

What I object to is guilt by association. Many of the groups now on the subversive list were not communist in the beginning but have been taken over & controlled by communists. The whole complexion has changed.

Eleanor Roosevelt to Harry S Truman
May 31, 1952

Mrs. Roosevelt, always known for her concern about racial minorities, was upset when Congress was considering an immigration restriction law known as the McCarran-Walter Bill. As usual, she did not hesitate to advise President Truman on her opinions, whether he asked for them or not. She was worried about how Asians would react to a bill that on the surface removed some restrictions against their immigration, but which she believed actually increased controls.

May 31, 1952

Dear Mr. President:

I try not to bother you too often but I am very much troubled at the moment about the McCarren-Walters Bill.[1] I realize that I can not possibly know much in detail about any legislation and this is a complex and technical subject.

However, I hear that this Bill would generally restrict immigration and make it more difficult than it now is. It would remove the barriers to naturalization for certain Asiatics and provide a small quota for a number of Asiatic countries which now do not have a quota.

Of course, the removal of racial barriers is all to the good but I understand that this legislation sets up a special classification for persons of Asiatic and Oriental ancestry and sets them completely apart from Europeans and others in a highly restricted category. I am told that it even defines a fifty percent blood test for persons of Asiastic ancestry no matter where born.

The people of Asia are just at present over-sensitive and very proud and I am afraid the enactment of such a bill with these provisions would be very unfortunate. I also think that the Russians would use it for plausible propaganda against us.

Most of us would like to see exclusionist bars go down but not in favor of new ones which would provide fresh evidence that we consider ourselves "superior" to the peoples of Asia.

This legislation may be before you any day for signature and if on mature consideration you think it is really bad, I hope you will veto it, though I realize I can not be familiar with it from every point of view. I am only writing you what my general feeling has been.

Very cordially yours,

Note

1. McCarran-Walter Bill. Named for Sen. Patrick A. McCarran of Nevada and Rep. Francis B. Walter of Pennsylvania.

Eleanor Roosevelt to Harry S Truman
draft, n.d.

Mrs. Roosevelt wrote this first draft of the letter she sent to President Truman on May 31, 1952. It is almost identical to the final one, but it sheds light on her thoughts.

[No date; it is a draft]

Draft

Dear Mr. President:

As a rule, I try to avoid becoming involved in any way with purely domestic issues and legislation before the Congress.

However, I have been hearing a great deal about certain legislation, which disturbs me very greatly, not only because of its domestic implications, but even more, because of its foreign implications. I refer to the pending Omnibus Immigration legislation, called the McCarran-Walter Bill.

I am not, of course, informed in any great detail concerning all the provisions of this legislation. Obviously I could not be. As I understand it, very few people are. It is a complex and technical subject which defies me, and most of us.

Nevertheless, I do hear that much is being made of the fact that this Bill which, as I hear it, would in general greatly restrict immigration and make it immensely more onerous and difficult, would remove the barriers to the naturalization of certain Asians, and provide a small quota for a number of Asian countries which now do not have quotas.

Of course the removal of racial barriers is all to the good. However, I also understand that this same legislation sets up a special classification for persons of Oriental-Asian ancestry, and sets them completely apart from Europeans and others, in a highly restricted category. It even defines a 50 percent "blood test" for persons of Asian ancestry no matter where born.

It seems to me that the Russians could make as good propaganda use of these provisions as of our present unfortunate exclusion provisions. I need not tell you how proud and sensitive the peoples of Asia are.

I think the enactment of such a Bill, with these provisions, would be most unfortunate. I would like to see the exclusionist bars go down, but not in favor of these new ones which would provide fresh evidence that we consider ourselves "superior" to the peoples of Asia. Such an enactment would in my judgment, have a terrible effect, coupled, as it is, with all the other restrictive provisions of this legislation.

I am writing these words to you because you may have this legislation before you for signature one of these days. I just want you to know of my views, being certain that you will want to consider all viewpoints on this matter.

Eleanor Roosevelt to Burt Drummond
May/June 1952

Burt Drummond of Buffalo, New York, could not let the Hiss case rest as far as Mrs. Roosevelt was concerned. He seemed too certain that he could change her views if she would just listen. Two years after the end of the case and after he had exchanged letters with Mrs. Roosevelt, he wrote to her again. He said he hoped she accepted the jury verdict of Hiss's guilt. Drummond believed that had Whittaker Chambers's entire story come out before the election of 1948, President Truman would have been defeated—then the future "would now be far more hopeful than it is, due to the crippled mentalities which have so long been at the helm in Washington." Again, Mrs. Roosevelt answered him—and most public personalities probably would not have—in a succinct letter. This is a draft written by Mrs. Roosevelt's secretary.

[Handwritten draft; no date except answering a letter of 5/25/52]
In ans to your letter one always accepts a court verdict till it is proven false, which has happened, however.

I do not think there are crippled mentalities in Wash on the whole. There are always a few anywhere. I do not believe the country has suffered more from Hiss than from Chambers who, on his own evidence, was a communist for a long period.

Eleanor Roosevelt to Adlai Stevenson

August 6, 1952

During the presidential campaign of 1952, Eleanor Roosevelt offered advice to Adlai E. Stevenson, a good friend and the Democratic nominee. She regularly tried to persuade him to accept advice from Bernard Baruch, a financier and political adviser, but like President Truman, Stevenson questioned an association with Baruch, whose reputation was not impeccable.

August 6, 1952

Dear Governor Stevenson:

I was asked by the two gentlemen whose letter[1] I enclose if I would forward it to you. I assure you that they want nothing after the campaign. They both have work to do and this is a purely altruistic offer on their part, so I think you are quite safe in accepting if you can use them.

The papers state that you are coming to New York City late in August. Will you forgive me if I make a suggestion to you? I have a feeling that Mr. Baruch would be very much flattered if you ask, as soon as possible, whether you could see him while you are in New York. This may seem to you a waste of time and of course, if you feel it is, I do not want you to consider this suggestion. However over the years Mr. Baruch gave some good financial advice to my husband and he has had long experience in organizing materials in two wars.

Unfortunately President Truman is so annoyed because Mr. Baruch would not give up his old rule of not coming out openly for a candidate and heading a financial committee for him that they exchanged unfortunate letters and President Truman felt that his information could be of no use to him.

You may feel exactly the same way but I have always found that while it took a little tact and some flattery to get on with the old gentleman I got enough information with valuable experience back of it to make it worth while. He is not always a liberal and you will not always agree with him but fundamentally he is sound and I think it is valuable to have some contacts with him, particularly unofficial ones.

With warm good wishes and appreciation of the fact that I am just adding one more headache to the many you probably have, believe me

Very cordially yours,

Note

1. Letter not available.

Eleanor Roosevelt to Harry S Truman
November 6, 1952

Shortly after the defeat of Adlai E. Stevenson by Dwight D. Eisenhower for the presidency in 1952, Mrs. Roosevelt wrote President Truman to thank him for having sufficient confidence to appoint her to the American delegation to the United Nations and to promise a report on a trip to Chile before Christmas. She took the opportunity to give her opinions on the electoral defeat and expressed her reservations about how much Eisenhower could do to end the war in Korea.

November 6, 1952

Dear Mr. President:

I will hope to get down to Washington some time before Christmas to report to you on my visit to Chile and on anything else that turns up in the General Assembly.

In the meantime I want to thank you for the many opportunities you have given me for service during your administrations.

I know that after the great efforts you put into the campaign it must be a keen disappointment to you but I think we were against impossible odds, especially the feeling many people had that they want their boys home from Korea. I am afraid General Eisenhower will not be able to fulfill the hopes of these people, and it may be difficult for him in consequence. I like your offer of your own plane to go immediately to Korea.

With every good wish

Very cordially yours,

Eleanor Roosevelt to Bernard Baruch
November 18, 1952

In 1952 Eleanor Roosevelt's favorite candidate, Adlai Stevenson, lost the presidential race to the popular hero of World War II, Dwight D. Eisenhower. Mrs. Roosevelt was not particularly impressed with Eisenhower and was not sure how good a president he would be. Some of her friends were urging her not to resign from her post in the United Nations, a position that she had held throughout the Truman administration. She believed resignation was proper since the power balance in American government was shifting and it would not be right to try to stay on in the UN under a Republican administration. She explained her rationale to her good friend, Bernard Baruch, and elaborated on what she saw her future role to be.

November 18, 1952

My dear Friend:

Thank you for your very kind letter.

It isn't within my hands to resign or not to resign. Each of us does that automatically and I think it would be highly unfair not to resign from the Human Rights Commission.

I want you to think over the problem in the following way. I have been able, because the President has always been willing to see me, to discuss with him at the end of every meeting or of any mission which I undertook, everything that had occurred. The State Department, which always received my report first, was glad to have me do this because they felt that frequently reports sent from the State Department go to secretaries and never reach the President. Therefore, I was able to get to the President what I thought the non-governmental organizations and the women of this country generally felt on a great many subjects, as well as the routine report of what had occurred and my opinion of what other nations felt.

This would be impossible with General Eisenhower, since I hardly know him and since I do not belong to the party that will be in power. If there were a number of American women being given important positions on the policy-making level in the United Nations, then I think it would be right to have representatives from both parties. But since the number of women is very limited, I think it is important that it be a woman who can reach the President with the point of view of the women and who also has the interests of the United Nations at heart.

Of course this does not mean that I shall take less interest or be less active but I think of good Republican women, Mrs. Bolton[1] or Mrs. Read,[2] who will do an excellent job.

I shall take as much as I can get in TV and radio programs and I shall feel free to criticize constructively. I think this is a good role for anyone to play.

I hope Governor Stevenson will be the leader of the party and help build up a good strong Democratic party which can play a fair and constructive role in opposition. I have spent many years of my life in opposition and I rather like the role.

I know how interested you always are in me and I am grateful to you for your interest but I am sure you will see the wisdom both for the women and representation of their interests and for the sake of the women's point of view in the UN getting good representation and appreciation by the President.

Affectionately and gratefully,

Notes

1. Frances Payne Bolton, Ohio Republican congresswoman.
2. Probably Mrs. Elbert A. Read, an Iowa civic leader.

Eleanor Roosevelt to Elizabeth Stevenson Ives
November 24, 1952

Shortly after the presidential election of 1952 in which Adlai Stevenson lost to Dwight D. Eisenhower, Mrs. Roosevelt wrote to Elizabeth Ives, Stevenson's sister. She was complimentary of Stevenson's campaign and complimented Mrs. Ives on her activity. Mrs. Ives responded with a laudatory letter and promised to try to see Mrs. Roosevelt when she and her husband came to New York in the future.

November 24, 1952

Dear Mrs. Ives:

I have not written to you before this because I know you have been deluged with letters, but I wanted to tell you how wonderful I think you and your brother were during the campaign. I think the outcome was almost more of a disappointment to you than it was to him because when you love some one you hate to see him lose.

The campaign was well worth while in that it started a process of education which I hope will continue for the next four years.

If you come to New York City at any time I hope you will let me know and that I may have an opportunity to see you.

Very sincerely yours,

Eleanor Roosevelt to Dwight D. Eisenhower
December 8, 1952

Shortly after Dwight D. Eisenhower was elected president in 1952, Mrs. Roosevelt decided to resign from her position as the American delegate to the Human Rights Commission of the United Nations. She wrote this letter to Eisenhower on December 8 and shared it with friends before mailing it to him. Upon advice, she decided to keep her resignation separate from her report on the commission. Therefore, the opening and closing paragraphs of this letter were deleted and used in another letter for her formal resignation. This letter stood as her report on the commission's work.

December 8, 1952

Dear Mr. President:

~~I am herewith tendering my resignation as the U.S. member on Human Rights Commission of the U.N.~~

~~I hope you will forgive me if I take this opportunity to say a few things about work of this Commission which I think you might like to know.~~

The subject of human rights has been receiving increasing attention and importance in the United Nations. The United Nations is drafting and proposing standards of action in this field. The United Nations can be effective in this respect, however, only to the extent these standards are supported and effectuated in individual countries. It is through action in each country that respect for the inherent dignity and worth of the human person will be achieved. In the United States we must continue to press ahead for the elimination of the discriminations which unfortunately still exist in our country. We are making progress in this respect, but we still suffer from too many discriminatory practices.

In spite of our inadequacies, the United States is at the forefront of the countries in the world in observing basic human rights and freedoms, and other countries accordingly look to us for moral leadership in this field in the United Nations. Our Declaration of Independence, Bill of Rights and Constitution are referred to by many as symbolic of the goal sought for all people throughout the world, and documents being drafted in the United Nations generally reflect their great principles. We have much to contribute, and we have in fact been contributing to the work of the Commission on Human Rights and other organs of the United Nations in the development of basic principles of fundamental freedoms and human rights.

There are a number of important matters now pending before the Commission on Human Rights. One of these is the completion of the two draft Covenants on human rights on which the Commission has worked since 1947.

It is anticipated that the Commission will complete its work on these two draft Covenants at its next scheduled eight-weeks session beginning April 6, 1953. Other human rights matters to be considered by the Commission at its 1953 session will include the reports of the United Nations Subcommission on the Prevention of Discrimination and Protection of Minorities, the draft Declaration on the Rights of the Child, local human rights committees, communications to the United Nations concerning alleged violations of human rights, and the United Nations Yearbook on Human Rights.

In the matter of the Covenants being drawn as treaties and having to be ratified by each nation according to their constitutional processes, none of us can be sure, of course, that when they are completed these treaties will be considered constitutional by our Senate. The members of the State Department who have worked on them have made every effort to have, at least the Covenant on Civil and Political Rights, in conformity with our Constitution. In any case, there is the possibility of making reservations on a document of this kind.

The members of the United States delegation who have worked on this, most of whom would of course aid a new appointee, believe strongly that the basic freedoms and human rights of all peoples everywhere must be respected in order that we may achieve international peace, justice and security. These goals are tied so closely together that it is illusory to seek one without the others.

~~I haven't had an opportunity to wish you well since your election but as I know how heavy your burdens will be, I want to do so at the present time.~~

Believe me,

Very sincerely yours,

Eleanor Roosevelt to "Sandy"
December 10, 1952

When Mrs. Roosevelt on December 8, 1952, drafted her letter of resignation and report on the UN Human Rights Commission to President-elect Eisenhower, she dispatched the letter to friends for comment. This letter to "Sandy," probably Durward V. Sandifer, State Department adviser to the U.S. delegation to the United Nations from 1946 to 1951, was also modified, explaining that she decided to separate her resignation from her report on the Commission's activities.

December 10, 1952

Dear "Sandy":

I am enclosing my letter of resignation to President-elect Eisenhower which <u>when the time</u> is ~~all~~ right, you will present<u>.</u> ~~at the proper time.~~

I am also enclosing a copy of what I have written on the basis of Jim Simsarian's[1] suggestions which he told me were also yours. I thought it over and decided that my letter of resignation should be just that, and that the report should be separate. ~~Having resigned I do not want to be in the position of giving advice until I am asked for it—when and if.~~

~~Please also tell me if you do not think this is right.~~

Very sincerely yours,

Note

1. An officer in charge of U.N. cultural and human rights affairs.

Eleanor Roosevelt to Dwight D. Eisenhower
December 15, 1952

After Mrs. Roosevelt conferred with friends, she sent a simple letter of resignation from the Human Rights Commission of the United Nations to President-elect Eisenhower. It was succinct and to the point.

December 15, 1952

Dear Mr. President:

I am herewith tendering my resignation as the United States Member to the Human Rights Commission of the United Nations.

I haven't had an opportunity to wish you well since your election, but as I know how heavy your burdens will be, I want to do so at the present time.

Believe me,

Very sincerely yours,

Eleanor Roosevelt's Introduction to Book about Bernard Baruch
[1953]

In 1953 Eleanor Roosevelt wrote a foreword to a biography of Bernard Baruch, Peace through Strength: Bernard Baruch and a Blueprint for Security *by Morris V. Risenbloom. She had long been a friend and confidante of Baruch's, and this relationship shows in this draft. This clearly is an early draft, since the final foreword published in 1953 is significantly longer and spells out in more detail Mrs. Roosevelt's respect for Baruch. She did not hesitate to praise Baruch even though many of her close associates never trusted him and never were willing to support the programs in which he was involved.*

I have always found Mr. Baruch to be a man who put his country above all personal considerations. He has an imaginative vision which gives him confidence that many situations can be met. If you do not know the answer, you will try to find the person who has the answer. This is a quality which my husband also had and I think it arises from confidence in dealing with people and with problems. All during his life I think Mr. Baruch has been very conscious of the welfare of the people as a whole.

I always found that in advising my husband he never for a moment lost sight of the effect any action would have on the lot of the working people, whether engaged in agriculture or in industry. For us, in the United States, he has filled a unique position. Many people listened to him and trusted him and his testimony before Congress has been valuable not only because of its effect on members of Congress but because of the attention given to it by the people as a whole which gave whatever he said immeasurable educational value. He has stressed with great foresightedness the value of preparedness. His recommendation on atomic energy still stands even after some years have elapsed as the wisest proposition yet made, even though the Soviets have not accepted it.

He has great vision for the future thinking in terms of the cooperative use of atomic power for peaceful purposes and the building up of underdeveloped areas. He sees in both of these things a way to establish a fuller life for all the people of the world and he hopes that eventually this troubled world will have both peace and freedom.

He was a friend and trusted adviser whose words were always listened to whether my husband was in Albany or in Washington. Around a president there will always be jealousies and stresses but Mr. Baruch always rose above them. To me personally he has been a much appreciated adviser and warm friend. He has served his country well in the past and I feel sure that his advice if followed will be a great service in the years to come.

This book contains many of his speeches and public statements which have the mark of long and deep thought so it is Mr. Baruch himself giving us the value of his mature judgement. It is a valuable book and one to be read with attention.

Eleanor Roosevelt

Eleanor Roosevelt to Walter Reuther

January 11, 1953

In 1953 Mrs. Roosevelt wrote to Walter Reuther, head of the Congress of Industrial Organizations (CIO) and one of America's major liberals and labor lead-

ers, suggesting that his union might wish to contribute toward the purchase of a set of paintings of the United Nations building. Mrs. Roosevelt felt close enough to Reuther to make such a personal request of him.

January 11, 1953

Dear Mr. Reuther:

There are some interesting paintings by Mr. Harold Weston which show the steel structure of the UN building. Mr. Duncan Phillips who is an art connoisseur, wrote the piece which I enclose about these paintings.

Several people have seen them including Senator Lehman. The UN should be very happy, I understand, to have them on the walls and it has been suggested that if the CIO were willing to undertake responsibility for half of the cost, the remaining funds would be contributed by individuals and some corporations. In fact I think Senator Lehman offered to contribute and several other people have done so.

I have no idea what you would think about this gift to the UN by groups of unions and individuals, but it might be a nice gesture. In any case I wish you would send someone in whom you have confidence to look at these paintings. Mr. Weston lives at the Wellington Hotel, 7th Avenue and 55th. Street and his studio is not far off, so the paintings could be seen without too much difficulty.

Very cordially yours,

Eleanor Roosevelt to the Nobel Prize Committee

January 29, 1953

Shortly after President Truman left office in 1953, Mrs. Roosevelt joined others in nominating him for the Nobel Peace Prize. Despite his failure to receive the award, Mrs. Roosevelt presented a good, if brief, case for him. This is an interesting turnaround from 1948 when certain people criticized her for not endorsing Truman for a term of his own. She corrected that oversight, but her support in 1948 seemed lukewarm at best. During the ensuing four years she worked more closely with him and came to respect him more. Thus, she gladly seconded his nomination for the peace prize.

January 29, 1953

Gentlemen:

I take pleasure in seconding the Honorable Harry S. Truman of the United States of America for the award of the Nobel Peace Prize.

Mr. Truman has performed a great service in preserving peace by a continuing and closely integrated policy of building the economic, political and spiritual strength of the Western World to meet, contain, and eventually to overcome the threat to Western independence, and to Western religion and culture, from Soviet imperialism. His record on the aggression in Trieste and in Teheran; his aid to Greece and his cooperation with the United Nations; his action on the Berlin airlift, and his support of the Marshall Plan; His stand in regard to Korean Communist aggression are all things that need no elaboration by me.

Mr. Truman patiently and successfully directed the United States in its new foreign policy of Western unity.

I think President Truman played a great role in promoting cooperation among nations and presenting measures that lead to peace.

Sincerely yours

Eleanor Roosevelt to Dwight D. Eisenhower
April 4, 1953

Mrs. Roosevelt continued to be concerned about the future of Israel, located as it was in the midst of hostile neighbors. Shortly after Dwight D. Eisenhower became president, she wrote this letter expressing her apprehensions about aid to Israel. She reveals here her belief that the Arabs were not espousing the causes of the "free world" and should be treated as equally as possible, but not at the expense of Israel.

April 4, 1953

Dear Mr. President:

I am a little troubled over the rumor that there is to be a change in our government's policy toward Israel. I recognize the fact that there must be equality of treatment by the government for Arab states and for Israel but I do not think it should be considered that, because Israel receives more money from private sources in this country, any aid from the government should be curtailed. We should take into full consideration on that through Mutual Security funds we have been helping with the task of resettling refugees in the Arab states and yet the Jewish refugees received in Israel are about equal to the number received in the Arab states.

I think we should in every way help the development projects and constructive work being done in the Arab states and yet we cannot forget the fact that the Arab states do not espouse the cause of the free world and that Israel does. If the Arab states would cooperate with Israel, they would go forward faster and some of Israel's difficulties would be solved.

When funds are quoted which are paid to the Arab states, the oil royalties are never included.

I think it is important that our aid be kept up for Israel and that in all legitimate ways we should equalize aid going to them and to the Arab states but I feel we should not do this by lessening aid that is going to Israel.

Very sincerely yours,

[*DDEL*]

Eleanor Roosevelt to Robert Wagner

September 16, 1953

In 1953 Robert F. Wagner ran for mayor of New York City. He was following in the footsteps of his father, Robert F. Wagner, who had been a senator from New York during the New Deal. Mrs. Roosevelt wrote the son a congratulatory letter after the primary.

September 16, 1953

Dear Mr. Wagner:

This is just a word of congratulations on your victory in the Primary yesterday. I don't think you will have any trouble defeating Mr. Riegelman[1] and I wish to extend my best wishes for a successful campaign. I know what the burdens are and how difficult your task will be. If there is anything which those of us who are in New York a great deal but who do not vote in New York, can do, you can count on us.

Very sincerely yours,

Note

1. Harold Riegelman, Republican candidate for mayor of New York City in 1953.

Eleanor Roosevelt to Mary McLeod Bethune

September 28, 1953

Mary McLeod Bethune, an African American woman, served in the New Deal in various capacities, especially in the National Youth Administration. In 1904 she founded the Daytona Normal and Industrial Institute for Negro Girls in Florida. It later merged with the Cookman Institute and became known as Bethune-Cookman College. The college regularly sought additional revenue. Mrs. Roosevelt, who used her status to assist the causes in which she believed, explained to Mrs. Bethune how she had acquired the donation of money. Roger Babson was a business forecaster, statistician, and author who had become quite famous in the late 1920s when he continued to predict a stock market crash. He also founded Webber College, a business college for women in Babson Park, Florida, where Mrs. Roosevelt spoke.

September 28, 1953

Dear Mrs. Bethune:

I am enclosing a check for $1,000.00 from Mr. Roger Babson.

When I was in Florida last year, I promised to make a speech for Mr. Babson on condition that he give you this amount!

With best regards,

Very sincerely yours,

Eleanor Roosevelt to W. Averell Harriman

November 19, 1953

Mrs. Roosevelt hoped that Harriman would financially support Bard College, an independent liberal arts college established in 1860 in Dutchess County, New York. She wanted Harriman to visit her at Hyde Park and then visit the campus to meet James Case, president of the college.

November 19, 1953

Dear Averell:

I can't remember whether I wrote you and I promised to do so, asking if you would be willing to see Mr. James Case who is president of Bard College.

I would love it if you could arrange to come to Hyde Park someday when you are in Arden and go over with me to visit the college. They are anxious to get interest and support financially. I think you will feel they are doing a good job and will be interested in what they have been able to accomplish.

Your daughter could tell you more about the college than I can because she was on the Board for a time.

I would be more than glad if you would let me know if perhaps the Saturday after Thanksgiving you and Marie[1] could drive up and lunch with me.

I am looking forward to having lunch with you the day after Thanksgiving. I like the King and Queen of Greece.[2]

Notes

1. Harriman married Marie Norton Whitney in 1930; she died in 1970.
2. King Paul and Queen Frederika of Greece visited the United States in the fall of 1953. On November 1 they visited Hyde Park, lunched with Mrs. Roosevelt, and placed a wreath on FDR's grave.

Eleanor Roosevelt to Robert Wagner

February 1, 1954

Eleanor Roosevelt wrote in February 1954 to congratulate Robert Wagner on his inauguration as mayor of New York City. She had been a longtime supporter of him and his father.

February 1, 1954

Dear Mr. Mayor:

I wish I could be with you this evening to express my appreciation for the fine work you have done for Israel Bonds. This tribute is richly deserved.

I hope your administration as Mayor of this City will be very successful and that you will give the City the kind of good government it deserves so that you may have the satisfaction of feeling you have accomplished a difficult but successful job.

Very sincerely yours,

Eleanor Roosevelt to W. Averell Harriman

June 8, 1954

Pare Lorentz, a motion picture director, author, and film critic who endorsed the Roosevelt presidency and headed the United States Film Service upon its creation, wanted to publish a history of President Roosevelt's life and times. In 1934 he had edited The Roosevelt Year: A Photographic Record, *published by Funk & Wagnalls Company. An enthusiastic Mrs. Roosevelt suggested that Harriman consult with Lorentz and with Isador Lubin, an American economist, educator, and former member of the New Deal "Brain Trust" who served as the industrial commissioner of the state of New York from 1953 to 1959.*

June 8, 1954

Dear Averell:

Pare Lorentz who has done a monumental work on Franklin and the whole period of history during his life, was in today and showed me where he has arrived. I think you and Isadore Lubin should see what Mr. Lorentz has done and he will gladly come in anytime, bringing the results of his labor with him. He has reached the point where he must think of a publisher.

To me his work is extraordinarily interesting as history, quite aside from any personal interest, and I would appreciate it if you could see him sometime soon. He tried a long while ago to talk to you about his work but something came up and he never did reach you, so I hope you will try to arrange to see him now.

Affectionately,

Eleanor Roosevelt to Winston Churchill

June 16, 1954

Mrs. Roosevelt congratulated Prime Minister Winston Churchill, her husband's friend and wartime ally, on the latest honor conferred on him by Queen Elizabeth II.

June 16, 1954

Dear Sir Winston:

I want to send you my warm congratulations on your latest honor. I know it means a great deal to be made a Knight of the Garter and I know you have a warm affection for your very lovely Queen, so it must be an added joy to have it conferred by her.

I hope that you and Lady Churchill are both much better. I hear of you sometimes from Mr. Baruch, and I hope that the clouds of misunderstanding which seem to gather now and then between our two countries will shortly be resolved.

With every good wish to you and Lady Churchill.

Cordially yours,

Eleanor Roosevelt to Roy Wilkins
n.d. [1955]

In 1955 the Senate debated a Federal Aid for School Construction bill that Mrs. Roosevelt and other liberals supported wholeheartedly. She had heard that the National Association for the Advancement of Colored People (NAACP) was planning to have an anti-segregation amendment attached to the bill while in the Senate Labor and Public Welfare Committee. She and Walter Reuther of the CIO worried that this might be a tactical mistake that could doom both the bill and the rider. Together they drafted a letter to Roy Wilkins, executive secretary of the NAACP, urging another strategy. Mrs. Roosevelt was a logical choice to write a statement, since she was a longtime supporter and board member of the NAACP. It is a lengthy and well-reasoned letter.

n.d. [1955]

DRAFT OF LETTER TO ROY WILKINS OF NAACP

Dear Roy:

Because of the importance of doing everything possible to assist in the implementation of the Supreme Court decisions and subsequent decrees ending segregation in the public schools, while at the same time making clear to the American people the NAACP's position in urging inclusion of specific Anti-Segregation language in the pending Federal Aid for School Construction Bill, we want to propose that the NAACP reconsider its position on one tactical and procedural matter, namely, the possibility of moving to attach the Anti-Segregation Amendment to the Bill after it has been reported out of the Senate Labor and Public Welfare Committee instead of insisting that it be added in that Committee before the Bill is reported out.

If such an Amendment is voted into the Bill in Committee, the Bill will then face these obstacles:

It will be difficult to have the Bill called up for debate. If a motion is made to make the Bill the pending business of the Senate, a filibuster would begin immediately against the procedural motion, not against either the Bill or the Amendment. If a cloture petition were filed and a vote had upon that petition, the votes against cloture might be increased by a combination of those who are opposed to federal aid and those opposed to an Anti-Segregation Amendment. Yet, neither the issue of the aid nor the issue of the Amendment would be squarely before the Senate. Thus the vote for cloture might be much smaller than a cloture vote conducted at a later stage, after the Bill itself had been made the pending business, and after the Anti-Segregation Amendment had been introduced, called up and debated.

It is our sincere belief that this approach of including the Amendment in the Committee's report will deny our friends who are dedicated to the objectives of the NAACP the opportunity to develop fully the substance of their arguments in support of our position of ending school segregation. Thus we will fail to awaken fully the conscience of the American people because the discussions will evolve essentially around technical and procedural matters instead of the principles involved.

On the other hand, if the Bill were to be reported out of Committee without the Anti-Segregation Amendment, but accompanied by statements of liberal members of the Committee specifically stating their intention to offer such an Amendment when the Bill becomes the pending business on the floor of the Senate, there would be no reason inherent in the bill itself for a filibuster against a motion to take up the Bill.

The proponents of the amendment would have opportunity to present to every member of the Senate, and to the American people, the complete case for insisting that such language is desirable and necessary in order to comply with the intent of the Supreme Court decisions and implementing decrees. This approach would provide the most effective opportunity to bring into sharp focus the immorality of school segregation and would afford our friends their greatest opportunity through public debate to mobilize the broadest possible support behind our efforts.

We believe that agreement by the NAACP to this degree of flexibility in tactics and procedure will strengthen our efforts to defend and implement the principles for which we are fighting.

Agreement by the NAACP upon this procedural approach will permit our tested and proven friends in the Committee to move ahead and, we believe sincerely, will best serve both our efforts to achieve complete school integration and maximum school construction.

Sincerely,
Mrs. Franklin D. Roosevelt
Walter P. Reuther

Eleanor Roosevelt to W. Averell Harriman
April 27, 1955

Believing that it was important to have a woman on the Federal Communica-

tions Commission, Mrs. Roosevelt contacted Governor Harriman to suggest that he put in a good word for Dorothy Moore Lewis, a broadcasting executive who had served as the coordinator of American broadcasts for the United Nations from 1948 to 1954.

April 27, 1955

Dear Averell:

I understand that Frieda Henneck is not going to accept another appointment to the F.C.C. I think it important that there be a woman on it, and Mrs. Dorothy Lewis who is over at the United Nations is very anxious to get it, and I think she is excellent.

She has not been active in either political party, and I do not think she is registered with any one, but for pure efficiency and general liberality, Mrs. Lewis could contribute a great deal.

So I am sending you the enclosed biographical material in the hope that if you can you will say a word for her.

With all good wishes,

Cordially yours,

Eleanor Roosevelt to Albert M. Bethune Jr.
September 22, 1955

Shortly after the death of Mary McLeod Bethune, the African American woman who had worked for the National Youth Administration and had founded a college in Florida, Mrs. Roosevelt received a letter from Mrs. Bethune's grandson. He explained his financial difficulties in some detail, emphasizing that some of the problems resulted from his grandmother's death, and asked Mrs. Roosevelt for a temporary loan of $350. Mrs. Roosevelt received many requests for help, and this was a standard reply. However, she inserted a sentence that seemed somewhat judgmental and harsh. Apparently she entertained second thoughts about the sentence and deleted it from her response.

September 22, 1955

Dear Mr. Bethune:

Thank you for your letter of the 21st.

I am sorry to hear of your difficulties but I fear I cannot lend you any money as I just do not have it at present to lend. ~~I remember, too, that your grandmother did not feel very highly about lending money.~~
With deep regret.

Very sincerely yours,

Eleanor Roosevelt to Walter Reuther

October 25, 1955

In 1955 the American Federation of Labor (AFL) and the Congress of Industrial Organizations (CIO) merged into a single labor union. The CIO had been an upstart union that had earlier challenged the AFL for ignoring the new industrial workers and instead concentrating on the skilled crafts. Walter Reuther, an unusual man in many ways, had led the CIO to a new position of leadership and respectability. This was especially significant since in its early years the CIO had been accused of Communist leanings and other unsavory characteristics. As the merger approached, the CIO published a souvenir book to catch the spirit of the CIO and to record its contribution to American life and progress. Reuther wrote Mrs. Roosevelt to ask her to contribute a letter, a fitting request considering that the CIO originated in the 1930s when her husband was president.

October 25, 1955

Dear Mr. Reuther:

I am very happy to send you these few lines of appreciation for what the CIO has meant to the development of Union Labor in the past few years.

Now that you are nearing your December first and second meeting before the merger of the CIO and AFL, I think the CIO deserves the thanks of all our citizens. It has set high standards of labor leadership. It has made it apparent that the leadership must recognize the responsibility of labor to the country as a whole. With its growing strength labor can no longer think only of its own desires. It must think of itself as a part of the whole picture of the economic life of the country. In some cases labor leadership has been ahead of management and it has shown more imagination in finding solutions to difficult situations than has the business world.

I hope that labor will continue to develop solutions to problems which take into consideration the good of all the people in our own country as well as the relationship of our own country to the world. I think a strong labor movement led by the ideals which have characterized the CIO in the past will be of great value to our country.

With particular appreciation of your own services and my very best wishes for your merger, I am

Very cordially yours,

Eleanor Roosevelt to Agnes Meyer

December 9, 1955

In December 1955 Adlai Stevenson entertained plans to run for the presidency a second time in 1956. Because he had been a reluctant candidate in 1952, he decided to be proactive this time. He considered appointing a committee of advisers on social issues, wondering if it should consist only of women. Mrs. Roosevelt wrote to Agnes Meyer, revealing her thoughts and conversation with Stevenson.

December 9, 1955

Dear Agnes:

Before I broached the subject of a new committee to Adlai Stevenson yesterday, he told me that he wanted to appoint a committee of advisers reporting to him and responsible to him, not to any of his other people, on education, health and welfare and he asked whether I thought it should be just a women's committee or include men. It seemed to me that it should be both men and women but that the women must be on an equal par with the men and that they should be nominated by a group of women whom I agreed I would try to consult with and clear through Mrs. Millicent McIntosh.[1] That seemed to please him very much and he said he would be glad to have the names as soon as possible, that he had not yet made up his mind when he would announce the advisory group.

I have called Mrs. McIntosh about this and she will do some thinking but she is counting on you to approach people and find out whether they will be willing to serve. I will call Sarah Blanding[2] over the weekend.

I hope this is going to work out well and that it seems to you to be going in the right direction.

Mr. Finnegan[3] talked to me about the organization of Democratic women, so their minds are running on the women and I hope by the early part of the New Year we will have something to say for all these efforts.

Affectionately,

Notes

1. Millicent Carey McIntosh, dean of Barnard College.
2. Sarah Gibson Blanding, president of Vassar College.
3. James A. Finegan, a Pennsylvania Democrat.

Eleanor Roosevelt to Agnes Meyer
December 14, 1955

When Mrs. Agnes Meyer received Mrs. Roosevelt's letter of December 9 regarding a Stevenson committee on social issues, she responded quickly, emphasizing that she strongly believed the committee should be all women since Stevenson's "campaign in '52 was far too masculine." She believed that if men were put on the committee it would downplay the role of women and the angle they hoped to achieve on the importance of certain issues to women. Mrs. Meyer wanted Mrs. Roosevelt to help her identify some names for the committee, including labor representatives. The former first lady disagreed with Meyer's thoughts about women on the committee.

December 14, 1955

Dear Agnes:

You have the same idea that Mr. Stevenson himself had because he originally wanted to have just women. A number of people with whom I have talked, however, feel rather strongly that we will really get more if we put in the best women we have in every field and include some top men. For instance, in mental health it is almost essential to have the Menningers.

I think you need not be afraid that the emphasis will not be on women. I agree with you that for political reasons women should be of major importance in this group.

I will try to think up some labor people. I have already made some enquiries.

Affectionately,

Eleanor Roosevelt to Nelson Rockefeller
No date except handwritten 1956

Because Eleanor Roosevelt strongly supported the United Nations, she did everything possible to obtain more support for the organization. In 1956 she wrote to Nelson Rockefeller, a leading Republican and potential presidential candidate in 1960, in his role as a member of the fund established by the Rockefeller brothers. The American Association for the UN regularly applied to the fund for support; this year she did more to try to assure funding.

[No date except handwritten 1956]

Dear Nelson:

The American Association for the UN has submitted through the proper channels our usual plea for support. When it comes before the fund which you brothers have established I would be so grateful if you would give it careful consideration and see whether this year you could give us some special help.

We would be deeply appreciative as we have a feeling that our organization efforts are beginning to bear fruit, but we need so much more follow-up done for the work in the field and more demands seem to be made on us every day for really giving the information on which public opinion can be based.

I hope you won't mind my writing you about this but I knew you would get our appeal before long.

Cordially yours,

Statements of Eleanor Roosevelt Supporting Adlai Stevenson
n.d. [1956]

During the presidential campaign of 1956, Mrs. Roosevelt wrote various statements of support for Adlai Stevenson. Three of these documents are reproduced here. The drafts have some penciled changes in that underlined words were added while those with strikeovers were deleted by her. The first document appears to be random thoughts that she may have shared with leaders of the party. Some of these comments apparently were just jotted down hurriedly. The second document is a more formal endorsement of Stevenson. The third one clearly is a draft of an introduction of Stevenson at a Democratic rally in Madison Square Garden in New York City.

[No date except 1956]

I am supporting Adlai Stevenson because I think he is the best candidate. I think he is, because he has taken the trouble to prepare himself. . . . Four years ago he was reluctant. Today he knows the world, and is no longer reluctant, and he knows what it will mean to be president of the United States. He does too, I think, have a very strong sense of obligation.

I think this is a very crucial year. We have had a good man and a fine general, but who does not know what it means to be a full time president. There has been leadership lacking. The greatest educator of the people of the United States should be the president. You think back, how much besides reassurance that it is a good world and not to worry, you have not been made to feel a part of the problem and I think that is essential for the president of the United States to do.

We have been negligent for too many years to weight the Vice President on both sides.[1]

Civil Rights:—the difference between the two platforms on Civil Rights

There are no longer situations which can be tried as though they are all by themselves. Almost every domestic issue has a facet that attaches itself to the world. 2/3 of the people of the world are colored, the white race is the minority. If we are to lead the free world we must give this 2/3 of the world a feeling that a democracy means something in the future which it has not meant in the past.

Mr. Stevenson is trying to paint in his speeches what he means by a new America.—the country going forward in the happiness and well-being of its people. The biggest reservoir of good will was obtained during the depression because all over the world the people who were also ex in poverty, saw a government that cared and was working for alleviation of the depression.

I did not feel we should insist on mentioning by name the Supreme Court decision [*Brown v. Board of Education of Topeka*, 1954].

We should do away in the Senate of Rule 22. Until we do away with that we can get no Civil Rights plank. The Democrats have a plank to get rid of that rule.

The Southern representatives accepted a change in the educational plank. Every American child should have the right to equal opportunity for full development etc., etc.,—Now! Every American child has the right <u>under the law of the land</u> to etc. etc.

Integration: You are not going to accomplish this change over night. In the North only one step must be taken. In the big cities the one step is housing must be integrated. The first step in the South is that there must be the protection of every citizen in his right to vote. This is a Federal right and the Federal Government has a right to supervise this.

Being a man of war does not necessarily mean you know how to fight the civilian battles.

Dollars for Stevenson: This is the democratic way of getting support. I would rather have a million dollars donated by a million people than by General Motors.

"As citizens of this democracy, you are the rulers and the ruled, the lawgivers and the law abiding, the beginning and the end. Democracy is a high privilege but also a heavy responsibility whose shadow stalks, although you may never walk in the dark.

"I say these things to you, not only because I believe them to be true, also because, as you love your country, I love my country, and I would see it endure and grow in light and become a living testament to all mankind of goodness and of mercy of wisdom."

When Governor Stevenson accepted the nomination for the presidency he stated his own position as a candidate and the record of the Democratic Party, which had selected him, in these words:

"I am not much concerned with partisan denunciation, with epithets and abuse, because the working man, the farmer, the thoughtful business man, all know that they are better off than ever before and they all know that the greatest danger to free enterprise in this country died with the great depression under the hammer blow of the Democratic party."

From that night in Chicago to the present Governor Stevenson has met the issue of the campaign with courage and conviction as he has continued to talk sense to the American people. I want you to listen again to his views on some of the issues. On communism at home and abroad he said: "Because I believe in freedom I am opposed to communism. And I think I know more about the Soviet Union than most of these self-appointed Republican custodians of patriotism ... we are opposing communism abroad, where its relentless pressure seeks further to narrow the area of freedom. We are opposing it at home where its agents and converts seek to undermine our society and corrupt our government."

On Korea—"Every one of us knows in his heart why we had to stand up and to fight in Korea. We all know that when the communists attacked across the 38th Parallel that was a testing point for freedom throughout the world. The men in the Kremlin thought they would be unopposed, and if they were the whole question of the future could be settled in one blow. If they had been allowed to conquer free people in Korea they could have picked away at the free world and engulfed more millions, piece by piece, one by one."

On corruption: "As a Democrat, as an office holder and aspirant for the greatest office on Earth, I have not nor will I condone, excuse or explain away wrong doing or moral obliquity in public office, whoever the guilty or wherever they are stationed. What's more I have had the satisfaction of firing and prosecuting a good many, and I mean from both parties."

On our American heritage and the responsibility of all the people to maintain our Democratic way of life:

Twenty years ago almost to the day, my husband, ~~Franklin speaking~~ <u>spoke</u>

from this same platform at another Democratic Rally in Madison Square Garden said:

"From the time my airplane touched ground at Chicago up to the present I have consistently set forth the doctrine of the present day democracy. It is the program of a party dedicated to the conviction that every one of our people is entitled to the opportunity to earn a living and to develop himself to the fullest measure consistent with the rights of his fellow men, You are familiar with that program. You are aware that it has found favor in the sight of the American electorate. This moment comes not from leaders of any group, of any faction, or even of any party. It is the spontaneous expression of the aspirations of millions of individual men and women. These ambitions have struggled for realization in different ways, on the farm, in the cities, in the factories, among business men and in the homes. These have found at length a common meeting ground in the Democratic program. Tonight we set the seal upon that program. After Tuesday we go forward to the great task of its accomplishment, and we trust, to its fulfillment."

In 1932, Franklin Roosevelt was a relatively unknown voice on the national political scene. He was running against a man who had been President for four years, and who prior to assuming that high office had won a world wide reputation for his great work in Europe. But the people, ~~however~~ nevertheless listened to my husband's voice and as you know the Democratic party won that election.

Today twenty years later there is a new voice of Democracy in our land— the voice of ~~Adlai E. Stevenson~~ our Democratic candidate for the President of the U.S. It is a voice that says the same thing in Virginia as it does in Harlem. It is a voice that talks sense to the American people. The Republicans claim that Governor Stevenson is talking over the heads of the people and his reply is—"The people are wiser, far wiser than the Republicans think." Governor Stevenson by not compromising and by stating his views on the vital issues of the campaign in clear and forceful language has won the ear and the heart of the American people.

This is a man who has sense of history and will use the best that he finds in history. He knows what Woodrow Wilson contributed and what my husband contributed but he knows new things have to be met in new ways and he has the courage and intelligence to meet those things in new ways.

We are tied to the old in the spirit in which met meet our problems but nevertheless we face forward as we meet the needs of the present.

With our candidate at the helm of our Ship of State we will make ourselves strong. We will work with other nations in the United Nations. We do not know the answers but we know we have a leader who can use the tools at hand. We will support him with our prayers and our work and God willing, he will lead us well.

Ladies and Gentlemen, Governor Adlai Stevenson

Note

1. Mrs. Roosevelt may have been referring to the need for stronger vice presidents. So many former ones were ill-equipped to become president. After Eisenhower's heart attack in 1955 and his declining health, Mrs. Roosevelt probably worried that he might not live out his second term, thereby putting Richard Nixon, the man she hated and feared, in the presidency for the remainder of the term. She thought both parties should nominate stronger vice presidential candidates fully prepared to assume the presidency.

Excerpts from an Interview
n.d. [1956]

During the presidential campaign of 1956, Mrs. Roosevelt did many things to support the candidacy of Adlai Stevenson. This is a short excerpt from an unidentified interview in which she commented on Vice President Richard M. Nixon and President Dwight D. Eisenhower.

[No date except 1956]

QUESTION: Mrs. Roosevelt, the Democrats have said that "A vote for Eisenhower is a vote for Nixon". Do you think this should be made an issue with the American people.

MRS. R.: I think it is an issue you have to face because at no time do any of us know what may happen to us, therefore we when we elect a president and a vice-president, we must be prepared to face the facts that the vice president may become president. That may happen to anybody at any time, and I think all of us should face that issue and know whether we are prepared to elect on that basis.

QUESTION: We have heard some criticism from both Democratic candidates about Mr. Nixon. Could you tell us how you feel about Mr. Nixon running for vice president?

MRS. R.: Yes, I know how I feel personally but I know that what I feel personally is probably a feeling that might not be shared by other people. I am told that Mr. Nixon is a very fine young man by Republican people whom I know, particularly young people, and that he has matured and grown in many ways. I happen to remember very clearly his campaign for the Senatorship.[1] I have no respect for the way in which he accused Helen Gahagan Douglas[2] of being a Communist because he knew that was how he would be elected, and I have no respect for the kind of character that takes advantage and does something they know is not true. He knew that she might be a Liberal but he knew quite well, having known him and worked with her, that she was not a Communist. I have always felt that anyone who wanted an election so much that they would use those means, did not have the character that I really admired in public life.

QUESTION: Mrs. Roosevelt, do you really think the present administration, and particularly President Eisenhower himself, wants prosperity only for big business and that he doesn't care about the little guy?

MRS. R.: Oh no! The President is a good man and he would always want to do the right thing as he saw it, but he has a great admiration for the achievement of the successful business man because he has never been a successful business man and you always admire what you really don't understand.

QUESTION: Don't you believe, though, that the big business man today realizes that he cannot be prosperous unless the man below him is prosperous too? He must have a market for his products.

MRS. R.: In words he would agree with you inasmuch as a big business has enormous power. Just go out and take a look at General Motors Research Center and come back and tell me if you do not think the power there and the real force that lies today in the management of these big businesses is tremendous, and you are apt to forget when you have that amount of power just exactly where your power stops.

Notes

1. In 1950.
2. Democratic congresswoman whom Nixon defeated in 1950 for the U.S. Senate.

Eleanor Roosevelt to Adlai Stevenson

January 11, 1956

In early 1956, Adlai E. Stevenson planned to enter the race for the Democratic presidential nomination for a second time. Long a supporter of his political ambitions, Mrs. Roosevelt wrote him often and gave him advice. In this in-

stance, she disagreed with her friend Agnes Meyer because Mrs. Roosevelt did not think an advisory committee should be composed of women alone. She also gave him encouragement about his son (Stevenson had three sons) who had been injured some time earlier. Mrs. Roosevelt had recently visited Bellingham, Washington, where she had been honored by the local Democrats. At her suggestion, he sent a telegram to Bellingham to commend them on honoring Mrs. Roosevelt and indirectly to give the local organization some encouragement in the upcoming presidential campaign.

Longview, Washington
January 11, 1956

Dear Mr. Stevenson:

I am sending you a copy of a letter which Mrs. Eugene Meyer sent to me which gives you suggestions of women for the advisory committee. Mrs. Meyer feels as you do that this should be only a woman's committee reporting directly to you. I still feel, however, that in spite of the desire to recognize the women, there ought to be some men on this committee where the man is undeniably better fitted for the field than a woman.

I hope all goes well with your boy. I saw that he had walked for the first time.

Thank you very much for your wire sent to Bellingham. The Democrats seem to be very enthusiastic there but of course they are far outnumbered by the Republicans in that area!

With kind regards,

Very cordially yours,

Eleanor Roosevelt to Harry S Truman

January 13, 1956

Events in the Middle East in 1956 proved quite volatile, which gave Mrs. Roosevelt the opportunity to write to former president Truman about the situation. She viewed the Soviets as a major threat to world peace and believed that the United States should exert stronger leadership in the region. Mrs. Roosevelt indicated in this letter that she planned to send Truman a statement that she would like for him to sign, but it apparently was not enclosed with the letter. It arrived in another envelope about a week later.

January 13, 1956

Dear Mr. President:

I am sure that you feel as I do that the situation in the Near East is highly critical, largely brought about through Soviet planning and action, and if they succeed in getting rid of our bases in North Africa and getting rid of Israel which is the only democratic area in the Near East which can make a stand against them, they will have a bridge to Pakistan, India, and the rest of Asia. Because I feel this way, I have listened to the suggestion from some of my friends in the Jewish community that a significant statement by a few people would carry more weight than some of the statements which are being made today with a great many signatures attached.

The enclosed statement has been carefully worked out and I am sending it to you, to Walter Reuther and to George Meany[1] hoping that you might all be willing to sign it if you think it is a wise move at this time. If there are any changes which you think wise, we would of course want you to make them. If you don't think it wise, you must of course, also let me know. I have great faith in your judgment and therefore would like to feel that I was not moving without your agreement in this matter.

Very cordially yours,

Note

1. Both labor leaders.

Eleanor Roosevelt to Richard Bolling
January 20, 1956

Richard Bolling, a congressman from Missouri, wrote Mrs. Roosevelt about a bill pending in the Rules Committee of the House of Representatives, of which he was a member. The bill concerned federal aid to education, but he was bothered by an anti-segregation rider, which he believed would kill the bill. Mrs. Agnes Meyer, a friend of Mrs. Roosevelt and the wife of the publisher of the Washington Post, had made a public statement in which she said she hoped that the National Association for the Advancement of Colored People (NAACP) would drop its demand for the rider to get the bill passed. Because Bolling had heard that Mrs. Roosevelt agreed with Mrs. Meyer, he asked her for a letter to that effect that he could publish in an effort to get the education bill approved. Mrs. Roosevelt explained her position in her answer.

January 20, 1956

Dear Mr. Bolling:

When the bill which you are now talking was brought before the Board of the NACCP last spring, Walter Reuther and I asked the Board to allow it to be brought out of committee without an amendment, stating that the Federal aid should only go to school construction in unsegregated areas. We had the promise of Senator Lehman and Hubert Humphrey[1] that as soon as it reached the floor of the Senate they would amend it. They asked that this be done in order that there would be an open debate on the Floor so the whole country would know what the argument was about and who the people were who were taking sides. Otherwise it would be killed in the Rules Committee and never reach the Floor and no one in the country would know anything about it.

The NAACP did not agree with our position at that time and therefore insisted that the rider should be attached in the Rules Committee.

The present situation is extremely difficult. I can understand Mrs. Eugene Meyer's position and I can understand that of anyone in the Congress because it looks as though in the Senate what would happen would be that if the amendment is attached to the Federal Aid for Schools Construction Bill, the Southern Senators will filibuster indefinitely, the Republicans will call the bill up immediately, and no other legislation will get through the Congress. The Republicans, therefore, will be able to characterize this Congress which is controlled by the Democrats as a "do nothing" Congress. In addition, the Congressional members themselves will have the onus of having prevented funds to reach the states in what is really a crisis in our schools, of having held up much important legislation in an election year of having kept men from being free to campaign early enough to put their party position clearly before the country. So I think if I were a member of Congress, I would feel obliged to vote for the bill and prevent the amendment from being introduced if possible. I am, however, not a member of Congress nor candidate for office. I have, therefore, an obligation, I think, to live up to the principles in which I believe. I believe that it is essential to our leadership in the world and to the development of true democracy in our country to have no discrimination in our country whatsoever. This is most important in the schools of our country. Therefore I feel personally that I could not ask to have this bill passed without an amendment since unless the situation becomes so bad that the people are worried about all education, I fear nothing will be done in the area of discrimination.

I am sorry this is not the kind of letter you will want to publish but I felt you should know my position as clearly as I could state it.

Very sincerely yours,

Note

1. Democratic senator from Minnesota.

Eleanor Roosevelt to Harry S Truman
January 21, 1956

Approximately a week after her letter on January 13, 1956, Mrs. Roosevelt sent the final draft of the statement on the Middle East to former president Truman for his signature. She appreciated his support. Mrs. Roosevelt also stated that since Truman's daughter, Margaret, indicated that her parents would be in New York soon, she would like to have them for a meal. On January 25 Truman returned the signed statement and declared that he and Mrs. Truman would be happy to have lunch with her.

January 21, 1956

Dear Mr. Truman:

I am enclosing the statement for you to sign which I have already signed, and it will then go when I hear from Mr. Meany and Mr. Reuther if they agree to sign, for their signature before going to the press.

I was very grateful for your letter about the Near East because it supports what I have been saying and gives me some real facts from people who are better fitted to observe than I am. I have just been speaking from my own observations and you have given me some valuable background which I can use.

I saw your very nice daughter last night at Mary Lasker's home and she looked lovely, but I am glad she does not have long to wait for a holiday since I really think her work has been pretty grueling on this radio show. She tells me that you will be here the end of the month and I am hopeful that you and Mrs. Truman and Margaret will come over to my little apartment for a meal one day. I would love it if you could come for lunch with me on February 3rd at one o'clock.

Many thanks for your letter and looking forward to the pleasure of seeing all of you.

Very cordially yours,

Eleanor Roosevelt to Adlai Stevenson
February 11, 1956

Bernard Baruch, a well-known financier who had involved himself in politics, and Mrs. Roosevelt were friends. She regularly tried to convince Adlai Stevenson

*to use Baruch's knowledge and influence. In 1956 as the presidential campaign
began to develop, she wrote to Stevenson, expecting that he would approach
Baruch for help. Mrs. Roosevelt hoped that Baruch would show Stevenson "how
Secretary Humphrey, can be put in a hole." At this point Mrs. Roosevelt still
addressed Stevenson as Mr. Stevenson.*

February 11, 1956

Dear Mr. Stevenson:

I have just spent a night with Mr. Baruch and he is very anxious that you
should ask to see him when he comes here in March or April. I think if you
write a little note now it would be a good thing. He tried to explain to me
some financial situations which he says he wants to tell you about because he
says he knows how to handle them and show you how Secretary Humphrey[1]
can be put in a hole. This is one of the areas in which I think he is extremely
useful, and at the moment he is rested and very alert and much better than I
have seen him in a long time. I think you will find talking to him extremely
enlightening and interesting.

I also saw Mr. Beckel[2] who is deep in Florida politics in Sarasota and he
begged me to ask you to go there. David Gray, my uncle, has a house in Sarasota
said to please ask you to come and stay with him. They feel that many of the
Eisenhower Democrats are ready to come back and that you should not ne-
glect that part of the state.

You have a very ardent democrat who worked for you in the last campaign in Mr. Frank Johnson who is at Rawlins[3] College, Winter Park, Florida.
He is losing his job because of his activities for the UN and for you but that
does not seem to upset him. I think if he does turn up, he would be enor-
mously appreciative if you would see him.

There is a Negro situation here which I think a little later on you will
have to think about seriously but at the moment I think the less you say the
better.

Very cordially yours,

Notes

1. Secretary of the Treasury under President Eisenhower.
2. A friend who was a member of the Democratic Party in Florida.
3. Rollins College.

Eleanor Roosevelt to Agnes Meyer
February 23, 1956

At the beginning of 1956, the Stevenson for President campaign began to get off the ground. Apparently, Stevenson wanted to appoint Mrs. Meyer chairperson of one of the campaign committees, but she remained reluctant to head any group. An important member of the Democratic Party, she would add as a chairperson considerable influence in the campaign. Mrs. Roosevelt wrote Mrs. Meyer explaining how she understood her thoughts and assessing the status of the campaign.

February 23, 1956

Dear Mrs. Meyer:

I quite understand your not wanting to be chairman of any committee. I think the Governor has every intention of naming such a committee and I will see what they think is the best way to use it when he is here the end of this month. .

I hope Nassau will be pleasant and that you will come home feeling refreshed.

It is difficult for me to evaluate how the Stevenson campaign is going but I would say that there begins to emerge a certain amount of organization and that there is an astonishing amount of willingness to be active on his behalf.

The Negro situation is a difficult one but his position is basically sound and will be so recognized when it is fully understood.

Affectionately,

Eleanor Roosevelt to Adlai Stevenson
April 11, 1956

In the early stages of the campaign of 1956, Mrs. Roosevelt, a Stevenson partisan for some time, tried to inform him of things she had observed with which he might not be familiar. During the primary season of 1956, Stevenson's major Democratic opponent was Sen. Estes Kefauver of Tennessee. In April Mrs. Roosevelt, believing that Stevenson needed to know several developments, wrote him a long letter in which she made her feelings obvious.

April 11, 1956

Dear Adlai:

I am really worried about one or two things that I think I should say at the present time. It seems to me that it is unwise to be attacking Mr. Kefauver as much as you have been doing. The things that need to be attacked are the issues that need to be made clear to the man in the street in the simplest possible terms. The people need to feel that you have done all the agonizing over how to meet situations, that you are sure of what you would do if you were starting it today. In a primary campaign I think these issues can be stated in a somewhat exaggerated way as far as one's certainty of how one intends to begin. It is obvious that no solution is certain and that you may have to change your approach but the people have turned to Eisenhower because they feel, simply because he said very little, that he knew the answers. Kefauver has so far said nothing worth listening to but he has said it in a way that makes the people feel he also is someone who has the answers. That is not quite honest but it is reassuring and many people need reassurance particularly when they don't want to have to think things out for themselves.

I also feel strongly that Mr. Finnegan should be mapping out his strategy and getting things set up for the convention so that he knows exactly whom he is counting on to make each move. This can't be done overnight but if not done before the convention you will not have the kind of organization that will be able to do the negotiation and the winning over of people and the actual carrying of votes. Mr. Finnegan should have his finger on every single state with a man and woman in each state dealing not only with the regular Democrats but with the volunteers, so that he pools the two together and they operate to complement each other.

You should be giving yourself to thinking out the speeches and the trips and where your strategic points are. You should have someone with you— someone who is more approachable than Sherman Adams[1] but who would act for you as he acts for the President, who would have the power and do the job. Otherwise you are not free. Everyone around you is devoted but I have a feeling that just because of their devotion they are not gauging well the public sentiment and giving you the reports. A Sherman Adams would see that he was getting the proper kind of reports from Mr. Finnegan and the same would be so of any other people working in the field. I get a feeling of a bad set-up on public relations, of an inferior public relations organizational job being done, and of your being pressed without the proper balance of information or the time to think of the things you ought to be thinking about.

The problems of today are serious enough. Nobody knows the answers but the people must feel that the man who is their candidate knows where he is going to begin, that he is not so tortured by his own search that he can't give them reassurance and security.

I think it is important to get this kind of organization started immediately.

This is not meant to be a discouraging letter but an encouraging one. If I did not think you could win, it would not be worth doing a good job.

With every good wish, and looking forward to seeing you on the 25th, and please forgive me if I have been too blunt.

Cordially,

Note

1. Former governor of New Hampshire and assistant to the president who served as White House chief of staff.

Eleanor Roosevelt to Channing H. Tobias
April 17, 1956

On April 11, 1956, Roy Wilkins, Executive Secretary of the National Association for the Advancement of Colored People (NAACP), gave a speech in Chicago, which was widely reported in the press. The press reports suggested that he was advocating that the NAACP and black voters shift from the Democratic Party to the Republican Party. Wilkins manifested displeasure by these reports, since he had used the words "if necessary" regarding the possibility of changing parties. On April 17 Mrs. Roosevelt wrote a letter to Channing H. Tobias, chairman of the board of the NAACP, tendering her resignation from the board of the NAACP.

April 17, 1956

Dear Dr. Tobias:

Since I do not have the time to attend full meetings and since I have come to feel that Roy Wilkins as Executive Secretary is taking a very unwise course politically I am tendering my resignation from the Board. I do not wish to be responsible for actions which I do not have the time to actually consider with the Board.

Very sincerely yours,

Eleanor Roosevelt to Channing H. Tobias

April 26, 1956

Because of her effort to resign from the board of the NAACP on April 17, Mrs. Roosevelt talked with Channing H. Tobias, a clergyman who chaired the NAACP board of directors, informing him that she would be willing to discuss with Roy Wilkins, the executive secretary, her concerns about his actions. Before they met in person, Wilkins sent her a four-page letter describing his ideas so that she would know his position before they saw each other. He stressed, particularly, how segregationists such as Sen. James O. Eastland of Mississippi controlled the Democratic Party. Following her receipt of the letter, she conferred with Wilkins. Then she wrote to Tobias to rescind her resignation.

April 26, 1956

Dear Dr. Tobias:

I have had a long talk with Mr. Roy Wilkins and I have pointed out to him why it would be wise for me to resign but I also understand the difficulties my resignation might bring on the organization. He assures me that he will remember to make very clear his meaning in what he says and writes. In addition, he will try not to be tempted by the picturesque phrase into saying something that might excite the emotions and actually might also be harmful. I feel, therefore, that with your help and close cooperation the Association will be non-partisan and a little wiser in its approach to certain questions.

I can't be at meetings for more than an hour as a rule, when I can go at all, but I will remain at least for the present time on the Board.

Very sincerely yours,

Eleanor Roosevelt to Adlai Stevenson

June 13, 1956

Following his victory in the California primary in 1956, Adlai Stevenson wrote Mrs. Roosevelt to thank her for her one-day appearance in California on his behalf. He mentioned that he thought the Republicans were trying to split the Democrats by saying that Averell Harriman of New York was the only true successor to the New Deal–Fair Deal. In her thoughtful answer to the letter, Mrs. Roosevelt confirmed the importance of the Harriman issue but opined that he should soon be removed as a challenge to Stevenson. As in other letters, she stressed the importance of good organization in all the states.

June 13, 1956

Dear Adlai:

I was so happy over the California results. One day did not mean much from me I fear, but the people there seem to have come to their senses which relieved me.

Your analysis of the Republican attitude is, of course, correct both on what they did for Kefauver and what they will undoubtedly do for Averell. They would like to see the party completely divided and I don't know that there is any way one can hold it together and live up to one's convictions, but somehow I think understanding and sympathy for the white people in the South is as important as understanding and sympathy and support for the colored people. We don't want another war between the states and so the only possible solution is to get the leaders on both sides together and try to work first steps out.

I have been asked by Mr. Butler[1] to come down to Washington in an effort to get a Civil Rights plank developed for the Convention which will not mean the South will walk out of the Convention.

I don't look forward to it because I have spent endless hours in the UN discussing over the value of words and I think that is what we will have to do in this case.

It is essential for the Democratic party to keep the colored vote in line, so you can't take away the feeling that you want to live up to the Supreme Court decision[2] and go forward, and that this can't be done in one fell swoop. Desegregation of schools in the South must follow a number of steps. Even in the North we have to desegregate housing before we can desegregate schools.

According to the papers this morning the meeting between Tom Finletter[3] and Carmine DeSapio[4] has produced a decision that you and Averell will not attack each other personally. I think you are right that there should be no defensive attitude on your part—simply a statement by your supporters of qualifications.

I am impressed in New York state by the undercover support you have and I feel sure that once released from Averell the great majority of the votes will come happily to you.

You have not in any [way] aggravated my burdens. I chose myself to do this because I felt it was important that we have a nominee in the Democratic party who had not only a chance of winning but a chance of giving us a good administration.

I will be going abroad on August 17th but I hope I shall hear before then that you are nominated, and I will be back on the 9th of September after the meeting of the World Federation of UN Associations.

If you come East at any time and want complete rest, I would love to have you come and stay with me but I don't want you to do it if it is just a case of adding another trip and another hectic night.

I would like to stress again the importance of Mr. Finnegan's concentrating on all the details of organization and coordination between regulars and the volunteers. Every move in the Convention should be planned and the people should be picked who are to speak and know beforehand what they are to do and what delegations are their responsibility.

Take a good rest now and get ready for the fight in the campaign which I know you will really enjoy.

Affectionately,

Notes

1. Paul Butler, chairman of the Democratic Party.
2. *Brown v. Board of Education of Topeka*, 1954.
3. Thomas K. Finletter, former secretary of the air force.
4. Carmine G. DeSapio, a New York political boss.

Eleanor Roosevelt to Ralph Bunche
July 16, 1956

Mrs. Roosevelt hesitated about traveling to Mississippi in response to a local National Association for the Advancement of Colored People (NAACP) request, and she asked for advice from Dr. Ralph Bunche at the United Nations, an African American, a diplomat, and winner of the Nobel Peace Prize in 1950.

July 16, 1956

Dear Dr. Bunche:

I am enclosing to you this correspondence because I think perhaps you can help me decide wisely. As you can see from my letter, I felt it was a mistake to go to Mississippi but if you think it would be wise, and I must say this young man's second letter is very persuasive, I will of course go. However, I am terribly afraid my visit would be followed by retaliations on the Negro people of the area, and then I would feel really guilty.

Eleanor Roosevelt and Dr. Ralph J. Bunche. (Courtesy of the Franklin D. Roosevelt Library)

I would be grateful if you would give me your judgment as to the right thing to do.

With appreciation for your help, and my good wishes,

Very sincerely yours,

Eleanor Roosevelt to Estes Kefauver

August 4, 1956

United States senator Estes Kefauver of Tennessee sought the Democratic presidential nomination in 1956 but bowed out after former Illinois governor Adlai E. Stevenson defeated him in several key primary contests. Mrs. Roosevelt supported Stevenson, and Kefauver's decision to release his delegates impressed her as she believed it would contribute to the unification of the Democratic Party, the first step toward harmony and victory in November.

August 4, 1956

My dear Senator,

I want to tell you how much impressed I was both by your statement and by your very generous and statesmanlike attitude.

I am sure that your move will strengthen the Democratic Party, and bring the nominations to quicker conclusion, and make it possible for a unified Party to win in November.

With my warm congratulations and respect,

Very cordially yours,

Eleanor Roosevelt to Adlai Stevenson

August 28, 1956

In the summer of 1956, Mrs. Roosevelt traveled through Europe with her grand-children, but she could not turn her thoughts away from the presidential election. She wrote this letter to Adlai Stevenson giving her views and making some subtle suggestions. The former first lady also evaluated the Republican campaign and found it wanting, but in the long run Eisenhower's popularity sustained him. Mrs. Roosevelt offered to campaign for Stevenson when she returned home.

Hotel Crillon, Paris
August 28, 1956

Dear Adlai:

I received a strange telephone message from San Francisco this morning. They called in the middle of last night but the boys refused to wake me up! This morning a Mr. Clarke[1] said he wanted my approval to raise funds by asking everyone who had Roosevelt dimes to donate them to the Democratic party campaign fund. At least that is what I made out of it. I told him I could give no approval at this distance on a move to raise funds for you, that you were the one who must be consulted but whatever you approved I would be willing to have done. I hope this was not putting too much on you but I had no way of knowing whether this was a good idea or whether the man was really someone you approved of having start this sort of movement.

I read in the papers of your trip with Estes Kefauver to see the leaders in different parts of the country which seems to me a good idea. At this distance Chicago[2] and San Francisco[3] seem a long way off and ten days over here make me feel I am in another world, so I hesitate to pass on certain observations but I do so in the belief that you will pay no attention to anything which you don't feel is valid.

Everyone I talked to feels that the crucial point in the election is to show people that prosperity will not come to an end if the Republicans are defeated. Somehow a group should make a study of our economic situation and then if possible the whole situation should be put into words of one syllable and the proposed plans equally simple. I have a feeling that the Republicans will sustain prosperity until after the election but that inevitably, whichever party goes in, a break will come after the election. This seems to me actually the one paramount point for the majority of people who care only about how good a living they are earning. The fact that some are not doing so well does not affect those who are still doing well, so the picture will have to be made clear and they will have to feel that everyone will eventually be affected.

I saw the Queen of Holland[4] and she talked to me about New Guinea and Indonesia, but there is time for that after I get home as it is tied up with our whole position on the colonial question. It will take some thinking through.

The Suez[5] situation does not look very happy to me. The Soviets have a knack for standing back and being enigmatic and letting us wonder what they will do while they shove somebody else to the fore, usually a weaker nation that would never dare stand up on its own. Mr. Dulles[6] piously talks about living up to the principles of the UN and ignores the UN when it might be useful at the start in making life easier by having all the nations involved instead of the 22 most interested ones.

I was much impressed in Denmark with the tiny garden holdings for factory workers outside the cities. The government and the city buys the land and sells it to a group (usually about 300) of factory workers. They build their own little camp houses and live there five or six months of the year. It might be helpful in combating juvenile delinquency.

Now we are in Paris, having a busy but, on the whole, pleasant time. I think the boys are enjoying it much more since Grania Gurewitsch[7] joined us. The three young ones seem to have a gayer time. We are off tomorrow on a four day motor trip in the North of France, then Friday night here, and Saturday to Geneva for a week. I will be (D.V.) at home in New York on September 9th and I hope to go to Hyde Park from the 10th to the 12th. I think I saw you were going to be in N.Y. about that time to speak. If you let me know, I would love to have a chance to talk with you and hear something of your plans and campaign preparations.

Tell Mr. Finnegan I will be glad if he will send me any dates he has lined up that he wants me to fill and also any suggestions of what he would particularly like me to cover in speaking. Since the Republican convention I feel more certain than ever that you can win. They seem to me empty and void of imagination or content. I saw today that Mr. Hall[8] is exhorting them not to be complacent. From what I hear I should think complacency was hardly allowable, though I would be glad if they would continue to feel that way!

With every good wish,

Affectionately,

Notes

1. A Stevenson supporter.
2. Site of the Democratic National Convention.
3. Site of the Republican National Convention.
4. Queen Juliana.
5. Under a 1954 agreement British troops were removed from the Suez Canal zone in June 1956. The next month, the U.S. and Britain withdrew offers to help finance the Aswan High Dam across the Nile River. This, along with several other factors, led Egyptian Gamal A. Nassar to take over the canal in July. Later, in October, a war began when Israel invaded Egypt. Britain and France attacked Egypt on October 31. The war ended on November 6 with a brokered peace by the United Nations.
6. John Foster Dulles, secretary of state.
7. Dr. David Gurewitsch's young daughter.
8. Leonard W. Hall, chairman of the Republican National Committee from 1953 to 1957.

Eleanor Roosevelt to Robert Wagner
September 10, 1956

In September 1956 Mrs. Roosevelt contacted Mayor Wagner of New York City to congratulate him on his decision to run for the United States Senate from New York. If he won, he would be repeating his father's career in the upper chamber.

September 10, 1956

Dear Mr. Mayor:

I see by the papers that you are going to make a run for Senator. I am delighted, and if there is anything at all I can do I will be glad to help. At this time I do not know how much time the Stevenson Committee will take, but I am sure they won't take all of my time.

With warm congratulations, and best wishes.

Cordially yours,

Eleanor Roosevelt to Adlai Stevenson

September 19, 1956

During the presidential campaign of 1956, Mrs. Roosevelt advised Adlai Stevenson on various occasions. This is a cover letter in which she passed along a succinct memo from Bernard Baruch and a longer document on health care. She wrote to Stevenson again the next day to comment further on the health-care issue. Baruch's note was brief. He essentially advised Stevenson to stay out of the South at the moment because the area was so annoyed with Eisenhower that Stevenson should do nothing possibly to antagonize the people there. Baruch also reported that the vice presidential candidate, Estes Kefauver, was doing well in winning back Democrats in Minnesota and other nearby areas. Baruch's belief that Stevenson had a winning chance demonstrated too much optimism.

September 19, 1956

Dear Adlai:

I am sure you have the information on the enclosed memorandum or Mr. Finnegan has it. However, Mr. Baruch asked me to pass it along and I do so.

I am also passing along a memorandum which is one of those I have received on health problems. I am adding a few words of my own.

Affectionately,

Eleanor Roosevelt to Adlai Stevenson

September 20, 1956

On September 19, 1956, Mrs. Roosevelt had sent Adlai Stevenson a brief note and indicated that she had enclosed a health plan that he might propose for implementation when he became president. The next day, she wrote him again to comment on the some aspects of the plan. The plan document is not available, but her attitude about government involvement in health care is clear. She also gave Stevenson some medical advice of her own.

September 20, 1956

Dear Adlai:

This memorandum of Esther Lape's is so very good that I hesitate even to add to it but I think you can spell out better the method of payment. For instance, it can be made clear that those with adequate incomes would simply have to appear to show they had had the examination and had carried out the necessary recommendations, but between three and ten thousand dollars where real illness can be an almost impossible burden there should be an arrangement with the doctors for a fixed sum for the examination and for the different categories of remedial care—these to be paid in full where the people were able to or in part by the locality, but below three thousand dollars to be paid in full by the locality. In a way, of course, this is meeting the cost out of taxation, in part at least, but the savings made in lessening the number of people in public hospitals, prisons and mental institutions would be great.

Medical care should mean, of course, dental care and mental health as well as the ordinary things included in medical care.

If we are going to say that the Democrats have a program for really making life better for everybody, this is one of the basic foundation spots. Education and housing come next.

I will try this out in speeches and if I find it is not well received you can stay clear of it. But I think something constructive as a Democratic program of action has to come before the people. Criticism is not enough.

I have some very remarkable cold tablets which, if you take them the minute you feel achey or any symptoms of cold, have always successfully stopped a cold for me. I would like to send you a bottle because Dr. Gurewitsch who prescribed them for me suggests that a cold for you might be a serious added burden. He recommends that I send you a bottle. If you want them, have your secretary call Miss Corr at TE 8-0330 and she will send them right on to you at the address given.

I am also enclosing a letter from Malcolm Ross who is a very reliable person. His idea is good.

Affectionately,

Statement of Support for Adlai Stevenson
September 25, 1956

This is a draft statement of Mrs. Roosevelt explaining her reasons for supporting Adlai Stevenson in his second run for the presidency. It specifically addresses the issue of civil rights and may have been intended for circulation in the South. The underlined words are those that she added and the strikeovers are ones she deleted.

September 25, 1956

I think Mr. Stevenson has a deep sense of obligation to live up to the Constitution and will feel that he must see that the law of the land is complied with. I also think he has imagination enough to feel that leadership in the White House can do something to make it easier for the Southern White people to see their position in the light of the world situation, and I am fairly certain he will call a meeting of leaders to confer with him and to settle on ~~out~~ some mode of procedure. No one can set an exact timetable but if we have a procedure which is being followed out and which is constantly moving forward there will not be a sense of frustration such as we now have.

Mr. Stevenson is sensitive to the feelings of people and this is one of the necessary qualities in meeting a situation of this kind. One must know how the Negro people in the US feel who have waited so long for their full rights as citizens, and yet one must also know how the Southern white people feel whose way of life is being changed, otherwise we may find ourselves involved in violence and bloodshed. The one thing we want to remember from the past is that violence and bloodshed may delay our ultimate objective, which is a spirit of peace and cooperation among all the citizens of the US.

I feel that Adlai Stevenson's sense of dedication to his task of a peaceful world and a united people in the US is a guarantee of the best steps being taken for civil rights and better and happier lives for all our people.

Eleanor Roosevelt

Eleanor Roosevelt to Adlai Stevenson
October 10, 1956

During the last month of the presidential campaign of 1956, Mrs. Roosevelt took another opportunity to encourage Adlai Stevenson and to give him advice. She regularly passed along letters and documents that she received from people, and she often advised him to consult with specific people, in this case Chester Bowles, former governor of Connecticut and ambassador to India. The former first lady also cautioned him about becoming too tired.

October 10, 1956

Dear Adlai:

The enclosed letter was sent to me by Pare Lorentz a man of imagination. I don't know if you ever saw his documentary films. One of them, "The River" is quite unforgettable. He is giving this purely to uphold your hand.

I hope you take a rest whenever you can. It troubles me that the grueling campaign you have taken must take so much out of you physically.

I had a talk with Chester Bowles and I think what he said about the third phase of the campaign and the need to tie the domestic issues into the foreign and show their inter-relationship, and his ideas for doing this, might be very useful to you. I hope you will be seeing him shortly. He always stimulates me and though you will have to weigh and sift what he suggests I think it is worth going through carefully.

I am not hearing any objection any more to your humor, so don't worry about that! Just let it come naturally.

If you can speak to the mass of people as though you were talking to any one individual in your living room at Libertyville,[1] you will reach their hearts and that is all that you have to bother about.

My very best wishes, and good luck!

Affectionately,

Note

1. Stevenson's hometown in Illinois.

Eleanor Roosevelt to Estes Kefauver
November 7, 1956

President Eisenhower's landslide reelection triumph in 1956 distressed Mrs. Roosevelt, but she accepted the people's decision. In a consolatory message to Kefauver, Stevenson's vice presidential running mate in 1956, she praised him for his magnificent campaign work and wished him well in his senatorial career.

November 7, 1956

Dear Senator Kefauver:

I am afraid nothing could have changed the landslide and the American people having spoken.

I hope you will continue to find your service in the Senate interesting for you will be needed there more than ever.

You made a magnificent campaign and I send you all good wishes for the future.

Very cordially yours,

Eleanor Roosevelt to Robert Wagner
November 7, 1956

Robert Wagner, mayor of New York City, attempted but failed to win election in 1956 to the United States Senate. As a close political associate of his, Mrs. Roosevelt expressed her regret at his loss.

November 7, 1956

Dear Mr. Mayor:

I was hopeful for a little while last night that you were going to be able to rise above the landslide for President Eisenhower but you made a magnificent showing and we will just have to hope for better luck in the future. I still feel the day will come when you will be following in your father's footsteps and taking Senator Lehman's place.

I grieve that you lost this time but you are doing fine work as Mayor and you made a good fight which must be some consolation.

I can't help feeling that the organization in the State and in the City has become very poor and perhaps some reorganization is indicated.

With warm good wishes to your wife and to you, and hopes for the future.

Very cordially yours,

Eleanor Roosevelt to Adlai Stevenson
November 7, 1956

The optimism of some and the hope of other supporters of Adlai Stevenson to reverse the results of the 1952 presidential contest failed to materialize in 1956. On the morning after the election, Mrs. Roosevelt sent Stevenson a note of condolence. Writing it as a close friend, she was not maudlin about the results. It was a practical message and one that Stevenson undoubtedly received with gratitude.

November 7, 1956

Dear Adlai:

Let me congratulate you on a magnificent fight. No one could have done more, but the love affair between President Eisenhower and the American people is too acute at present for any changes evidently to occur. I think in spite of the responsibility you felt, it is probably a relief to be relieved of it. Now you can enjoy your grandson and the boys and devote yourself to your own interests and feel at least that the weight of the world is not exclusively on your shoulders. None of us can, I fear, escape some sense of responsibility but we will all of us be able to do less.

I thought your message to the president was fine. I did not call you because I knew you would be overwhelmed with messages and I hoped that when you did go to bed you would have your first good night's rest in a long time.

I think you will be cleaning up neglected work for sometime but before long do take a real rest and holiday. If you are in these parts, please come and see your very devoted friend and admirer,

Eleanor Roosevelt to Agnes E. Meyer
February 8, 1957

After talking with former Illinois governor Adlai E. Stevenson, the Democratic presidential nominee in 1952 and 1956, Mrs. Roosevelt conceded her fondness for him and said that she believed he would enter international law, but she remained distressed by the loneliness of his personal life. She outlined these feelings to Stevenson's close friend, Agnes E. Meyer.

February 8, 1957

My dear Agnes:

I had an hour with Adlai and I think he has pretty well decided to go back into law and try to do international law which will take him travelling and give him a much wider field of interest. What really bothers him is the loneliness of his personal life and the actual sordid details of running a farm and a house when he is not there most of the time. Yet he wants to keep the farm for the boys who are at home and also for the married boy. I told him I wished he could find the right person to marry but for heaven's sake not to marry just for the sake of being married! He is going to the meeting in San Francisco and will suggest his plan. I have written Mr. Butler that I back it but that I can't be at the meeting.

I am so fond of Adlai and he does seem rather helpless and lost. Perhaps he will pull out of this in time, and I think your friendship means a great deal to him. Those of us who are really fond of him will just have to keep in touch with him as much as we possibly can.

I am glad you like what I wrote about the cultural center and I hope it turns out to be all that you want it to be.

Let me know when you come to New York. I will be away from the 10th of February through the 18th, and I will be in Washington, D.C. for the conference of the American Association for the UN on March 3rd to the morning of the 5th. I shall hope to see you then.

Affectionately,

Eleanor Roosevelt to Sam Rayburn

August 7, 1957

Mrs. Roosevelt possessed a myriad of interests, as evidenced by this letter in which she urged the speaker of the House of Representatives to do what he could to remove obstacles to a bill to provide for the humane slaughter of animals. Sam Rayburn answered her letter two weeks later to say that the session was running so long that he doubted that the bill would be brought up quickly. He did feel it would be considered in the new session in January.

August 7, 1957

Dear Mr. Speaker:

I am told that the Humane Slaughter Bill, which has excited a great many of my friends to action, is being held up in the House by Mr. McCormack[1] and I have been asked if I would please speak to you & ask you to speak to him so that it might come to the floor as my friends feel fairly sure it will be voted on favorably. I understand also that a small group of Jewish Rabbis feel that the Bill does not take care of their particular situation adequately, but others think it does, so I hope this can be cleared up.

With my good wishes,

Very cordially yours,

Note

1. A Massachusetts Democrat who later became speaker.

Eleanor Roosevelt to Lyndon B. Johnson

August 17, 1957

In this somewhat critical letter to the Senate majority leader, a Texas Democrat, Mrs. Roosevelt felt compelled to write about civil rights legislation and the attitude of some Southern Democrats on this heated subject. Her remarks in her newspaper column had disappointed Johnson, but Mrs. Roosevelt understood his strategy in trying to pass a civil rights bill and reiterated her position in her

response to his letter of August 12, in which he had offered some strong state-
ments regarding her attitude and choice of words.

August 17, 1957

Dear Senator Johnson:

I am sorry that you are disappointed in my support but you must realize that I understand very well your extremely clever strategy on the Civil Rights Bill. You may not have been "trying to fool the people" but you chose the one point on which good people might have some qualms and you built on that and that is why you have a goodly company of people with you. The end result, however, is that the Bill with this amendment will do very little since the "qualified voter" still has to qualify according to the laws of the states and none of you have touched on that particular point at any time. I have said that it is better to accept this bill than to have nothing and even the NAACP agrees on that but it would be fooling the people to have them think that this was a real vital step towards giving all our people the right to vote or any other civil rights.

I doubt if the Republicans ever really intended to do anything along this line but I can't say that I really believe the Democrats have intended to do much either, particularly those of you who come from Southern states or borderline states as Texas is.

I admire your ability as a leader. You have certainly done a remarkable piece of work and I know how persuasive you are but it is easier to look at actual results when you sit at a distance and are not really affected by what happens one way or another, and that is what I have been doing. I hope you pass the Bill and I shall say that it is better because it will at least show the world that we have moved a little but it will be a very little towards that fundamental right of every citizen—the right to vote.

Now may I add that I have pointed out in a column which will come out on Tuesday that I fully expect that as Senate Leader you will cooperate with Senator Knowland[1] and put back many of the foreign aid cuts, if not all. If the House Bill were approved there would be real harm done to the UN programs and foreign aid all the way down the line would suffer. I have said in this column that you and Senator Mansfield[2] are too statesmanlike to allow this to happen though it is a perfectly natural desire to want to show up the Republicans in their leadership. You would not allow this desire to influence you in your decision as to the real good of the country.

I hope I am correct in believing this and I am sorry to have caused you disappointment for, like everyone else, I find you a delightful and persuasive person and I have a great admiration for your ability, but on the Civil Rights issue I am afraid I must hold to my opinion.

Very cordially yours,

Notes

1. William F. Knowland, a California Republican, held a seat in the United States Senate from 1945 to 1959.

2. Michael J. "Mike" Mansfield, a former professor of history and political science at Montana State University, served as a United States senator from Montana from 1953 to 1977, when President Jimmy E. Carter appointed him ambassador to Japan. A Democrat, Mansfield was Senate majority leader in the Eighty-seventh through the Nineth-fourth Congresses.

Eleanor Roosevelt to Lyndon B. Johnson

January 31, 1958

Mrs. Roosevelt praised Senator Johnson's recent speech on outer space and international control and invited him to address the March conference of the American Association for the United Nations.

January 31, 1958

Dear Mr. Senator:

The American Association for the United Nations has a two day conference for some 90 organizations which cooperate with it every year. This year the conference will be held in Washington from Sunday, March 9th through the 10th.

We were so impressed by your speech the other day on outer space and international control that we wonder if you would be willing to address the conference on Monday afternoon, March 10th. If you feel that you might be able to do this, Mr. Clark Eichelberger, our Executive Director, will be in touch with you the latter part of next week.

I am so glad you took the attitude you did. It seemed to me the first real sign of leadership that we have had from anyone.

Very cordially yours,

Eleanor Roosevelt to W. Averell Harriman

June 20, 1958

The former first lady wrote to New York governor Harriman, a diplomat and Democratic politician, that she and some liberals regarded Thomas Finletter as the best Democratic senatorial nominee that year. Worried that the popular Nelson A. Rockefeller would obtain the Republican gubernatorial nomination, she stated that she wanted Harriman to win and the state represented in the United States Senate by someone of Herbert H. Lehman's stature. Lehman represented New York in the upper chamber from 1949 to 1957.

June 20, 1958

Dear Averell:

I was so sorry that I could not wait and attend the dinner given for you for the Young Democrats in Syracuse on the 14th because I would like to have heard your speech. I would also have liked to have had a chance to talk with you about something which has been on my mind.

In talking with the liberals with whom I rather frequently come in contact, I have a feeling that if we hope to keep them in line this autumn our best nominee would be Tom Finletter and therefore I have said that I thought he would be the best candidate we could name. The Democrats, particularly the old leaders in the state, may prefer some of the other men who have been mentioned and may think just because this is a Democratic year they can have whoever they want elected. However, if Nelson Rockefeller heads the Republican ticket and if we are interested in seeing the state of New York represented by a man of integrity and knowledge, I have a feeling we had better try for the best candidate. I know that all kinds of difficulties and situations will come up before you and I know all the old problems that crop up but I thought I ought to write you what my own judgment was in this matter since I want to see you win and I want to see the state of New York represented in the Senate by someone who can hope to gain stature along Herbert Lehman's lines.

With my best wishes and regrets that I was not able to hear you on the 14th,

Affectionately,

Eleanor Roosevelt to W. Averell Harriman

August 19, 1958

In an unmistakably frank letter to Governor Harriman, Mrs. Roosevelt expressed her concern over the gubernatorial campaign in New York and her determination that Harriman control Carmine G. DeSapio, a former New York secretary of state and political boss. She indicated that it would be difficult for her to work diligently for Harriman's reelection if she concluded that DeSapio, rather than the governor, guided the New York State Democratic Party.

August 19, 1958

My dear Averell:

I read the story in Friday's New York Times in which it is said that you have told your friends that you support Mr. Finletter for the nomination for US Senator but that you would accept Mr. Murray[1] if the political situation is such that Mr. Finletter cannot be nominated. You already have a Lieutenant-Governor who is a Roman Catholic and you will probably have another Catholic running. This article gives the impression that this is one of the things felt to be essential in the nomination for the US Senate. Frankly, I think it would be a mistake. I believe we must keep a balance, and the predominance of any one religion in the candidates is a mistake. Also, you know as well as I do that you can control Mr. DeSapio if you make up your mind to do so. I know this is hard for you to do but the man you decide to have for the US Senate will be nominated.

You say that the Liberal party has put pressure on you. I would suggest that the Liberal party is the least important factor in the pressures exerted at the present time. It is the liberals in the Democratic party that are going to be upset if they think, as many of them do, that what you have done by permitting this article to be written is to give the "kiss of death" to Mr. Finletter's nomination, because the moment you say you will accept an alternative you imply that you are subservient to the bosses. Many liberal Democrats in this election are weighing the question of whether they will vote for you or for Nelson Rockefeller—both of you suffer under the same difficulty, that of not really knowing the game sufficiently well to play it on the level of the bosses. You have the advantage because many people feel that you have learned something about this game during your time in office and this is a Democratic year, but from what I hear it might be quite possible that Democratic liberals, not wanting to vote for the Democratic candidate for the US Senate, will shed also the Democratic governorship because they will think the responsibility is yours.

I am afraid I am being rather brutal but I would rather tell you now what I hear than wait until after the race is over. I told you a long while back that I thought you would win and I still think so, given a feeling among Liberal Democrats that you can control DeSapio and the other leaders and that you will stand and work for the candidates that you really think are the best for the job for which they are nominated.

There is considerable criticism just now of Nelson because people have felt that he is compromising on principles in order to get the support of the organization in his party. If this becomes equally true in both parties, then where do the liberals put their trust?

I hated to have to fight you for the nomination in Chicago but I believe that Adlai was actually the best fitted for that nomination. I certainly will not fight you openly in this State but it would be hard to work for you if I felt that the party was guided by DeSapio and not by you.

My very best wishes,

Always affectionately,

Note

1. Thomas E. Murray Sr., Democratic candidate for U.S. senator from New York in 1958.

Eleanor Roosevelt to W. Averell Harriman

November 5, 1958

Although pleased with Democratic victories in the off-year elections in 1958 and the party's enlarged control of Congress, Mrs. Roosevelt regretted Governor Harriman's defeat for reelection. She consoled him by mentioning his good service to the state and reminding him that an individual can express himself freely out of office.

November 5, 1958

My dear Averell:

I want to tell you how deeply I regret the fact that you were not re-elected. You gave the state good service and I hope you will feel rewarded for what you have done in public service and find much more of interest to do in the years to come.

I am afraid it was the convention in Buffalo and DeSapio's campaigning upstate where he is not liked, which brought about the final result, but it may well be that nothing could have made a change. People are unpredictable.

There is one wonderful thing about being out of office. One is much freer to express oneself and one has the feeling that one can do whatever one wants to do and that is certainly a satisfaction.

With my best wishes to you and Marie,

Affectionately,

Eleanor Roosevelt to John F. Kennedy
December 18, 1958

Eleanor Roosevelt always said what she thought and that often brought responses, both favorable and unfavorable, from public figures. One such example concerned Sen. John F. Kennedy of Massachusetts, who had begun to build a national campaign for president after his almost successful bid for the vice presidency at the 1956 Democratic National Convention. Kennedy heard in 1958 that Mrs. Roosevelt had made a statement on a national television news program that Kennedy's "father had been spending oodles of money all over the country and probably has a paid representative in every state by now." Kennedy asked her to identify her informant or if she would be willing to name any such representative and any example of spending on his father's part. She did not disavow her earlier comments.

December 18, 1958

Dear Senator Kennedy:

If my comment is not true, I will gladly so state. I was told that your father said openly he would spend any money to make his son the first Catholic President of this country, and many people as I travel about tell me of money spent by him in your behalf. This seems commonly accepted as a fact.

Building an organization is permissible but giving too lavishly may seem to indicate a desire to influence through money.

Very sincerely yours,

Eleanor Roosevelt to John F. Kennedy
January 6, 1959

Sen. John Kennedy continued to be sensitive to charges that his father was spending money in large quantities around the country to secure the presidential nomination for his son. Mrs. Roosevelt had repeated in her daily column common wisdom she had heard to this effect. Eleanor Roosevelt disliked Kennedy's father, Joseph P. Kennedy, and thought that Senator Kennedy had not taken a strong enough stand against McCarthyism. When Kennedy objected to her using this information, he contacted her again in December 1958 asking her to issue a clarification about the rumors. To put this matter to rest, she wrote a statement that took up about half of her newspaper column for January 6, 1959, dealing with this matter. The relevant portion of the column is reprinted below.

Eleanor Roosevelt and President John F. Kennedy. (Courtesy of the Franklin D. Roosevelt Library)

January 6, 1959

Dear Senator Kennedy:

I am enclosing a copy of my column for tomorrow and as you will note I have given your statement as the fairest way to answer what are generally believed and stated beliefs in this country. People will, of course, never give names as that would open them to liability.

I hope you will feel that I have handled the matter fairly.

Very sincerely yours,

Excerpt from Mrs. Roosevelt's *My Day* column for January 6, 1959

A few days ago I received a letter from Senator John Kennedy telling me that I had been completely misinformed as to the fact that his father had any paid representatives working for him in any state of the Union, or that Mr. Kennedy senior has spent any money around the country on Senator Kennedy's behalf.

My statement to the Senator had been that it was commonly accepted as a fact that these things had been done. And that while it was obligatory on anyone to build up an organization if they wished nomination or election, in any case an extravagant use of money to achieve these results was not looked upon with favor.

"I am certain no evidence to the contrary has ever been presented to you. I am aware, as you must be, that there are a good many people who fabricate rumors and engage in slander about any person in public life. But I have made it a point never to accept or repeat such statements unless I have some concrete evidence of their truth.

"Since my letter to you, I assume you have requested your informants to furnish you with more than their gossip and speculation. If they have been unable to produce concrete evidence to support their charges or proof of the existence of at least one 'paid representative' in one state of the Union, I am confident you will, after your investigation, correct the record in a fair and gracious manner . . ."

Since my information came largely from remarks made by people in many places, I think I should give my readers Senator Kennedy's own statement. That is the fairest way I know of dealing with a situation of this kind.

Eleanor Roosevelt to John F. Kennedy

January 20, 1959

While John F. Kennedy was developing his campaign for the presidency in 1960, the issue of his father's influence and money continued to plague him. In January 1959 he wrote Mrs. Roosevelt in response to a column she had written in which she mentioned that Kennedy had "paid representatives" throughout the country working to make him president. He asked Mrs. Roosevelt to reveal the names of her informants or at least identify some of the paid representatives, knowing that her informants could give no such names "because I have no paid representative." Mrs. Roosevelt answered him candidly but with tact as she tried to deal with his controversial presidential candidacy.

January 20, 1959

Dear Senator Kennedy:

In reply to your letter of the 10th, my informants were just casual people in casual conversation. It would be impossible to get their names because for the most part I don't even know them.

Maybe, like in the case of my family, you suffer from the mere fact that many people know your father and also know that there is money in your family. We have always found somewhat similar things occur, and except for a few names I could not name the people in the case of my family.

I am quite willing to state what you decide but it does not seem to me as strong as your categorical denial. I have never said that my opposition to you was based on these rumors or that I believed them, but I could not deny what I knew nothing about. From now on I will say, when asked, that I have your assurance that the rumors are not true.

If you want another column, I will write it—just tell me.

Very sincerely yours,

Eleanor Roosevelt to John F. Kennedy

January 29, 1959

During the exchange of correspondence in early 1959 regarding Mrs. Roosevelt's comments about Sen. John F. Kennedy and the influence of his father, Joseph P. Kennedy, she wrote this brief telegram to chide him for being thin-skinned.

Telegram, January 29, 1959

MY DEAR BOY I ONLY SAY THESE THINGS FOR YOUR OWN GOOD I HAVE FOUND IN LIFETIME OF ADVERSITY THAT WHEN BLOWS ARE RAINED ON ONE, IT IS ADVISABLE TO TURN THE OTHER PROFILE.

MRS. ELEANOR ROOSEVELT

[*JFKL*]

Eleanor Roosevelt to Mary Clark Rockefeller

May 7, 1959

In a letter to Governor Rockefeller's wife, the first lady of New York, Mrs. Roosevelt was delighted to learn that individuals were compiling a history of the old executive mansion in Albany. She pledged her cooperation and willingness to answer questions, recalling some of the official parties, receptions, and changes that had occurred when she and her husband occupied the home.

May 7, 1959

Dear Mrs. Rockefeller:

I will ask the library at Hyde Park to send you a selection of photographs if they have them, taken during the years in Albany. I am very much afraid there may not be many but there may be a few and I will be very glad to have you use them.

I am delighted that a history of the old executive mansion in Albany is being compiled and I am very happy to answer your questions.

My husband and I were more or less alone by the time we went to Albany, except for holidays. My daughter, Anna, was already married, my son James was in college and Franklin and John were in Groton. Elliott was also at school and later married. In the holidays many of them came to Albany but as a rule we went to Hyde Park for the holidays, so, except for the fact that Jimmy had pneumonia, there were very few of them who spent any length of time in the Mansion in Albany.

We had a number of official parties. The ones I remember best were the New Year's receptions and the parties for the Legislature and the press. I had a number of teas for groups of people coming to Albany or for organizations—sometimes just women, sometimes mixed groups. My husband regularly entertained members of the legislature at stag dinners and used the evenings as briefings on his programs. We had a number of official dinners for the Court, for different legislative leaders and of course we had a great many out of town guests. I remember one party when Admiral Byrd[1] came back from one of his trips and was given a decoration by the state.

We had a movie machine and showed movies sometimes in the evenings.

We made only one change in the grounds. We turned the greenhouse into a swimming pool and had a very small greenhouse. We did very little inside the Mansion—some painting but very little change in the rooms was made.

I found the old house attractive and I did not mind its location. I liked my neighbors though I have to agree that at certain religious festival times the noise was sometimes a little distracting as the weather was usually warm and the windows were open! At that time there was a Roman Catholic orphanage nearby and at Christmas time we always had a party for the orphans—a custom started by Al Smith. This, I understand, has been discontinued.

With very best wishes for the success of your enterprise,

Very cordially yours,

Note

1. Richard E. Byrd, an American rear admiral and explorer of the Arctic and Antarctic, between 1928 and 1957 did more than any other person to direct the exploration of the bleak, frozen continent of Antarctica.

Eleanor Roosevelt to Walter Reuther

May 25, 1969 [1959]

After two failed presidential campaigns, Adlai Stevenson considered the possibility of trying for a third nomination. Walter Reuther, a leader of the AFL-CIO, wielded influence in the Democratic Party, and his support was considered valuable by many candidates, especially of the more liberal variety. When Mrs. Roosevelt heard that Reuther planned to come out for John F. Kennedy, she endeavored to talk him out of an early endorsement. No doubt Mrs. Roosevelt was more optimistic about Stevenson's chances than she should have been, given his track record and the popularity of the young John Kennedy. The letter is dated 1969, but this is clearly a typographical error and should be 1959.

May 25, 1969 [1959]
CONFIDENTIAL

Dear Walter:

Someone has told me that you plan to come out shortly for Senator Kennedy for President. I have a feeling, judging from the mail which comes in each day, that there is a greater and greater demand for Adlai Stevenson—the feeling being that we need a more mature man with more knowledge of the world in the next four years.

I wonder if you would not consider waiting until the Convention to find out what Stevenson's chances are before making your decision.

I know this is perhaps difficult for you to do but I thought I might suggest it since it seems to me that a Stevenson-Kennedy ticket is probably the strongest ticket we can have in the fight against Nixon, or, if the situation should change in the Republican Party, against Rockefeller.

I hope you will forgive me for even trying to make this suggestion to you, and I look forward to seeing you on Memorial Day.

Very cordially yours,

Eleanor Roosevelt to Lyndon B. Johnson

June 2, 1959

Relations between Mrs. Roosevelt and the Johnsons had improved considerably by the summer of 1959 as Johnson was making plans to capture the Democratic presidential nomination in 1960. On Memorial Day he visited Hyde Park and delivered a speech for the occasion. Mrs. Roosevelt appreciated his sojourn and remarks.

June 2, 1959

My dear Senator:

I want to thank you many, many times for coming up to Hyde Park on Memorial Day. It was a tremendous ordeal and the weather was very hot, but I can only tell you that all of us, including your small audience, deeply appreciated the effort you made and the very fine speech you delivered. On all sides I was told that this was the most successful Memorial Day Service that had ever been held. You were very kind, and I just want to say that only you could have made me really glad that President Truman could not come!

Please tell your wife how much I appreciated her coming with you.

I hope now that you have found the way when you are at leisure you will let me know and come up for a longer time, so that you can really enjoy seeing the Memorial. All you have to do is write me a little ahead of time.

With renewed thanks and warm good wishes to you and Mrs. Johnson.

Very cordially yours,

Eleanor Roosevelt to Harry S Truman

August 12, 1959

In 1959 Mrs. Roosevelt contacted former President Truman about the dropping of the atomic bomb on Japan and the use of nuclear power during peacetime. She had agreed at the time that he had to use the atomic bomb on Japan in 1945. Although she harbored reservations about the second bomb that destroyed Nagasaki, after visiting there, she understood why it had to be done. Mrs. Roosevelt expressed her desire for the banning of nuclear weapons even though peaceful uses of this power might be possible.

August 12, 1959

Dear Mr. President:

Thank you very much for the explanation which I shall pass on to the people who asked me.

As you know, I have always said that you had no choice but to use the atomic bomb to bring the war to an end. For a time I was disturbed at our having used it in Nagasaki but after being in Japan and seeing the defenses and talking with one of our representatives who had been a prisoner of the Japanese and who explained that unless there had been a second demonstration the Japanese would have felt they could defend themselves which would have resulted in the destruction of the whole of Japan and the loss of millions of our own men, I realized that you had this knowledge and that you could make no other decision than the one you made. I have since written this publicly a number of times. I would give a great deal, however, now if we could come to an agreement for stopping the whole use of atomic energy for military purposes. I know that certain experiments have to go on in order to continue the development for non-military purposes but they should be done in such a way, if possible, as to protect the human race from fall-out. I realize the differences in opinion among scientists as to how much is harmful and unharmful, but if we are going to advance, this is an area where we should succeed in getting this knowledge used for peacetime uses successfully.

Your last paragraph touches on a point that I have thought on very often. We have such short memories that now we behave as though Germany and Japan had always been our best friends, and I sometimes wish we really remembered who was responsible for starting World War II. I have a feeling that we should have some fresh thinking on our whole peacetime situation.

If you are in these parts, I hope you will let me know. I would still love to have a long talk with you.

With kind regards to Mrs. Truman and the hope that she is feeling better.

Cordially,

Eleanor Roosevelt to Lyndon B. Johnson

January 23, 1960

Worried that Vice President Richard M. Nixon, whom she regarded as ruthless, would win the presidential election of 1960 due to Democratic divisions and the prosperity issue, Mrs. Roosevelt urged the establishment of a peace agency as an appeal to women and young voters to vote Democratic.

January 23, 1960

Dear Senator Johnson:

I was sent a bill which was introduced the other day by a Congressman from Florida in the House, urging the establishment of a peace agency. This is in many ways similar to the idea for a peace agency presented to the Advisory Council at the last meeting.

I feel very strongly that this idea will make a real appeal to women and young people, and no matter who our candidate is we do not have a chance of meeting Nixon unless we can get a majority of the women's vote and of the young people's vote. The feeling is that the Democrats are lagging in their interest in peace and are afraid to take many of the steps that need to be taken, so I urge you in the hope that you will be able to work out something beyond this bill which has been introduced to the Advisory Council idea, which is based probably on sounder facts, and really do something about it.

A year ago I thought that the Democrats would really win the coming election. I cannot bear to think of Nixon's being the President of the US but I think it is very probable that he will be. He is well organized and ruthless, and the Democrats have allowed themselves in many areas such as New York City to be dominated by boss rule and an amount of dishonesty is coming out in their various relationships to their positions and the work they do which gives people a very good reason for not returning them to power. I think in New York City we can easily find ourselves defeated even for the mayorality.

There is no question that the Republicans are trying to capitalize and be the "apostles of peace and prosperity", and unless we manage to change the situation quite forcibly in the next few months, I am afraid we are in for a Nixon victory.

I know you will say I am being an "apostle of doom" but I am looking very hard for some one thing that might catch the imagination of women and youth and help our party to keep their vote, or gain their vote, in the next election.

With my good wishes,

Very cordially yours,

Eleanor Roosevelt to Lyndon B. Johnson
January 29, 1960

In an endeavor to attract African American voters to the Democratic side, Mrs. Roosevelt complained about the weaknesses in the civil rights bill under consideration by the House Rules Committee. She regarded as absolutely essential certain features in the final bill, offering her help if necessary.

January 29, 1960

Dear Senator Johnson:

I am writing you because from all reports the "House Rules Committee" has at present a very weak civil rights bill and there is danger that this is all that will be approved.

There are three things that I think absolutely essential in any civil rights bill: 1. The implementation of the Supreme Court order[1] for desegregation everywhere in our country. I realize that time was given and that we have wasted time. I think this could have been begun in the first grade and the percentage increased year by year so that when these first graders reached high school they would be unconscious of what had happened. Unfortunately, this has not been done, and I think we should begin and do it immediately. 2. I think the Attorney General must have the power to move in all cases of civil rights violation. 3. I think the proposal to have federal voting registrars in areas where Negroes are denied the right to vote, is essential.

If it would help at all, I would be delighted to stop off in Washington on my way back from the West Coast on February 11th. If my plane is on time, I would get in at 3:30 p.m. but I could safely say I would be at the Senate by 4:30 if you cared to see me for a few minutes. I will then go back to the airport and come on to New York.

I think it absolutely necessary that we make a Democratic record on this bill. The Negroes are going over more and more to the Republicans, and those that we can count on as Democrats need a real achievement on the part of the Democrats to point to as a reason for backing the Democratic party.

With every good wish,

Very sincerely yours,

Note

1. The case of *Brown v. Board of Education*, 1954.

Eleanor Roosevelt to Sam Rayburn
February 27, 1960

During the election year of 1960, Congress considered a new civil rights bill. Mrs. Roosevelt, always concerned about the rights of African Americans, wrote to Sam Rayburn, speaker of the House of Representatives. Perhaps because Rayburn was an old-time southern politician from Texas, she may have believed that he needed special encouragement.

February 27, 1960

Dear Mr. Speaker:

This is just to tell you how pleased I was that the Civil Rights issue is now being discussed.

I hope that in backing the civil rights legislation you will see to it that the Bill will contain the following provisions:

1.Back the Supreme Court's desegration decision with a positive program for assisting school districts to move ahead with desegration.

2.Give the Attorney General the power to move in all cases of Civil Rights violations.

3.Assign Federal Voting Referees-Registrars to areas where Negroes are denied the right to vote.

In delaying the passage of a strong Civil Rights Bill we are repudiating the very principles on which our democracy was founded. I am confident that you will do what you can to stop this delay.

With every good wish.

Cordially,

[SRL]

Eleanor Roosevelt to Walter Reuther

April 25, 1960

In the months preceding the Democratic convention of 1960, the primary campaigns around the country heated up considerably, especially in the contest between two senators, John F. Kennedy and Hubert H. Humphrey of Minnesota. Mrs. Roosevelt and Walter Reuther worried that serious conflict in the primaries might hurt the party in the November election. In that regard she had contacted Humphrey but had no impact on him. She also mentioned a person who was seeking a real estate loan from the AFL-CIO and told Reuther that she knew nothing about such loans, but that this particular man had a good reputation.

April 25, 1960

Dear Walter:

I called Hubert Humphrey the other day but had absolutely no effect upon him. He and Kennedy both seem to feel they have no chance in the nomination unless they go on with these primaries. There is a chance they may be less enthusiastic after the West Virginia primary, though this is only a chance!

A Mr. Anthony Cucolo who built the Storm King highway years ago and knows all the New York State, West Point, and highway people, came and asked me to give him a letter of introduction to you and Jim Carey. He tells me that it is a practice for unions to loan money on real estate and that he wants to apply for a loan in this manner. I know nothing about this and can only vouch for the fact that he has been a successful and resourceful contractor, and as far as I know he has a sense of responsibility for his workers and for his community, and is an honest person.

Very cordially yours,

Eleanor Roosevelt to Agnes E. Meyer
June 6, 1960

At first Mrs. Roosevelt entertained no plans to attend the Democratic National Convention in Los Angeles, but eventually others, including Paul M. Butler, chairman of the Democratic National Committee, persuaded her to participate in the proceedings. Her memorable speech at the podium before the delegates was a shining moment, and the respect with which Democrats cheered and greeted her attested to her enormous popularity.

June 6, 1960

Dear Agnes:

I had made up my mind firmly not to go to the Convention, but Anna Rosenberg has today made a plea that I go out after the first day or two, and she says Paul Butler wants me particularly to make a speech which may be of some help on the Platform. By that time I feel I will not be interfering too much with my boys, and I will go out from Wednesday to Friday afternoon.

My old friends, Mr. and Mrs. Hershey Martin,[1] with whom I nearly always stay when I go out to Los Angeles, made an appeal to me to please stay with them, so I will go to them. However, I would be glad to know how I can get in touch with you at the earliest possible time after my arrival, so please send me your telephone number so I can find out where you are.

I was very much interested in your speech to Labor and thought it excellent.

I am enclosing a letter from a colored man whom I do not know but who sent me an article which he had written on Adam Clayton Powell.[2] I don't know why he turned against Powell but he certainly did give us plenty of information in the article. Whether he can be of any value to anyone, I don't know but I am sending you his letter in case you hear of someone who wants a man of this kind. I will tell him that I have forwarded his letter to a friend but will not give your name.

With affectionate thoughts and warm thanks for your kind offer of hospitality.

Affectionately,

Notes

1. Mrs. Hershey Martin was Myris Chaney, a professional dancer who was introduced to ER in the early 1930s. ER's employment of her to supervise the children's physical fitness program at the Office of Civilian Defense incensed congressional critics. Chaney married Hershey Martin, a band leader, in 1943.

2. Adam Clayton Powell Jr., a political and religious leader of the Harlem area of New York, served in Congress from 1945 to 1971. His private life disappointed many people and resulted in his being denied his seat in the House in 1967, but he won the special election to fill the vacancy. He did not claim the seat, but he won again in 1968 and returned to Congress until 1971.

Eleanor Roosevelt to Edmund G. Brown

June 10, 1960

Edmund G. "Pat" Brown, a Democrat, served as governor of California from 1959 to 1967. He supported Sen. John F. Kennedy for the Democratic presidential nomination in 1960. Concerned about international events, especially foreign relations with the Soviet Union in the nuclear age and Cold War, Eleanor Roosevelt wanted former Illinois governor Adlai E. Stevenson, the Democratic presidential standard bearer in 1952 and 1956, to be the party's nominee again in 1960 due to his experience and qualifications in domestic and foreign affairs. She hoped for a Stevenson-Kennedy ticket, believing that it would be the strongest slate to put up against the Republican presidential aspirant, Vice President Richard M. Nixon. In this letter to Governor Brown, written approximately a month prior to the commencement of the Democratic National Convention in Los Angeles, Mrs. Roosevelt sought to persuade Brown to head a California delegation pledged to Stevenson.

June 10, 1960

Dear Governor Brown:

I know that in California there is a good deal of support for Governor Stevenson, and therefore I thought you might like to see what I had written. I feel that this ticket is the strongest we can put into the field, and I hope very much that you and your delegation will come to agree with those of us who feel strongly that in this world crisis this is the best way for us as Democrats to serve our country and the world.

Very cordially yours,

Eleanor Roosevelt to Joseph P. Lash

June 15, 1960

Joseph P. Lash, an author and editor, first met Mrs. Roosevelt in 1939 on a train ride to Washington, D.C. This began a long, intimate friendship between Mrs. Roosevelt, Lash, and Lash's wife, Trude. In fact, to Mrs. Roosevelt, Lash seemed like a devoted son. After serving in the army during World War II, Lash directed Americans for Democratic Action (ADA) from 1946 to 1949. From 1950 to 1961 he was the United Nations correspondent for the New York Post, a position that put him in constant touch with Mrs. Roosevelt. His most famous book, Eleanor and Franklin: The Story of Their Relationship, *based on Mrs. Roosevelt's private papers and published by Norton in 1971, won the Pulitzer Prize in Biography in 1972, the National Book Award, and the Francis Parkman Prize presented by the Organization of American Historians. Mrs. Roosevelt once said, "The thing that counts is the striving of the human soul to achieve spiritually the best that it is capable of, and to care unselfishly not only for personal good but for the good of all who toil with them upon the earth." Lash concurred with her philosophy. In this letter, the former first lady confided her views on politics in 1960 to Lash.*

June 15th

Dearest Joe

Your letters & your mother's postcards have been a joy & today's says Trude arrived early but the party must have made her rise above it for it sounds delightful.

How crowded things must be! Perhaps just Denmark is that popular!

I did my 2 commencement addresses last week & Walter Reuther & family spent Sat.-Tue in H.P.[1] even tho I was gone to Amherst all Tuesday. Franklin came up to dine Sat. night & I wished for you. Walter feels we are lost unless Stevenson & Kennedy agree before the convention that whichever one can't win will throw his votes to the others which means if Kennedy starts a band wagon he'll win. Reuther's arguments that unless they are agreed they will elect the Republicans as Johnson will bring his disciplined votes to Symington's[2] & Adlai to stop Kennedy that means no Catholic or Negro vote for Adlai & a Rep. victory—Petitions are being circulated now in every state for Adlai. Finally I've agreed to go out Monday a.m. July 11th & if I have to I'll stay till Friday.

Meantime I was in Hartford last night for Mrs. Auerbach's conference, in Newark for bonds tonight & Sat for an evening speech in Miami! Home Sunday!

There are endless people who want to be seen, no peace as yet! All my love & good luck.

E.R.

Notes

1. Hyde Park.
2. First secretary of the air force from 1947 to 1950, Stuart Symington, a Missouri Democrat, served in the United States Senate from 1953 to 1976. He unsuccessfully sought the Democratic presidential nomination in 1960.

Eleanor Roosevelt to Michael V. DiSalle

June 21, 1960

Gov. Michael V. DiSalle of Ohio was an early supporter of Sen. John F. Kennedy of Massachusetts for president in 1960. He headed the Ohio delegation to the Democratic National Convention pledged to vote for Kennedy on the first ballot. If Kennedy did not win the nomination on the first roll call, Mrs. Roosevelt urged Governor DiSalle, who held office from 1959 to 1963, to join with her and others in shaping a Stevenson-Kennedy ticket as the best possible choice and most qualified team. She enclosed some information that she had composed dealing with the advantages of selecting Stevenson.

June 21, 1960

Dear Governor DiSalle:

I know that your State is bound in the first ballot for Jack Kennedy but if by chance he is not nominated on the first few ballots I hope that you may decide to join some of the rest of us who believe that Stevenson is our best nominee, and hope for a Stevenson Kennedy ticket.

I am enclosing a little statement which was not fully carried in the newspapers, which I made, and I thought you might be interested in reading it.

Very sincerely yours,

Eleanor Roosevelt to Agnes E. Meyer

June 21, 1960

After conversing with Democratic senator A.S. Mike Monroney of Oklahoma, Mrs. Roosevelt, who strongly supported Stevenson for the presidential nomination in 1960, decided that, until the votes began to change, it would not be wise to place Stevenson's name in nomination for the presidency if the outcome would produce for him a poor and embarrassing tally.

June 21, 1960

Dear Agnes:

In thinking over my conversation with you and Mike Monroney, I think it would be better if Adlai's name was not put before the Convention until it is clear that the votes are beginning to change. I did not realize that the galleries would be so controlled as the Senator told me last night, by Mr. Butler's having carefully issued tickets to the big subscribers. This will certainly make a complication and it is better that the first few ballots should go by. There is, of course, a chance that Kennedy will be nominated, but if that is a really good chance it is going to happen in any case, I think, and it would be a mistake to put Stevenson's name in nomination and then have a very poor showing even from those who are not delegates, and as this is going to be so carefully controlled we had better not take any chances. This is going to be a convention where one is going to have to work by ear all the way through and I hope that wiser heads than mine will be directing it!

Affectionately,

Eleanor Roosevelt to Gustav Ranis

July 9, 1960

Born in Germany, Ranis became a naturalized United States citizen in 1952 and earned a Ph.D. four years later from Yale University. In 1960 he was joint director of research at the Institute of Development Economics in Karachi, Pakistan. He later accepted a position as professor of economics at Yale University in Connecticut. He and Mrs. Roosevelt formed a lasting friendship through their common interest in government and economic development. In this letter, Mrs. Roosevelt updated Ranis on her life and the political situation in the United States prior to the Democratic National Convention. Without question she was a woman whose political and social ideals were ahead of their time.

July 9, 1960

Dear Gus:

I was so glad to hear that your wife[1] had her baby and that all is going well. How nice, too, that you are going to be able to meet each other in Europe in August. I think you were wise in deciding to return to Yale in the autumn. Is there any chance that in your travels in Europe you might be in Poland between September 1st and 10th when the World Federation of the UN Associations meets there? If so, I hope you will look up the US delegation as I hope to be there with them in Warsaw.

I got out to the Democratic Convention[2] Sunday the 10th. I doubt very much whether I can do anything and I am not too hopeful of Stevenson's nomination but certainly we will not give up, and we will try very hard to persuade Mr. Kennedy that his future will be benefited if he will run with Stevenson and run later in first place himself.

Senator Lehman was delighted over the victories the reform group had in New York in the last primaries. I was very pleased for him as it looks now as though we will gain a great many of the leaders next autumn in New York City, and we will hope to work later in the Bronx.

I hope to see you in the autumn but I imagine you will be living in Yale. My best wishes to your wife and the baby and with affectionate greetings to you.

Affectionately,

Notes

1. Ray Lee Finkelstein.
2. In Los Angeles.

Eleanor Roosevelt to Adlai E. Stevenson

August 11, 1960

In a post-convention letter to Adlai E. Stevenson, Mrs. Roosevelt once again revealed her affection for and appreciation of the former governor and two-time Democratic presidential candidate. She also revealed that she planned to discuss the upcoming campaign with Senator Kennedy and ascertain the goals he hoped to achieve if elected to the nation's highest office. Mrs. Roosevelt still showed some skepticism of the youthful Democratic presidential nominee, who had chosen Sen. Lyndon B. Johnson of Texas as his vice presidential running mate.

August 11 [1960]

Dear Adlai,

At first I wanted to return your check but I'll take it because it is you & I know it will make you happier. I'll give David Gurewitsch $500 & I'll try to use mine in ways you will approve of & which will be useful.

I'm seeing Kennedy on Tuesday & I hope he'll not talk only about getting the vote in Nov. but also about what he hopes to achieve if elected. He's got a hard fight here & in California & I wish people who meet him didn't feel he is such a cold & calculating person.

I go abroad Aug. 22nd & return Sept. 14th. Do let me know if you are to be here after that.

Every good wish, my thanks & my love.

Eleanor Roosevelt.

Eleanor Roosevelt to Mary Lasker

August 15, 1960

In her letter to Sen. John F. Kennedy on August 16, Mrs. Roosevelt revealed that several people had expressed interest in the results of the meeting she had with him on August 15. When she wrote Kennedy, she promised to enclose a copy of the letter that she sent to Mary Lasker. Lasker ran interference as an intermediary between Eleanor Roosevelt and John F. Kennedy in 1960, attempting to soothe their differences and seek an accommodation. Although personally he might have severed his ties with Mrs. Roosevelt, Kennedy clearly recognized in 1960 that the former first lady was of political value, and he sought to mend their relationship. Kennedy made an impression on Mrs. Roosevelt and she chose to endorse him, but her heart was still with Adlai Stevenson.

August 15, 1960

I had my talk with Senator Kennedy yesterday—an hour alone during lunch, and at the very end he called in Mr. Walton[1] for a few minutes before going over to address the Gold Ring Club.

I want to report that at the airport he was met by a very large group and the enthusiasm was great. I did not go myself to meet him but sent Edna and David.[2] Edna circulated among the people and asked them if they were Democrats or just curiosity seekers. Almost invariably they answered that they were

Democrats. The enthusiasm at the big house was tremendous, and I think he made a very good speech on the expansion of Social Security.

I did not ask the Senator for any definite promise as I felt that this would be almost impossible. But I told him that he needed the Stevenson votes in New York and California and that he had to carry these two states or he would be in trouble because he probably could not hold the Solid South.[3] This was brought about by his telling me that he had not realized before the fragmentation of the Democratic party and the fact that the majority in Congress did not give the leadership that holds the party together, and that since my husband's time there was no unity. The newly elected governor of Florida[4] came in to see him and said: "I want you to know that I am a conservative. I am against integration, and I am for the Right-to-Work law". Whereupon Kennedy said: "Why don't you join the Republicans?"!

I gather that his understanding of the difficulties of the campaign that face him have matured him in a short time. He told me that he had phoned Adlai this past week and asked for him to set up a small group to do research in the area of foreign policy. I told him that this was not enough, that he would have to give the people who were for Adlai the assurance that they were working together. All of us know that unless Adlai felt their philosophies were similar he would not accept the Secretary of State post. Therefore, I felt that he had to prove by working in the campaign and appearing on the same platforms, and perhaps by references and quotation, that there was close cooperation. Bringing both Chester Bowles and Adlai in whenever he could would mean that these were the men he was counting on for advice. He agreed and said he would try to do this.

We then spoke about Chester Bowles and he said he had asked Chester not to resign.[5] I had a letter Saturday from Chester in which he gave me his reasons for resigning. He said he thought Adlai was the best man for the Secretary of State post, that he (Chet) would rather be in the executive than in the legislative branch, so he would rather work for Kennedy than be a candidate for Congress.

Kennedy likes Chester Bowles and finds him easy to work with. He also seems to realize that his own mind is so quick he may perhaps be hasty in making decisions, and he needs Adlai there.

Now I have no promises from the Senator, but I have the distinct feeling that he is planning on working closely with Adlai. I also had the feeling that here was a man who could learn. I liked him better than I ever had before because he seemed so little cocksure, and I think he has a mind that is open to new ideas.

I agreed that I would go on the citizens committee here as honorary chairman, and that I would do what I could here. Whether I would take any trips or become more involved would depend on whether or not I was happy with the way he progresses as a person in the campaign.

My final judgment now is that here is a man who wants to leave a record (perhaps for ambitious personal reasons as people say) but I rather think because he really is interested in helping the people of his own country and mankind in general. I will be surer of this as time goes on, but I think I am not mistaken in feeling that he would make a good President if elected.

Notes

1. William Walton, a lifelong friend of Kennedy.

2. Born in Switzerland in 1902, Dr. Arno David Gurewitsch, who taught at the Columbia Presbyterian Medical Center in New York City for thirty-four years, was Mrs. Roosevelt's personal physician from 1945 to 1962. She developed a close relationship with Gurewitsch and his wife, Edna Schwartz Perkel, an artist, whom he married in 1958. There was little that Mrs. Roosevelt did not share with them during her final years. Gurewitsch accompanied ER for some fifteen years around the world and often photographed her with international dignitaries. The care he administered probably proved instrumental in allowing Mrs. Roosevelt to maintain a strenuous schedule in the 1950s.

3. Most southern states had traditionally voted Democratic since 1877, but some Republican candidates, notably Herbert Hoover and Dwight D. Eisenhower, had broken the electoral lock on the South. In 1960 Kennedy, a Roman Catholic, campaigned on a platform containing a liberal civil rights plank.

4. C. Farris Bryant.

5. Chester B. Bowles, a Democratic congressman from Connecticut from 1959 to 1961, did not seek renomination in 1960. He served as undersecretary of state in 1961 and as ambassador to India from 1963 to 1969.

Eleanor Roosevelt to W. Averell Harriman

August 16, 1960

Cognizant of the dangers in limiting human relations solely to the industrial world, the former first lady invited Harriman to become a member of the board of trustees of the Puerto Rican Cultural Center in New York City, where people could meet together in friendship and attempt to resolve mutual problems.

August 16, 1960

Dear Averell:

Some time ago I had the privilege of endorsing, with you, Governor Munoz Marin of Puerto Rico and Mayor Wagner, the Puerto Rican Cultural

Center—a place where New Yorkers and Puerto Ricans would meet together in friendship and would work together toward solving mutual problems.

Your statement was so excellent that I attach it to this letter and would call your attention to the new name—Puerto Rican Cultural Center, Inc.

The purpose of this letter is to urge you to join with me, and some thirty others as listed on the enclosed folder, and become a member of the Board of Trustees of the Puerto Rican Cultural Center. Most of the members are personal friends of yours.

We have secured a fine corner at Fifth Avenue and 110th St. for the building and are now soliciting $500,000.

The present tragic situation in Cuba and in other parts of Latin America, shows the great danger in limiting human relations to the industrial world. Our Cultural Center proposes to bring our two peoples into a closer understanding.

The high regard in which the Puerto Ricans hold you will make your Board membership especially valuable and we look forward to your early acceptance. Dr. Inman[1] is still the Executive Secretary and will be glad to call at your convenience to tell you more about the present situation. I hope you will soon advise me that you will join with me on the Board.

Yours cordially,

P.S. As I will be in Europe, would you please reply to me at The Puerto Rican Cultural Center, Inc. 420 Lexington Ave. New York 17, N.Y. (Room 1634)

Note

1. Samuel Guy Inman, executive secretary of the Puerto Rican Cultural Center in New York City.

Eleanor Roosevelt to John F. Kennedy

August 16, 1960

After John Kennedy received the Democratic nomination for president in 1960, he made a pilgrimage to Hyde Park to see Mrs. Roosevelt. She was a very important person in the party and in the country, and he sought her support in the campaign. This was a special issue since she had been rather critical of him and the role of his father in the two or three years leading to the campaign. From all reports, she found the young man charming. He wrote her a thank-you note for seeing him, and she responded the next day.

August 16, 1960

Dear Senator:

I want to thank you for coming to see me at Hyde Park last Sunday. It certainly was a busy day for you, but I am very grateful for the chance you gave me for this talk.

I had been asked to report to several people on our talk and I thought you would like to know what I said to Mary Lasker. I enclose a copy of my letter to her. A similar letter has gone to Ruth Field,[1] and I have reported verbally to Agnes Meyer, Anna Rosenberg and Mr. Bob Benjamin[2] who came to see me after spending the evening with you and some of the business men, and who is planning to raise some money for your cause here in New York. He counts on the above mentioned ladies to help in his smallish money raising dinner which he hopes to have in September.

Franklin[3] will tell me how you felt about our time together and what you would really like me to do. In the meantime, I will be at a press conference tomorrow for the NY Citizens Committee, and I will speak to a group of workers in the Citizen's Committee in the Bronx at the invitation of Robert Morgenthau, who is in charge of the Committee in the Bronx, before the 22nd when I go abroad.

I will be home the evening of September 14th, and I would be grateful if before I leave you could ask Franklin, Jr. to tell me if there is anything outside of this state that you really need me to do.

If you possibly can, I think it would be wise to call Anna Rosenberg before she leaves for Europe on August 22nd and ask for her help. She will be twice as anxious to work for you if she feels that you personally have contacted her and consider her help important.

With my good wishes,

Very sincerely yours,

Notes

1. A Stevenson loyalist.
2. Robert Benjamin, chairman of the Democratic Advisory Council.
3. Franklin D. Roosevelt Jr.

Eleanor Roosevelt to John F. Kennedy

September 27, 1960

*After having reservations about John F. Kennedy and supporting Adlai Stevenson
for the Democratic nomination in 1960, Eleanor Roosevelt threw her complete
support to Kennedy in the election campaign. In September 1960 Mrs. Roosevelt
sent Kennedy her evaluation and critique of the first presidential debate. She
summarized the comments of people who had been at her house the night before
to view the debate.*

September 27, 1960

Dear Senator Kennedy:

I watched with great interest the debate last night, and I had a number of
interesting people with me. Senator Benton[1] whom you know, thought it a
simply wonderful performance. He thought you were both very good and
that on the whole you did better than Mr. Nixon. I am so prejudiced against
Mr. Nixon that I dare not trust my own opinion, but I am going to tell you
what some people felt.

One person said to me that he felt you spoke a little too fast and had not
yet mastered the habit of including your audience at every point by saying "I
hope you agree with me, or my feeling is that you, the people to whom I am
speaking, will feel, etc."

Someone else said they thought you appeared a little too confident. I did
not agree with this, but I thought should tell you.

It was felt that Nixon would appeal to the pity for the underdog which is
prevalent in the American people, by seeming to be "humbler." I never have
this feeling about Nixon, so I am a bad judge on this particular case.

On the whole, I think it was a milestone for TV as a really good way to
campaign because it reaches so many people and gives them a chance to evaluate the ideas, the knowledge, and the personalities of the candidates. Unfortunately, however, television does not give the impression one gets from really
talking to the individual himself, and this is perhaps one of the reasons why
campaigning in person is still important. But, on the whole, I think these debates, judging by the first one, are definitely an advantage to you.

I am looking forward to seeing you.

Very sincerely yours,

Note

1. Sen. William Benton of Connecticut.

Eleanor Roosevelt to Peter Kamitchis

October 21, 1960

A little over two weeks before the presidential election of 1960, which occurred on November 8, Mrs. Roosevelt answered a letter she had received from the daughter of Peter Kamitchis, a writer and editor for numerous publications who became one of Mrs. Roosevelt's friends. Kamitchis expressed disillusionment in having to choose between Vice President Richard M. Nixon, the Republican presidential standard-bearer, and Sen. John F. Kennedy of Massachusetts, the Democratic presidential contender. Mrs. Roosevelt disagreed with his assessment of the contest and gently scolded him for his attitude. There was no question in her mind but that Kennedy was more honest than Nixon and would make a better president. She recalled in particular the spirited, unprincipled campaign methods Nixon had employed to defeat the ten-year veteran congressman from California, Horace Jeremiah "Jerry" Voorhis, a liberal Democrat, in 1946, which began Nixon's political career and instantly skyrocketed him to the national spotlight. Mrs. Roosevelt profoundly distrusted Nixon, and her instincts proved correct when Nixon resigned the presidency in 1974, shunned by conservative factions within his own party. One wonders what Mrs. Roosevelt would have thought had she lived long enough to witness Vietnam and Watergate.

October 21, 1960

My dear Peter:

I had a letter from your daughter the other day and I am glad she is having such a good time at college. Around election day I will see if she can come over to Hyde Park and bring her room mate. Up to that time I am very little in Hyde Park because I am working hard for the Democrats.

I am surprised that you have such an indefinite feeling about voting. It has always seemed to me that one had to vote for the party when one could not vote for the individual. As a matter of fact, in the present contest I think there is no comparison between Mr. Nixon and Mr. Kennedy. The one is really honest and the other has never been honest. I have watched Mr. Nixon ever since the campaign against Jerry Vorhees and I have distrusted him heartily.

As you know, I wanted Mr. Stevenson as our nominee but I have grown as I watch Mr. Kennedy and talk with him, to have a great respect for his mind and ability and his truthfulness of purpose in wanting to be a good public servant. I don't think it is a choice of the least of two evils. I think we will have a good President in Mr. Kennedy who will take the advice of the best people around him and who will be honest with the people. To say he would not make mistakes would be silly. Anyone would make mistakes with the problems that lie ahead of us.

With every good wish to you and the family.

Affectionately,

Eleanor Roosevelt to John F. Kennedy
October 24, 1960

During the presidential campaign of 1960, one of the issues involved American relations with Cuba, a real concern since Fidel Castro had taken over that island nation less than a hundred miles from American shores. Mrs. Roosevelt did not hesitate to give the candidate advice and remind him of the impression that she and others had of Kennedy's intentions regarding Cuba. The letter she refers to is not available. Mrs. Roosevelt let her feelings about Richard Nixon show in this letter.

October 24, 1960

Dear Senator Kennedy:

The enclosed letter has come to me and I think it is the way quite a number of people feel.

I thought I understood you to say during the last debate that you did not intend to act unilaterally but with the other American states. Since this is not fully understood, I pass the letter along to you because I think it would be unwise for people to have the impression that you did expect separately to interfere in the internal affairs of Cuba.

Things at present look as though they are going pretty well. I cannot, of course, ever feel safe till the last week is over because with Mr. Nixon I always have the feeling that he will pull some trick at the last minute. On the whole, things look pretty good, however. In the meantime, good luck!

Very cordially yours,

Eleanor Roosevelt to Jacqueline Kennedy
December 1, 1960

Shortly after John F. Kennedy won election to the presidency in November 1960, his wife, Jacqueline Bouvier Kennedy, gave birth to their second child and first son, John F. Kennedy Jr. Mrs. Roosevelt sent a congratulatory letter and also mentioned some of the difficulties of life in the White House.

December 1, 1960

Dear Mrs. Kennedy:

I waited this long to write you because I knew what a deluge of mail and gifts you must have had, but I cannot refrain from sending this line of congratulations on the birth of your first son. May he bring you and your husband much happiness and may he be a strong and sturdy little boy.

I know well that there will be difficulties in store for you in this White House life but perhaps also you will find some compensations. Most things are made easier, though I think on the whole life is rather difficult for both the children and their parents in the "fish bowl" that lies before you.

For both of you I wish every possible success and happiness, and may you feel well and strong before the inauguration.

Very sincerely yours,

Eleanor Roosevelt to John F. Kennedy

December 19, 1960

When John F. Kennedy invited Mrs. Roosevelt to attend his inauguration and sit with the family on the stand, she wrote him to decline the offer, explaining her reasons. This letter reveals her concern over her health. She also took this opportunity to comment favorably on his appointment of his brother, Robert F. Kennedy, to his cabinet as attorney general.

December 19, 1960

Dear Senator Kennedy:

I very much appreciate your kind letter, and certainly I intend to be at the inauguration ceremonies. However, my recollection is that your family sits around you in the stand, and directly behind the Cabinet members. I would not like to take anyone's rightful place, and it would be much better if I sat directly below on the benches where I could hear and see you because I am so deaf that unless I am in front of a person it is very difficult for me to hear what they say.

I hope you will forgive me for making this suggestion, but I remember how difficult it was to get everyone into the inaugural stand, and I will be with friends, so you will not have to worry about me, and I shall look up at you with every good wish for you in my heart on that strenuous and busy day.

You are most kind to ask me to review the parade from the stand in front of the White House but here again I think I will have to ask you to let me off, for if the weather is bad I would not be able to be there as I am anxious not to catch cold just at that time.

I know only too well all the strain that will be on you and Mrs. Kennedy that day and I do not want to add to it in any way. When things quiet down a little, or even before that time, if there is anything I could do for either of you I would, of course, be glad to come down and see you or help you in any way. But please do not have me on your mind. I assure you that I fully understand all the troubles that will be yours over the inauguration day period.

All your appointments interest me very much. They are excellent so far. I am only worried that you may find Congress giving you trouble over having a relative in the Cabinet or in any post about you. This is highly unfair but I remember how difficult they made it for Franklin when he took Jimmy in and how hard it was for both of them. I hope my forebodings will not come true. I certainly hope for both of you (because I know that this post is important in enforcing civil rights) a chance to go through with your program unmolested as far as possible.

Needless to say, I think of you every day because you are always in the papers, and I think of you with great understanding always as well as with sympathy and admiration.

Very cordially yours,

Eleanor Roosevelt to John F. Kennedy
January 24 [1961]

Shortly after his inauguration as president, Mrs. Roosevelt sent a congratulatory message to President Kennedy on his remarks. Her handwritten note was on a notepad from the Arizona Inn in Tucson, Arizona, and the envelope was postmarked on January 25, 1961.

Jan. 24th [1961]

Dear Mr. President:

I wanted to tell you how I felt about your Inaugural address. I think "gratitude" best describes the kind of liberation I felt after the speech which you gave. I have re-read your words several times & I am filled with thankfulness. May we all extend to your leadership & make your task easier.

With all good wishes to you & your wife.

Cordially yours

[*JFKL*]

Eleanor Roosevelt to John F. Kennedy
February 6, 1961

Mrs. Roosevelt rejoiced to have a Democrat in the White House again, even though she had earlier reservations about John F. Kennedy. She wrote this letter to compliment him on his proposal for the creation of the Peace Corps. She also informed him that she planned to feature the Peace Corps on her next television program.

February 6, 1961

Dear Mr. President:

I was deeply impressed by your fine State of the Union message. I was particularly glad that you were able to include your proposal for a national "Peace Corps". (?) I have been very much interested in the possibilities for useful service overseas which can be developed for people in this country and most particularly our young people.

I am preparing a television program on the national "Peace Corps" as the next in the "Prospects of Mankind" series which I have been making for National Educational Television. These programs, which are designed to stimulate interest and further understanding of important world issues as they relate to Americans, are carried by over fifty educational stations throughout the country and by commercial stations in New York and Washington.

With warmest personal regards,

Sincerely,

[*JFKL*]

Eleanor Roosevelt to John F. Kennedy
February 13, 1961

Shortly after John F. Kennedy became president, Mrs. Roosevelt wrote to the new chief executive to support the possible nomination of Mrs. Mary Dublin

Keyserling, a prominent social worker, to head the Children's Bureau. Keyserling, wife of economist Leon Keyserling, was assistant to ER at the Office of Civilian Defense, serving as chief of the Research and Statistics Division. Later she was director of the Women's Bureau in the Department of Labor under President Lyndon B. Johnson.

February 13, 1961

Dear Mr. President:

I have a long letter from Dr. Martha Eliot[1] on the subject of the Children's Bureau and in the course of it she says that she understands that Mrs. Mary Dublin Keyserling is being considered as head of the Children's Bureau. She adds that Mrs. Keyserling has "broad concerns for all people and is devoted to the idea that there must be a central bureau or office in which all health and welfare interests of children can continue to be focussed. Since she speaks and writes well on the economic issues she might be acceptable all round".

I have no idea whether you are really considering Mrs. Keyserling but I thought as Dr. Martha Eliot was once head of the Bureau I might pass on this opinion of hers.

Very sincerely yours,

[*JFKL*]

Note

1. A social worker who served on the faculties of both Yale and Harvard Universities and who served as chief of the Children's Bureau, which was eventually incorporated into the Department of Health, Education, and Welfare, today's Health and Human Services Department. She was credited, along with Dr. Edward Park of Yale, with developing a cure for rickets.

Eleanor Roosevelt to John F. Kennedy
March 2, 1961

After John Kennedy became president he taped an introduction for a film that Mrs. Roosevelt was doing. She wrote to thank him for the courtesy and for appointing her to the United Nations delegation for a short session. Because Adlai Stevenson was the new ambassador to the United Nations from the United States, his influence can be seen in her appointment. Mrs. Roosevelt was complimentary to Kennedy, and she closed with a request to meet with him without revealing her purpose.

March 2, 1961

Dear Mr. President:

I am most grateful to you for having taken the time to do the film for the Prospects of Mankind introduction yesterday, and I want also to thank you for having nominated me to the delegation at the United Nations for the coming short session. There is really no committee work that I can do but Adlai Stevenson seemed to think it might be useful to the atmosphere generally, particularly with the new African delegates, if I was on the General Assembly for the plenary meetings. I am grateful to him and to you for your feeling that I might be of use.

You were more than kind to take the extra time yesterday to let me have a glimpse of the children and of the perfectly lovely redecorating that you are doing in the White House. It is so light and bright and airy, and I hope you will find it a pleasant place to live. With all the responsibilities and aggravations that are bound to come your way, it does make a difference if one's surroundings are pleasant and cheerful.

I have wanted to have a chance to talk with you for a few minutes if you were free and it did not inconvenience you. I will be in Washington for the taping of the Prospects of Mankind next Sunday, March 5th. From two o'clock on it looks to me as though I would be on the job but unless you are going away, if you had a few minutes that morning or late in the afternoon I would be very grateful if I might come and see you.

Very sincerely yours,

Eleanor Roosevelt to John F. Kennedy

April 10, 1961

After serving on the United States delegation to the United Nations, Mrs. Roosevelt expressed her appreciation to President Kennedy for giving her this opportunity.

April 10, 1961

Dear Mr. President:

This is just to thank you again for the appointment as delegate to the United Nations.

I don't think I have been very useful but I think I accomplished what Adlai wanted in just appearing at the UN.

With my warm good wishes,

Very cordially yours,

Eleanor Roosevelt to John F. Kennedy
April 13, 1961

After Mrs. Roosevelt wrote President Kennedy to express her approval of his proposal for the Peace Corps, he appointed her to the National Advisory Council of the Peace Corps. His action pleased her considerably.

April 13, 1961

Dear Mr. President:

I very much appreciate your kind letter of the 10th regarding my acceptance to serve on the National Advisory Council of the Peace Corps.

This is an opportunity for service that I am glad to have, and I appreciate it being offered to me.

You were indeed kind to write and I want to thank you warmly.

Very cordially yours,

[*JFKL*]

Eleanor Roosevelt to John F. Kennedy
April 18, 1961

Robert M. Morgenthau, the son of Henry Morgenthau Jr., who had served for eleven years as secretary of the treasury for Franklin D. Roosevelt, was a friend of John F. Kennedy. When the president named the young Morgenthau an assistant United States attorney for the southern district of New York, a delighted Mrs. Roosevelt wrote this letter to inform Kennedy of her pleasure.

April 18, 1961

Dear Mr. President:

I have just come back from attending Robert Morgenthau's swearing in and I want to thank you for nominating him and to tell you that I feel sure he will do the best possible job. He worked very hard in the last campaign and it was due to him that in the Bronx we had a great increase in the Negro and

Puerto Rican vote. Mr. Buckley[1] would never have taken the trouble to do this.

    With many thanks for what you have done for Bob Morgenthau,

Very cordially yours,

[*JFKL*]

Note

  1. Charles A. Buckley, Bronx County Democratic leader from 1953 to 1967.

Eleanor Roosevelt to Robert F. Kennedy
April 18, 1961

Mrs. Roosevelt actively supported people in whom she believed. Shortly after the Kennedy administration began, she wrote Robert F. Kennedy, the attorney general, to thank him for appointing Robert Morgenthau to the Justice Department and to recommend an acquaintance for a newly created judgeship.

April 18, 1961

Dear Mr. Attorney General:

    I have just been to Robert Morgenthau's swearing in and it reminded me that I had not thanked you for giving him this opportunity for service. I am sure he will do his best to give good service and I think it is a fitting reward for his very hard work in the campaign.

    While I am writing you, I understand there will be a bill creating six new judgeships, and I have been asked by the new county chairman of Dutchess County to suggest that Joseph Hawkins of Poughkeepsie, who was previously our County chairman, would be a very good appointee for one of the judgeships. He is a well trained lawyer with many years of experience. He took what was practically a non-existent party in Dutchess County and produced some very good Democrats with hard work and some inspiration from Gore Vidal[1] who ran for Congress in that area.

    As you know, we are overwhelmingly Republican but we cut the vote tremendously in the last year—all, I think, due to Joseph Hawkins' good work.

    I hope you will consider Mr. Hawkins' name which will, I am sure, come to you from our new county chairman, Albert L. Hecht, 1 Washington St. Poughkeepsie, NY.

    The building of a Democratic party in these up-state counties is a long and wearisome business but I feel sure with perseverance and good organization it can be done, and recognition will give heart to new people and make them redouble their efforts.

With my good wishes,

Very sincerely yours,

Note

1. Eugene Luther Gore Vidal, one of the best-known literary figures in America, has written numerous novels, plays, essays, and reviews. He was the Democratic Party's candidate for the United States House of Representatives in the Twenty-ninth District of New York in 1960. He served on the President's Advisory Committee on the Arts from 1961 to 1963. His father was director of Air Commerce under FDR.

Eleanor Roosevelt to Sam Rayburn

May 8, 1961

Mrs. Roosevelt had long been a friend and supporter of Walter Reuther in his work for organized labor. This letter to Speaker of the House Sam Rayburn was on a letterhead entitled "Committee for Walter Reuther 25th Anniversary of Democratic Trade Unionism." Mrs. Roosevelt and United States Supreme Court justice William O. Douglas signed the letter. The list of names on the letterhead revealed an impressive lineup of Americans from every walk of life.

May 8, 1961

Dear Mr. Speaker:

A number of friends of Walter Reuther have organized a small committee to make an appropriate recognition of his twenty-five years in the labor movement.

It was back in the spring of 1936 that the United Automobile Workers, assembled in convention at South Bend,[1] joined up with the CIO[2] and began its role as a union dedicated to the public interest as well as to the welfare of its own membership. It was at this same convention in 1936 that Walter Reuther was elected to the Executive Board of the Auto Workers, from which post he went on to top leadership in the union. Now, twenty-five years later, he has built a record of democratic trade unionism second to none.

Many of the great advances in working conditions obtained across the collective bargaining table originated in Walter Reuther's resourceful mind and came to fruition through his determination and courage. Many of the great legislative advances in working conditions have resulted from his efforts in both the legislative halls and the political arenas. But at least as important as Walter Reuther's struggle to obtain a fuller life for the workers of America has been his deep belief that the labor movement must advance with, and not at the expense of, the remainder of the national and international community. To this end, he has worked tirelessly to improve the lot of Americans in all walks of life. To this end, too, he has been the leader in trade union efforts to make our nation cognizant of its international responsibilities and to make the abundance of America available to hungry peoples everywhere.

On June 15 we will present Walter Reuther with a bound volume of letters of appreciation from persons he has known in the United States and throughout the world. We are sure that he would want a letter from you included in that volume. So will you please send a letter (please do not fold it) to Walter Reuther for inclusion in the volume. Please write your letter to Walter as soon as possible and mail it in an envelope addressed as follows:

Mr. Justice William O. Douglas
United States Supreme Court
Washington 25, D.C.

In any event, please be sure we receive your letter by the end of this month as we want your letter, appropriately bound with the others, for presentation to Walter on June 15.

Sincerely yours,

Mrs. Eleanor Roosevelt
Honorary Chairman

William O. Douglas
Chairman

[SRL]

Notes

1. South Bend, Indiana.
2. Congress of Industrial Organizations.

Eleanor Roosevelt to Robert F. Kennedy

June 18, 1961

People regularly contacted Eleanor Roosevelt when they thought she could help them in some way. Surprisingly for such a public and busy person, she often responded. This letter deals with two cases of alleged discrimination, which she passed along to the new attorney general, Robert Kennedy. The letters and the case mentioned in her letter have not survived, but her letter reflected her constant interest in the protection of individuals.

June 18, 1961

Dear Mr. Attorney-General:

Enclosed is all the material I have on Ralph N. Jackson. I hope it will help you to make your decision.

I am also enclosing another case where the man feels very strongly that he has been discriminated against because of his race. If there is anything you can do about it, I am sure it would be appreciated.

I have no personal knowledge of this case and only pass it along in case it should prove to be an injustice which you would want to have brought to your attention.

The enclosed letter to the President will give you an idea of what the case is all about, and also the necessary serial number and information for review.

With many regrets that I have to disturb you,

Cordially yours,

Eleanor Roosevelt to John F. Kennedy
July 3, 1961

When the Memorial University of Newfoundland in Canada opened in 1961, President Kennedy appointed Mrs. Roosevelt to represent him at the ceremony. She was flattered, but she wondered how well she could stand in for him at the occasion.

July 3, 1961

Dear President Kennedy:

I am deeply honored that you have designated me your Personal Representative to participate in the ceremonies incident to the opening of the Memorial University of Newfoundland at St. John's on October 9th, and I want to thank you warmly. It would be for me a great privilege to represent you. However, I would like to point out that I must return home on October 10th and it seems to me you might like to have your representative stay for that day as it seems to be an important one in the scheme of events.

I will be more than happy to accept your assignment provided you do not feel you would like to appoint someone who can remain for the entire ceremonies.

With my warm good wishes,

Cordially yours,

[*JFKL*]

Eleanor Roosevelt to Robert F. Kennedy
July 15, 1961

Time and again, Mrs. Roosevelt did what she could to help people. In this case she asked the attorney general to look into charges of communism at Highlander Folk School, an old alternative school in Tennessee for labor people. She believed they were not Communists, but had no way of knowing. Mrs. Roosevelt asked Kennedy to look into the matter. She also enclosed another letter, which has not survived, indicating that she would like him to investigate the matter detailed therein.

July 15, 1961

Dear Mr. Attorney-General:

Highlander Folk School has been a controversial school for many years. In Tennessee they insisted that the classes and the people attending them were somehow contaminated with Communism, but I think they were far more concerned with the fact that these classes were for working union people and integrated. I have never felt that either the colored or the white people were communists but this does not mean that I am right. You have undoubtedly much better ways of finding out than I have. However, I feel I have an obligation to send you this letter from Myles Horton[1] to me and to Reinhold Niebuhr,[2] simply for your information. I hope that you will have some way of looking into the rights of this situation and not allow an opportunity which has existed for labor people to be wiped out unless there is real reason based on fact to do so.

I am also enclosing a rather remarkable document from Mrs. Byron House of Little Rock, Arkansas. I hope you will find time to read it and perhaps if you can help them that you will do so because I think these women have shown great courage.

Very sincerely yours,

Notes

1. Myles Horton ran the Highlander Folk School in Monteagle, Tennessee, which Mrs. Roosevelt supported enthusiastically. This school trained union organizers. Horton actively participated in meetings of the Southern Conference for Human Welfare.

2. Theologian and philosopher.

Eleanor Roosevelt to John F. Kennedy
July 22, 1961

Mrs. Roosevelt was always willing to advise presidents, especially Democratic presidents, about things that concerned her. In this letter she worried that the average person was not bonding with Kennedy and that he should make a more direct effort to communicate with the people. She brought up the Fireside Chats of her husband as a model, advising the president on how to improve the quality of his voice. Mrs. Roosevelt apologized for intruding, indicating that she heard the general public and he might not have that opportunity. In this regard, she acted as his eyes and ears among the public—the same as she had done for her husband.

July 22, 1961

Dear Mr. President:

I hope you will forgive me if I seem presumptuous, but I am concerned because I feel that there is not as yet established a real feeling among the people that you are consulting them and that they must react and carry on a dialogue with you on such subjects as you choose to bring before them.

I was in the middle part of NY State the other day, talking to some newspaper people and they said that though their papers ran stories about you every day as lead articles, they did not find that the people generally were discussing you among themselves and making it a personal matter where they stood on this or that one of your projects.

I listened during a rather long drive which I took to your last press conference and decided that it did not take the place of fireside chats. The questions asked were asked by men and women of good background and were much too sophisticated for the average person to understand. I think the people are anxious to have you talk to them on one question at a time and explain it fully and ask for their reactions and understand that their answers will be analyzed and considered.

I wish you could get someone like my old teacher (probably her daughter) to help you deepen and strengthen your voice on radio and TV. It would give you more warmth and personality in your voice. It can be learned, and I think it would make a tremendous difference.

Your statement in your press conference that you hoped members of Congress would use parliamentary means to bring the education bill out on the floor and that then you felt the votes would be found to pass it, may prove to be correct but I doubt it unless you can get it across to the people how important this bill is, and they communicate with their Congressmen.

I know I am wishing an awful lot of work on you but we have never needed leadership more and we never needed closer ties between the President and the people to inform them of the world situation and to make them face the present situation.

I apologize for taking up your time, and I feel I should also apologize to all your many advisers who probably understand the whole situation far better than I do, but I do get the reaction, and have the reaction, of the ordinary man in the street, and I think this may be one of the things which it is hard for you to get.

With my warm good wishes,

Very cordially yours,

Eleanor Roosevelt to John F. Kennedy
July 26, 1961

On July 25, 1961, President Kennedy delivered a radio and television speech in which he called for more military expenditures to meet threats from the Soviet Union in Berlin and other places. The New York Times reported comments from several places about how nervous Kennedy seemed on television. Mrs. Roosevelt wrote to congratulate him on the stand he had taken and also to give him advice about his voice.

July 26, 1961

Dear Mr. President:

I listened to your speech last night with great interest and I found it moving and exciting. I felt that you conveyed the intensity of your own concern, but I still feel there is too much strain on your throat which should be completely free. Please try to take some lessons in breathing and projection because in the long run it will be useful in saving you time and effort.

The column which I have written today will, I hope, not offend you because I have a great sense of admiration for your willingness to shoulder the responsibilities you have to accept, and certainly no one should understand better than I do what a lonely business these decisions are.

I liked your appeal to us at the end of the speech, and I hope it had a real effect. On one person I spoke to this morning I know it had. This particular person said she thought each one of us as individuals should send you everything we could possibly save, to use in the defense you felt necessary, so you moved the people and that is a great achievement.

A copy of my column is enclosed just in case you want to see what I said for public consumption.

With every good wish,

Cordially,

Eleanor Roosevelt to John F. Kennedy

September 9, 1961

One aspect of the Cold War activities revolved around obtaining tractors to ship to developing countries, which was believed might help convince them that democracy represented the best way. The effort to get the tractors failed, but Mrs. Roosevelt nevertheless expressed pleasure to have served on the committee.

September 9, 1961

Dear President Kennedy:

Thank you very much for your kind letter regarding the Tractors for Freedom Committee. I was happy to serve on the Committee and I am only sorry that our efforts were unsuccessful.

With appreciation for your thought in writing and my warm good wishes.

Cordially,

[*JFKL*]

Eleanor Roosevelt to John F. Kennedy

October 18, 1961

In the fall of 1961 President Kennedy sent Mrs. Roosevelt as his representative to a meeting in Newfoundland. She wrote him a short note commenting on her personal reaction.

October 18, 1961

Dear Mr. President:

I have not written you to report on the trip to Newfoundland.

You were most kind to send me as your representative, and going in a government plane certainly made the trip very comfortable.

It is a long time since I have "endured" red carpets and inspecting honor guards, and I am quite sure I enjoy life better outside the official functions than I do inside, so I am quite glad I do not have to return very often!

With my warm thanks for your kindness,

Very cordially yours,

Eleanor Roosevelt to John F. Kennedy
November 2, 1961

Mrs. Roosevelt always supported the United Nations and sought peace. When she joined a Quaker committee to sign a Declaration of Conscience and Responsibility, she kept her promise to write President Kennedy. Her understanding of world affairs, as reflected in this letter, is deep and profound.

November 2, 1961

Dear Mr. President:

I have this day signed for the American Friends Service Committee a Declaration of Conscience and Responsibility, and one of the things I had to promise to do was to write to you.

In your speech to the United Nations you were very forthright in saying that we must really work for peace. I think one of the ways of working for peace is to really think through what we think is right and stand for it in our national policy. For years now we have been reacting to other countries, particularly Germany and the Soviet Union. When we displeased Germany we changed, when Russia did something we reacted to what she had done. We are now seeing the usual pressures being put on our government by certain scientists, by the Pentagon and by a great many groups who have come to think that any kind of conciliatory gesture is appeasement and cannot have any effect on the Soviet Union. I wish we could throw off all ideas of appeasement and think through what it means if, because the Soviet Union has put on the show she has just finished, our national security requires us to do the same thing. The inevitable merry-go-round that will result can lead us nowhere, it seems to me, except to disaster in the long run.

This Declaration of Conscience and Responsibility pretty well says what I am beginning to feel it is essential for many of us to say if we are going to negotiate when we come to discussing Berlin. There will have to be some give and take and in the present frame of mind of most of the country any kind of giving will be appeasement. Yet I can think of a considerable amount which should be thought about very carefully.

Germany started two world wars. She occupied and devastated part of Poland, Czechoslovakia and Russia. These countries cannot have forgotten. They must have a certain amount of fear in watching Germany's rise to economic power, and this fear is understandable. I would think that we would have enough fear so we would not want to give Germany nuclear weapons, even though it is cloaked by the fact that she is a member of NATO and only receives NATO weapons.

There has been no formal acceptance of the Oder-Neisse line,[1] yet it was little enough for Germany to pay for the damage she had done.

I would think it might well be considered of mutual interest to obtain withdrawal of troops on either side for a demilitarized central Europe. I realize that it would be considered that we were weakening NATO by not having Germany in, and therefore weakening our western defense, but if we get equal concessions on the other side, is this perhaps not a good way of beginning disarmament? Negotiations must go on, and that means give and take, and we had better be preparing our people not to look upon anything which pleases both sides as appeasement on our part.

You have done much to strengthen the United Nations. I hope we can do even more, and I hope we can make a beginning in the development of world law.

I would not have bothered you with this letter but it was one of the things we were asked to do if we signed the Declaration. I want to add that if there is anything I can do to help you prepare the people for future steps which you want to take, I would be more than happy to do so.

Very cordially yours,

Note

1. The Oder and Niesse Rivers served as the boundary between Poland and East Germany after the end of World War II in 1945. East Germany recognized the boundary in 1950, but West Germany held out until 1970, and it remained a sensitive political issue for many years.

Eleanor Roosevelt to John F. Kennedy

December 12, 1961

Protection of civil liberties constituted a vital cause to Mrs. Roosevelt. In this letter, she wrote to President Kennedy asking him to intercede on behalf of a former communist who was serving a federal prison sentence.

December 12, 1961
Los Angeles, Calif.

Dear Mr. President:

A plea to sign a petition in behalf of Junius Scales has just been sent to me. However, I prefer to write you directly about this case rather than sign the petition.

Junius Scales is in a federal prison serving a six-year sentence at this moment. He was convicted under the "membership" clause of the Smith Act,[1] and the Supreme Court[2] upheld this action. When he entered Lewisburg Prison,[3] Scales had been out of the Communist Party for over four years. He left the Party of his own accord.

In a democracy the fate of an individual is important. Therefore, it seems to me to be a great pity to allow a man to suffer for no purpose whatsoever.

I am sure, if you look into this case, that you will agree this man is deserving of compassion, so I urge you to do what you can to get a commutation of sentence for Junius Scales.

With my warm good wishes to you, Mrs. Kennedy and the children[4] for every happiness at Christmas and in the New Year,

Very cordially yours,

[*JFKL*]

Notes

1. The Alien Registration Act of 1940 made it a crime to advocate the violent overthrow of the United States government.
2. In 1951.
3. In Lewisburg, Pennsylvania.
4. Caroline and John Junior.

Eleanor Roosevelt to John F. Kennedy
December 23, 1961

During the administration of John F. Kennedy, he took several opportunities to appoint Mrs. Roosevelt to special committees and commissions. This is Mrs. Roosevelt's response to her appointment as chairman of the President's Commission on the Status of Women.

December 23, 1961

Dear Mr. President:

Many thanks for your kind letter of the 15th.

I am delighted to serve as Chairman of the President's Commission on the Status of Women, and want to thank you for your invitation to do so.

I am indeed sorry about your father's illness[1] and that your burdens at Bermuda[2] had to be heavier.

With every good wish to you and the family for the New Year.

Cordially,

[*JFKL*]

Notes

1. Joseph P. Kennedy had suffered a stroke.
2. President Kennedy flew to Bermuda for a brief conference with British prime minister Harold MacMillan on December 21 and 22, 1961.

Eleanor Roosevelt to John F. Kennedy
February 1, 1962

Mrs. Roosevelt's activities throughout her life probably qualified her to receive the Nobel Peace Prize, although there was no specific dramatic action or event to justify it, as was true in the case of others. President Kennedy's nomination of her for this prize was something that many people would have expected.

February 1, 1962

Dear Mr. President:

I have learned through Mr. Lee White and Mr. Abba Swartz[1] that you have sent a letter nominating me for the Nobel Peace Prize in 1962. I am overcome by such an idea and I must frankly tell you that I cannot see the faintest reason why I should be considered. Of course, I am grateful for your kindness but I shall not be surprised in the least if nothing comes of it but my gratitude to you for having thought of this gesture will be just as great.[2]

With my warm good wishes,

Very cordially yours,

[*JFKL*]

Notes

1. Members of the prize committee.
2. Linus C. Pauling, an American scientist, received the Nobel Peace Prize in 1962 for warning of the dangers of radioactivity in weapons.

Eleanor Roosevelt to John F. Kennedy
April 7, 1962

During the last year of her life, Mrs. Roosevelt continued her busy role in many activities. She was involved in the 1962 cancer crusade, and she convinced President Kennedy to join her in a television program launching the campaign.

April 7, 1962

Dear Mr. President:

I just want to put into writing my deep appreciation for your gracious participation in the television program launching the 1962 cancer crusade.

The telecast was very well received from all I have heard, and I have been informed that the crusade got off to a very good start this year.

With gratitude and warm thanks for the fine support you have given this life-saving activity.

Very cordially yours,

[*JFKL*]

Eleanor Roosevelt to John F. Kennedy
June 11, 1962

Mrs. Roosevelt addressed issues that concerned her. Many of those related to the United Nations and her role in the American Association for the UN (AAUN). In the summer of 1962, she expressed to President Kennedy her concern and that of the AAUN for military testing in outer space.

June 11, 1962

Dear Mr. President:

I presided at the last Board meeting of the American Association for the UN and the Board decided to try to ascertain through someone in Washington close to the administration, if not through you yourself, what the real future might be as regards testing 500 miles in outer space. We felt strongly that this might lead to the Russian feeling that this was in direct contravention to your speech before the United Nations in which you said we should keep military experiments out of outer space.

We are really deeply troubled about this, and a delegation from our Board will meet with Mr. Bundy[1] next week. I hope you will ask Mr. Bundy what the result of this was as I think we may represent a position which may be rather strongly brought out.

I perfectly understand the pressures that the Pentagon and probably some of the scientists are bringing on you, but I do feel that such action on our part is really a challenge to the Russians to feel complete freedom to do anything they desire in this area. Perhaps you would be glad of a little opposition. In any case, I hope this does not give you any further difficulties.

Very cordially yours,

Note

1. McGeorge Bundy, special assistant for national security affairs.

Eleanor Roosevelt to John F. Kennedy
June 20, 1962

Mrs. Roosevelt championed various causes, including the concern about high-altitude testing of nuclear weapons. In the summer of 1962 President Kennedy had responded to her letter about such tests. This was a thank-you note to the president for his listening to her arguments and for his courtesy to a delegation from the American Association for the United Nations.

June 20, 1962

My dear Mr. President:

Please accept my sincere thanks for your letter of June 16 in reference to high altitude testing.

We appreciate the fact that you have taken a great deal of time to give us such a full explanation of your position. We feel that we now understand the situation much better.

I am most appreciative for the courtesy shown the delegation from the American Association for the United Nations and want to again thank you for your letter.

With all best wishes,

Very cordially yours,

[*JFKL*]

Eleanor Roosevelt to John F. Kennedy
June 22, 1962

John Kennedy had earlier appointed Mrs. Roosevelt to chair the Commission on the Status of Women. When the commission met in Hyde Park, New York, he sent a letter of encouragement. Mrs. Roosevelt wrote to thank him for his consideration. •

June 22, 1962

Dear Mr. President:

It was more than good of you to take time from your busy schedule to send such a warm letter to me on the occasion of the meeting of the Commission on the Status of Women at Hyde Park. All of us appreciated having your good wishes and were heartened by your willingness to work in every way possible to obtain an equalization of employment opportunities in all areas.

The meeting was a most successful one and I hope our findings will prove useful.

With my warm thanks and good wishes,

Very sincerely yours,

[*JFKL*]

Eleanor Roosevelt to John F. Kennedy
July 27, 1962

Near the end of her life, Mrs. Roosevelt planned to attend a ceremony at Campobello, where she and her husband had maintained a summer home. Since she had heard that Kennedy might come for the event, she invited him to lunch and to have the opportunity to visit with the prime minister of Canada, John G. Diefenbaker.

July 27, 1962

Dear Mr. President:

I understand there is a chance that you may come up to Campobello for the opening of the bridge and that the date is now set for August 13th. I will be very happy if you and any members of your immediate party would come to a buffet lunch at my cottage which Mr. Hammer[1] has kindly loaned me for a week. So far I have had no definite arrangements set by the local committee and I would not, of course, interfere with anything they intend to do, but I will invite the Prime Minister of Canada and the head of the local committee just on the chance that this is what they would like me to do. I hope that such informality will suit your convenience as well, and I look forward to the pleasure of seeing you.

Very cordially yours,

Note

1. An art dealer from New York City, who owned the house at Campobello where Mrs. Roosevelt was staying.

Eleanor Roosevelt to John F. Kennedy

August 15, 1962

John F. Kennedy did not attend the dedication of the bridge at Campobello as Mrs. Roosevelt had wanted. Nevertheless, while still in Campobello she wrote the president to suggest that the island might become a memorial to her husband, hoping that the United States government might consider buying the house they had owned earlier and donating it to the Canadian government.

Campobello Island

Dear Mr. President:

I want to write you about your suggestion that this Island might become an international F.D.R. memorial. I imagine this would have to be an act of the Canadian government and I think it would be a perfectly delightful idea. I am told on the Island here that there has been some talk of it in the Canadian Council. If this should happen, I have been wondering whether the American government might not purchase from Mr. and Mrs. Victor Hammer this house and grounds that belonged to my husband and make it a gift to the Canadian government to use for joint conference purposes in the summer months. Some organization interested in holding joint conferences on the many subjects that are of interest to us both might run and sponsor some of these, and there is ample room in the house for twelve or fourteen people to stay at a time and be very comfortable. With the new bridge, there will be undoubtedly more facilities for housing guests than there have been before. At present there is only one very modest little inn but I don't think it will be very long before modern motels will grow up in every direction.

It would be nice to feel that the house might be an F.D.R. Memorial Conference site because he was interested in friendship between Canada and the US and made considerable efforts to promote it.

I don't know whether you will even consider this suggestion but it is one that I think might be really useful.

With many thanks for your kind reference to the bridge and the Island and hoping some day you will see it, for it is really very beautiful.

Very cordially yours,

Eleanor Roosevelt to Agnes E. Meyer
August 28, 1962

Shortly before her death, Mrs. Roosevelt admitted that she had not been feeling well that summer and hoped that Mrs. Meyer would visit her at Hyde Park.

August 28, 1962

Dear Agnes:

I don't know if you are home yet but I hope you are back and enjoying Westchester County because I would love to have you drive over to Hyde Park someday for lunch with me. I long to see you but I have been quite miserable this summer, with the result that I am finding it hard to get my strength back and I am staying at Hyde Park this month pretty steadily.

Could you come on Monday, September 10th at one o'clock?

With much love and looking forward to seeing you.

Affectionately,

Eleanor Roosevelt to Robert F. Kennedy
September 21, 1962

Mrs. Roosevelt continued as an active public figure almost to the day she died. Less than two months before her death she was planning a new series of one-hour television programs on "The American Experience." She sent a letter to

Robert Kennedy, hoping he would appear on the first program, which, fittingly, concerned the matter of civil rights for African Americans.

September 21, 1962

Dear Mr. Kennedy:

I would like to invite you to appear with me on the first program of my new series of one-hour television discussions for Metropolitan Broadcasting. In "The American Experience," we will examine vital contemporary issues in historical perspective. The subject of the first program is "The Negro and Civil Rights," and we plan to record it on Tuesday afternoon, October 23, in the New York studios of WNEW-TV.

I would especially like to have you join me for this discussion because of your fine work as Attorney-General in the field of civil rights. We are also inviting John Hope Franklin, author of the study "Civil Rights in the United States—1863 to 1963," Barry Bingham, publisher of the Louisville Courier-Times, and the Reverend Dr. Martin Luther King, Jr.

I hope that your busy schedule will permit you to appear with me. After I hear from you, Henry Morgenthau, Executive Producer of the series, and Paul Noble, Producer, will be in touch with your office.

Sincerely,

Eleanor Roosevelt to Martin Luther King Jr.
September 21, 1962

Committed to equal rights for all Americans, Mrs. Roosevelt closely followed the civil rights movement and the marches for freedom. Just six weeks before her death, she was making plans to appear on television on "The American Experience" to explore the topic of African Americans and civil rights. Although in failing health, which prevented her appearance on the show, Mrs. Roosevelt made no mention of her illness in a letter to Dr. King inviting him to participate in the televised discussion. It was one of her last letters, a fitting conclusion for a person who had given generously of herself so that others would enjoy better lives.

September 21, 1962

Dear Dr. King:

I would like to invite you to appear with me on the first program of my new series of one-hour discussions for Metropolitan Broadcasting. In "The American Experience," we will examine contemporary issues in historical perspective. The subject of the first program is "The Negro and Civil Rights," and we plan to record it on Tuesday afternoon, October 23, in the New York studios of WNEW-TV.

I would especially like to have you join me for this discussion because of your leadership in the field of civil rights. We are also inviting Attorney General Robert Kennedy, John Hope Franklin, author of the study "Civil Rights in the United States—1863-1963," and Barry Bingham, publisher of the Louisville Courier-Times.

We are offering an honorarium of $50.00 plus expenses to our guests. I hope that your busy schedule will permit you to appear with me. After I hear from you, Henry Morgenthau, Executive Producer of the series, and Paul Noble, will be in touch with your office.

Sincerely,

Eleanor Roosevelt to John F. Kennedy
September 27, 1962

Less than a month before her death, Mrs. Roosevelt remained active in causes that were close to her. In this letter she wrote President Kennedy to ask him to be the honorary chairman of the building and development program for Wiltwyck School, a school for troubled young people of which she was one of the founders.

September 27, 1962

Dear Mr. President:

As you may know, for almost a quarter of a century, the Wiltwyck School for Boys has been an important spokesman for children in need. Nonsectarian and interracial in its program, the School serves as a unique residential treatment center for deprived, neglected and disturbed children all under the age of twelve, helping these youngsters to become useful, happier and more productive citizens.

I am a founder of Wiltwyck, have been a member of its Board of Directors for many years and know first hand of the vital work it is doing. It has pioneered in the residential treatment of emotionally upset youngsters who are too disturbed to remain in the community. I need hardly tell you how serious is the plight of children whose homes have been broken by death, divorce, desertion, and other stresses that disrupt normal family life.

Through the total treatment program of Wiltwyck, I have become tremendously impressed with what can be done to meet their urgent needs and to help reconstruct their lives.

Because I know intimately about the vital work of Wiltwyck, I have agreed to serve as Chairman of its building and development program.

I would be grateful if you would help this urgent effort by lending your name as an Honorary Chairman. It would also be helpful if you would send us a statement concerning the need for treatment centers like Wiltwyck. The enclosed material describes the work of the School.

Thank you very much for your assistance. Your statement will be of great value to all of us who are interested in the future of our nation's number one asset, its children.

Cordially,

[*JFKL*]

Editor's note: Signed by Mr. Shep Sterling due to Mrs. Roosevelt's illness.

Eleanor Roosevelt to John F. Kennedy
October 2, 1962

Approximately a month before her death, Mrs. Roosevelt had been quite ill. President and Mrs. Kennedy sent flowers and their good wishes. This is her note of thanks and reflects her plans to be active again shortly. That was not to be.

October 2, 1962

Dear Mr. President:

I want to thank you and Mrs. Kennedy for the lovely flowers and for your thought of me. It was more than good of you to have me on your mind and I am deeply appreciative.

The cause of my fever has been discovered and I should shortly be back on my regular schedule.

With every good wish to you both,

Very cordially yours,

[*JFKL*]

Bibliography

Selected Published Primary Source Material on Eleanor Roosevelt and Her Writings

Asbell, Bernard, ed. *Mother & Daughter: The Letters of Eleanor and Anna Roosevelt.* New York: Coward, McCann and Geoghegan, 1982.

Black, Allida M., ed. *Courage in a Dangerous World: The Political Writings of Eleanor Roosevelt.* New York: Columbia Univ. Press, 1999.

Chadakoff, Rochelle, ed. *Eleanor Roosevelt's My Day: Her Acclaimed Columns, 1936-1945.* New York: Pharos Books, 1989.

Emblidge, David. *Eleanor Roosevelt's My Day: Her Acclaimed Columns, 1945-1952.* Vol. 2. New York: Pharos Books, 1990.

————. *Eleanor Roosevelt's My Day: Her Acclaimed Columns, 1953-1962.* vol. 3. New York: Pharos Books, 1991.

Lash, Joseph P. *Love, Eleanor: Eleanor Roosevelt and Her Friends.* Garden City, N.Y.: Doubleday, 1982.

Miller, Kristie. "A Volume of Friendship: The Correspondence of Isabella Greenway and Eleanor Roosevelt, 1904–1953. *Journal of American History* 40 (summer 1999): 121–56.

Roosevelt, Eleanor. *The Autobiography of Eleanor Roosevelt.* New York: Da Capo Press, reprint edition, 1992.

Roosevelt, Eleanor. *On My Own.* New York: Harper, 1958.

Streitmatter, Rodger, ed. *Empty Without You: The Intimate Letters of Eleanor Roosevelt and Lorena Hickok.* New York: Free Press, 1998.

Index

Acheson, Dean G., 72, 73, 76, 77, 78, 133, 152, 153, 174, 175

Adams, Henry, 15, 16

Adams, Sherman, 211, 212

African Americans, 30–31, 31, 32, 48–49

Agnew, Ella G., 31

Alien Registration Act of 1940, 273

Allenswood School, 5–6

American Association for the UN (AAUN), 198–99, 226, 277, 275–76

American Bar Association, 130

American Civil Liberties Union, 114

American Federation of Labor (AFL), 196

American Friends Service Committee, 114, 271

American Labor Party, 98

Americans for Democratic Action (ADA), 245

American Student Union, 152

American Volunteer Group (Flying Tigers), 51

Amsterdam News, 138, 144

Anderson, Mary, 40, 42

anti-Catholicism, 4

antilynching bill, 48

Arthurdale, New Jersey, 27–28

arts and crafts, 36–37, 37–38

Asia, 127

Asian immigration, 176–77, 177–78

atomic bomb: Truman's use of, 176, 238–39

atomic war: drift toward, 140

Auerbach, Mrs., 246

Austin, Warren R., 101, 102, 105, 165

Aylward, Mr. and Mrs. Robert, 118

Babson, Roger, 190

Baker, Newton D., 16, 17

Balfour, Arthur J., 105

Balfour Declaration, 105

Bard College, 190

Barkley, Alben W., 141, 142

Baruch, Bernard, 192; book introduction, 185–86, letters to, 26–27, 27–28, 120–22, 180–86; praise of, 185–86; Stevenson advised to consult, 179, 208–9; Stevenson receives his letter of advice, 220; Truman urged to consult, 63–64

Beckel, Mr., 209
Benes, Eduard, 71, 72
Benjamin, Robert, 253
Benton, William, 254
Berlin, 271–72
Bernadotte, Count Folke, 122
Bernadotte Plan, 122
Bethune, Albert M., Jr.: letter to, 195
Bethune, Mary McLeod, 42, 43, 195;
    alleged communist ideas of, 175;
    letter to, 189–90
Bethune-Cookman College, 175, 190
Bevin, Ernest, 125, 127
Biddle, Francis, 52
Bingham, Barry, 280, 281
black community: proposal for, 163
Blanding, Sarah Gibson, 197
Bohlen, Charles E., 105, 106, 107
Bok, Edward, 19
Bok Award, 20
Bolling, 206–7
Bolton, Frances Payne, 181, 182
Bowles, Chester, 251; praise as ambas-
    sador, 173–74; elected governor of
    Connecticut, 128; housing program,
    129; John Kennedy's relationship
    with, 250; letters to, 128–29, 162–63,
    174–75; Stevenson advised to confer
    with, 222–23
"Brain Trust," 191
Brown, Edmund G., 244–45
Brown v. *Board of Education of Topeka*,
    200, 214, 215, 241
Bryan, William Jennings, 15
Bryant, C. Farris, 250, 251
Buck, Pearl, 34–35, 39–40
Buckley, Charles A., 263
Bunche, Ralph: advice sought, 215;
    letter to, 215–16; photo of, 216
Bundy, McGeorge, 276
Butler, Nicholas Butler, 35, 36
Butler, Paul M., 214, 215, 225, 243, 247
Byrd, Harry F., 100

Byrd, Richard E., 236, 237
Byrnes, James F., 73

California: conflict within Democratic
    Party, 79–81
Campobello, 278
cancer crusade, 275
Carey, James B., 64, 86, 243
Carlin, George A., 61
Carter, Alice, 20
Carter, Jimmy, 228
Case, James, 190
Castro, Fidel, 256
Catholic Church: controversy with,
    135–36, 137–38; Herbert Lehman
    and public school aid opposition,
    134; on New York politics, 137–38
Catlin, Edward Gordon, 117
Catt, Carrie Chapman: condolences on
    death of Franklin Roosevelt, 59–60;
    letters to, 21–22, 22, 24, 25, 59–60
Chamberlain, George F., 16, 17
Chambers, Whittaker, 178
Chaney, Myris (Mrs. Hershey Martin),
    244
Chapman, Oscar Littleton, 72, 73
Charlton, Louise, 66
Chennault, Claire L., 51
Chiang Kai-shek, 65, 173
Chiang Kai-Shek, Madame, 34, 51; Chi
    Omega award, 50; letters to, 43–44,
    45, 45–46, 46–47, 49–50, 50, 51, 52–
    53, 117–18, 128; photo of, 43;
    speaking activities, 48, 49, 50
Chi Omega, 50, 86–87
Chou-en-lai, 161
Churchill, Lady, 192
Churchill, Winston, 58, 166; American
    leadership attitude, 166; sends
    condolences, 56; election defeat, 61–
    62; as Knight of the Garter, 192;
    letters to, 56, 58, 61–62, 139–40,
    155–56, 192; Franklin Roosevelt's

relationship with, 84; television-radio invitation, 139–40, 155–56; advises Truman on, 58

civil liberties, 200–01, 221–22; Arizona restrictions, 52; Kennedy asked to protect, 273; television program on, 279–80, 280–81

civil rights bill: 1957 bill, 226–28; 1960 bill, 241–42; weakness of, 240–41

civil rights report, 91

Civil Service Commission, 130, 131

Clapp, Elsie Ripley, 26, 27

Clarke, Mr., 217

Clay, Lucius, 149, 150

Clinton, Hillary Rodham, 7

Cohen, Benjamin V., 122, 165

Cold War, 100–102, 102

colonialism: U.S. association with, 153–54

Commission on the Status of Women, 277

Committee for Amnesty, 114

communism: in Asia, 127, 146; clemency for former communists, 273; fear of, 88; and Highlander Folk School, 267; Stevenson's policy, 201

communists: anti-communist activities, 151–53; Republicans and Catholic votes, 137–38

Congress of Industrial Organizations (CIO), 86, 186, 196, 264, 265

conscientious objectors, 113–14

Cook, Nancy, 23–24, 26, 27, 28

Cookman Institute, 190

Cooley, Mr. and Mrs., 14

Cornell, Katherine, 87

corruption: Stevenson's policy on, 201

Costigan, Edward P., 29

Costigan-Wagner Antilynching Bill, 29

Cox, Edward E., 100

Cox, James M., 18, 19

Craig, May, 110

Cuba: ER on, 256

Cucolo, Anthony, 243

Cummings, Homer S., 29

Currie, Lauchlin M., 44, 45, 46

Cutting, Mrs. Bronson, 13–14

Czechoslovakia, 71

Daniels, Jonathan, 40, 42, 81–82, 83–84, 95

Daniels, Josephus, 14–15, 81

Davis, John W., 19, 20, 22

Daytona Normal and Industrial Institute for Negro Girls, 190

Declaration of Conscience and Responsibility, 271–72

Declaration of Human Rights, 8

Delano, Fredric (FDR's uncle), 15

Delano, Laura (FDR's aunt), 82

Democratic National Convention: in 1960, 243–43

Democratic Party, 6; in California, 79–81; in Dutchess County, 263–64; weakness of, 103, 106

DeSapio, Carmine G., 214, 215, 229–31

Dewey, Thomas E., 92, 93, 119, 120, 121

Dickerman, Marion, 23–24

Diefenbaker, John G., 277, 278

Dies, Martin, Jr., 38, 39, 88

Dies Committee, 88–89

DiSalle, Michael V. 246

discrimination, 49, 207, 266

Dix, John A., 13

Dombrowski, James, 66

Dornbush, Adrian, 38

Douglas, Helen Gahagan, 79, 80, 152, 153, 204

Douglas, Lewis, 76, 77, 78, 111, 112

Douglas, Melvyn, 152, 153

Douglas, William O., 54–55, 264–65

Dow, Stephen Olin, 36, 37

Drummond, Burt, 142–43, 178

Dubinsky, David, 137, 138

Dulles, John Foster, 3–4, 218, 219

Eastland, James O., 213

Eccles, Marriner Stoddard, 92, 93
Eden, Anthony, 166, 169
education: federal aid to, 135, 206–7
education bill, 269
Education of Henry Adams, The, 15
Eichelberger, Clark M., 172, 228
Eisenhower, Dwight D., 3, 182, 203,
    224, 251; appeal of, 170–71, 175; big
    business attitude, 204; Chi Omega
    speech, 86–87; congratulates, 60; as
    a Democrat, 128; Human Rights
    Commission resignation, 184–85;
    letters to, 54, 60, 86–87, 116–17,
    123–24, 140–42, 149–50, 156–57,
    172–73, 182–85, 185, 188–89;
    unhappy with his reelection, 223;
    SHAPE commander, 167; Stevenson
    defeat, 180; soldiers' concerns, 67;
    television-radio appearances, 123–
    24, 140–42, 156–57
Eisenhower, Mamie Doud, 141, 142
Eisler, Gerhart, 151
*Eleanor and Franklin: The Story of Their
    Relationship,* 245
election of 1912, 13
election of 1944, 54–55
election of 1946, 74–75, 75
election of 1948, 92–93, 97–99
election of 1958: in New York, 228–29,
    229–31
election of 1960, 240, 241, 242
Eliot, Martha, 260
Elizabeth II, Queen, 192
England. *See* Great Britain
ERP. *See* European Recovery Program
    (Marshall Plan)
European Recovery Program (ERP),
    106–7. *See also* Marshall Plan
European social structure: postwar
    conditions, 69

Fair Employment Practices Commis-
    sion (FEPC), 145–46
Farley, James A., 83–84

federal aid to education, 206–7
Federal Bureau of Investigation (FBI),
    88, 157
Federal Communications Commission,
    194–95
Federal Council of Churches, 114
Federal Emergency Relief Administra-
    tion (FERA), 30, 31, 152
Federal Theatre Project, 152
Ferguson, Edith, 14
Ferguson, Isabella Selmes, 13–14, 15–
    16
Ferguson, Robert H., 13, 16–17
Field, Ruth, 253
Finegan, James A., 197, 211, 215, 219,
    220
Finkelstein, Ray Lee, 248
Finletter, Thomas K., 214, 215, 229, 230
fireside chats, 268–69
Flanagan, Hallie, 151
Flynn, Edward Joseph, 97–99, 135, 136
food: limited supplies in Europe, 124–
    25
foreign aid, 64–65, 227
Foreman, Clarke, 66
Forrestal, James Vincent, 72, 73, 93,
    98–99, 104
France, 124–25, 160, 167–68
Franco, Francisco, 74
Franklin, John Hope, 280, 281
Frederika, Queen, 191
Freedom Crusade, 150
Fritchie, Barbara, 58–59
Fuller, Lenore, 38

Gandhi, Mohandas K., 173–74
Gelders, Joseph, 66
Germany, 68, 72–73
Glass, Meta, 88
Golden, John, 121
government: role of central, 141
Gracie, Anna Bulloch, 18, 19
Graham, Frank P., 65–66
Gray, David, 20, 21, 72

Gray, Maude (ER's aunt), 14, 20, 21, 23, 24
Great Britain, 64–65; Arab armaments, 93; conditions in, 68–69, 125–26; Palestine withdrawal, 95–96; uncooperativeness of, 133; world leadership of, 125
Greenway, Jack, 13
Gross, Ernest, 165
guilt by association, 175
Gunther, John, 144–45
Gurewitsch, David, 9, 219, 221, 249, 251
Gurewitsch, Edna, 249, 251
Gurewitsch, Grania, 218

Hall, Leonard W., 219
Hall, Mary Ludlow (ER's grandmother), 5
Hamilton, Alice, 87
Hammer, Mr. and Mrs. Victor, 278
Handicraft Cooperative League, 37–38
Hapgood, Charles, 38
Harding, Warren G., 18
Harriman, W. Averell, 61, 65, 77, 124, 190, 214, 214; 1958 election, 230–231, 231; letters to, 147–49, 149, 190–91, 191–92, 194–95, 228–29, 229–31, 231, 251–52; photo of, 148; presidential favorite son, 174; on Puerto Rican Cultural Center, 251–52; and Franklin Roosevelt papers, 162
Hawkins, Joseph, 263
health care: in 1956 campaign, 220–21
health of ER, 279
Hecht, Albert L., 263
Helm, Edith, 158
Henderson, Joseph W., 131
Henneck, Frieda, 195
Hickerson, John D., 159, 160
Highlander Folk School, 66, 267–68
Hiss case, 142–43, 152, 153, 178
Hitler, Adolph, 3

Hobby, Oveta Culp, 42, 43, 51–52
Hoover, Herbert, 6, 251
Hoover, J. Edgar, 157–58
Hopkins, Harry L., 30, 40–42, 54, 61, 77, 163
Horton, Myles, 66, 267, 268
House, Byron, 267
House Un-American Activities Committee (HUAC), 3, 38–39, 88, 139
housing, 129
Howe, Louis, 19, 20, 21
Howe, Mary, 18
HUAC. *See* House Un-American Activities Committee
Hull, Cordell, 21, 22
humane slaughter of animals, 226
Human Rights Commission, 111, 159; Eisenhower report, 183–84; meeting of, 66–68; resigns from, 181, 182–83, 185; reports to Truman on, 132–33
Humphrey, George M., 209
Humphrey, Hubert H., 207, 242
Humphrey, Robert L., 143

immigration: proposed restriction of, 176–77, 177–78
India, 161, 173–74
Inman, Samuel Guy, 252
integration: Stevenson's policy on, 200–201
International Labor Organization (ILO), 71, 72
International Red Cross, 160
Interstate Commerce Commission, 130
Isaacs, Rufus Daniel, Lord Reading, 16
Israel, 99–100, 110–12, 115–16, 118–19, 188–89, 205–06
Israel Bonds, 191
Ives, Elizabeth Stevenson, 182

Jackson, Ralph N., 266
Japanese-American Citizens League, 52

Japanese-Americans: women desire to enlist in WAAC, 51–52
Japanese internment, 39–40
Japanese Student League, 52
Jehovah's Witnesses, 114
Jessup, Philip C., 159, 160, 165
Jewish state. *See* Israel
Jews: status of, 64–65
John Birch Society, 153
Johnson, Herschel V., 84, 85
Johnson, Hiram W., 13, 14
Johnson, Leon E., 163
Johnson, Lyndon B., 97, 245, 360; and AAUN, 228; civil rights bill, 227–28; Hyde Park speech, 238; letters to, 96, 226–28, 228, 238, 249–40, 240–41; peace agency, 239–40; honors Franklin Roosevelt, 96; vice presidential candidate, 248
Jones, Olga A., 26, 27
Jowitt, William A., 111, 112
Juliana, Queen, 169, 218, 219
Julius Rosenwald Fund, 66

Kamitchis, Peter, 255–56
Kefauver, Estes, 158, 175, 214, 210–11, 217, 220; letters to, 216–17, 223; 1956 loss in election, 223; 1956 campaign withdrawal, 217
Kefauver Committee, 158
Kellogg-Briand Pact, 18
Kennan, George, 147
Kennedy, Jacqueline Bouvier, 256–57
Kennedy, John F., 242, 255; Edmund G. Brown supports, 244; Campobello bridge dedicated, 278; on cancer crusade, 275; criticism of family, 232, 235; DiSalle supports, 246; inaugural address, 258–59; letters to 232, 232–34, 234–35, 235, 252–53, 254, 256, 257–58, 258–59, 259, 259–60, 260–61, 261–62, 262, 262–63, 266–67, 268–69, 269–70, 270, 217–72, 273, 274, 274–75, 275, 275–76, 276–77, 277, 277–78, 278–79, 281–82, 282; on Memorial University of Newfoundland, 266–67, 270–271; Morgenthau appointment, 262–63; Nobel Prize nomination, 274–75; Peace Corps advisory council, 262; Peace Corps congratulations, 259; personality, 249; photo of, 233; on Reuther's support of, 237; speaking techniques advice, 268–69, 269–70; television debate critique, 254; television program introduction, 260–61; UN appointment, 8, 260–61; as vice president with Stevenson, 248; visit report, 249–251, 253; on Commission on the Status of Women, 274; Wiltwyck School support, 281–82
Kennedy, John F., Jr., 257
Kennedy, Joseph P., 3, 232–34, 235, 274
Kennedy, Robert F., as attorney general, 257–58; letters to, 263–64, 265–66, 267–68, 279–80; and McCarthy, 3; television appearance, 279–80
Kerr, Florence Stewart, 40, 42
Keyserling, Leon, 260
Keyserling, Mary Dublin, 259–60
Khan, Zufrulla, 168
King, Harry Orland, 13
King, Joan Carol, 136
King, Martin Luther, Jr., 280, 280–81
Knight of the Garter, 192
Knowland, William F., 227, 228
Knox, Frank, 89, 90
Korea, 146, 151, 160–61, 180, 201
Ku Klux Klan, 29, 2
Kung, Dr. and Mrs. H.H., 53
Kung, Madame, 46

Labour Party (England), 62
LaFollette, Mary, 38

Landis, James McCauley, 40, 42
Lansing, Robert, 15
Lape, Esther E., 23, 220
Lash, Joseph P., 9, 152, 245–46
Lash, Trude, 245
Lasker, Mary, 208, 249–51, 253
Latin Americans: policy toward, 121
Lattimore, Owen, 46, 47
League of Nations, 18–19
League of Women Voters, 6, 49
Leahy, William D., 76, 77, 78
Le Hand, Marguerite "Missy," 21
Lehman, Herbert, 135, 137, 174, 187, 207, 224, 229; letter to, 133–34; reform activities in New York, 248
Lenroot, Katharine F.: photo of, 25
Levermore, Charles H., 19, 20
Lewis, Dorothy Moore, 195
Lewis, Fulton, Jr., 152, 153
"Little White House," 81, 82
Lloyd, Selwyn, 166, 169
Lloyd George, David, 16, 17
Lodge, Henry Cabot, 20, 21
Lorentz, Pare, 191–92, 222
Lovett, Robert, 82, 83, 88
loyalty tests: Truman's policy on, 82–83, 87–88
Lubin, Isador, 191–92
Luce, Clare Booth, 147
Luttrell, Geoffrey, 13–14
lynching, 26

MacArthur, Douglas, 159, 162–63
MacMillan, Harold, 274
Mansfield, Michael J. "Mike," 227, 228
Mao Zedong, 117, 128
Marin, Munoz, 251
Marshall, George C., 102, 103, 106, 112, 116, 122, 126, 127, 128; in cabinet a second time, 160; letters to 82–83, 88–90, 99–100, 100–102, 104–5, 106–7, 110–12, 114–16; Marshall Plan, 80–81
Marshall, Hugh N., 151–53

Marshall Plan, 80–81, 91, 147. *See also* European Recovery Program
Martin, Mr. and Mrs. Hershey, 243, 244
Martineau, Muriel Robbins, 16
Masaoka, Mike, 52
Masaryk, Tomas G., 71, 72
Mason, Lucy Randolph, 66
Massey, Vincent, 117
McAdoo, William Gibbs, 19, 20, 21
McCarran, Patrick A., 177
McCarran-Walter Bill, 176–77, 177–78
McCarthy, Joseph, 3, 146, 153, 157
McCarthyism, 232
McClane, G. Warren, 94, 95
McFarland, Carl, 131
McIntosh, Millicent Carey, 197
Meany, George, 206, 208
memorial for FDR: proposed at Campobello, 278–79
Memorial University of Newfoundland, 266–67, 270–71
Meyer, Agnes E., 205, 206, 207, 253; on health and request for a visit, 279; letters to, 135–36, 197, 198, 210, 225–26, 243–44, 247, 279; reluctant to head Stevenson committee, 210
Middle East, 91–93, 99–100, 121–22
military influence in government, 92
military preparedness, 146
minimum wage, 30–31
"Missouri Gang," 120
Molotov, Mr., 113
Monnet, Jean O.M.G., 160, 167
Monroney, A.S. Mike, 247
Morgenthau, Henry, 280, 281
Morgenthau, Henry, Jr., 262
Morgenthau, Henry, III, 156
Morgenthau, Robert M., 253, 262, 263
Mundt-Ferguson Bill, 146
Murphy, Carl, 175
Murray, Arthur, Lord Elibank, 159
Murray, Thomas E., 230, 231
Murrow, Edward R., 174, 175

Mussolini, Benito, 3
"My Day," 7, 145–47, 233–34

NAACP, 26, 29, 144; anti-segregation amendment, 193, 206–7; resignation from board attempts, 94–95, 138, 212; travel to Mississippi for, 215
Nagasaki, 176
Nassar, Gamal A., 219
National Association for the Advancement of Colored People. *See* NAACP
National Association of Manufacturers (NAM), 131, 132
National Committee for a Free Europe, 149–50
National Labor Relations Act (NLRA), 131, 132
National Labor Relations Board (NLRB), 131, 132
National Youth Administration, 189
Neal, Claude, 29
Nehru, Jawahralal, 161, 173–74
Niebuhr, Reinhold, 267
Nixon, Richard M., 3, 237, 239–40, 244, 254, 255, 256; fear of, 203, 203–4; and Helen Gahagan Douglas, 79–80
Nobel Peace Prize, 274–75
Nobel Prize Committee, 187–88
Noble, Paul, 280, 281
nuclear testing in space, 276, 276–77
nuclear weapons, 238–39

O'Day, Caroline Love Goodwin, 21, 23
Oder-Neisse Line, 272
O'Donnell, John, 152, 153
O'Dwyer, William, 135, 136, 137
Office of Civilian Defense, 7
Osburn, William Church, 36
outer space, 228

Pajus, Mr., 72
Palestine, 95–9, 104–5, 108, 115–16, 126

Park, Edward, 260
Parmelee, Maurice, 39
Patterson, Robert Porter, 72, 73
Paul, King, 191
Pauley, Edwin W., 79–81
Pauling, Linus C., 274
peace agency, 239–40
Peace Corps, 259
Peace Through Strength: Bernard Baruch and Blueprint for Security, 185
Pearson, Drew, 121
Pegler, James Westbrook, 152, 153
People's Century, The, 44
Pepper, Claude D., 76, 77
Pera, Joan H., 145–47
Perique, Shakespeare, 28–29
Perkel, Edna Schwartz, 251
Perkins, Frances, 87, 121, 122; letters to, 24, 119–20, 130, 130–32; photo of, 25
Peron, Juan, 74
Philippines, 126
Phillips, Duncan, 187
Pickett, Clarence E., 27, 28
Poland, 71
Potsdam Conference, 62
Powell, Adam Clayton, Jr., 243, 244
presidential debate, 254
President's Commission on the Status of Women, 274
prisoners of war, 160–61
Progressive Citizens of America (PCA), 89, 90
public school aid: Catholic opposition to, 134
Puerto Rican Cultural Center, 251–52

race question, 154
Ranis, Gustav, 247–48
Rayburn, Sam, 226, 241–42, 264–65
Read, Mrs. Elbert A., 181, 182
Read, Elizabeth F., 23
Reading, Lady, 86, 87
Reading, Lord, 16

Reagan, Ronald, 171
Reedsville, West Virginia, 27
religion: on teaching of, 143
Reston, James, 95, 96
Reuther, Walter, 64, 205, 206, 245;
    honors him, 264–65; on Kennedy
    endorsement delay, 237; letters to,
    186–87, 196, 237, 242–43; Wilkins
    letter, 193, 194
Richards, Fleetwood, 96, 97
Riegelman, Harold, 189
Risenbloom, Morris V., 185
Roberts, Owen J., 114
Roberts Commission, 114
Rockefeller, Mary Clark, 235–37
Rockefeller, Nelson, 198–99, 229, 230
Rogers, Edith Nourse, 50
Rollins College, 209
Romulo, Carolos, 121, 122
Roosevelt, Alice Lee (TR's daughter), 17
Roosevelt, Anna (ER's daughter), 14,
    123, 236
Roosevelt, Anna Hall (ER's mother), 5
Roosevelt, Archibald B. "Archie," 17
Roosevelt, Edith Kermit Carow (TR's
    wife), 17
Roosevelt, Eleanor
—, China: on civil war in, 65; on
    friendship with, 44, 45, 45–46, 46–
    47; on health of Madame Chiang,
    46, 46–47; on situation in, 45–46,
    161; on speech by Madame Chiang,
    48; hopes to visit region, 52–53
—, Civil rights, 2; American Bar
    Association actions, 130; Arizona
    legislation restricting, 52; on
    immigration restriction, 176–77,
    177–78
—, Communists: on fear of, 88–90; on
    "guilt by association," 176; in labor
    unions, 86; on loyalty oaths, 82–83;
    on security risks, 39; on situation
    with Soviet Union, 81

—, Democratic Party, 103, 106; conflict
    in California, 79–81; in Dutchess
    County, 263–64; 1946 election, 75;
    1948 Truman endorsement, 119–20,
    122–23; 1948 prospects, 107; 1948
    election, 9, 97–99; 1960 primaries,
    242; 1960 election, 239–40; on
    Stevenson support in 1952, 169–70,
    199–203; Stevenson 1956 campaign
    committee, 205; Stevenson advice
    on 1956 campaign, 210, 211–12,
    213–15, 217–19, 222, 233; 1956
    Stevenson support, 221–22;
    Stevenson student support of, 170–
    71; on Stevenson women's 1956
    campaign committee, 197, 198;
    Stevenson on good 1956 campaign,
    224–25; nomination of Stevenson at
    1960 convention, 247; support of
    DiSalle for Stevenson in 1960, 246
—, Education: seeks support for Bard
    College, 190; donates money to
    college of Bethune, 190
—, elections: 1946 election, 75; 1948
    election, 9, 97–99; on 1948 endorse-
    ment of Truman, 122–23; on 1948
    Truman candidacy, 119–20; 1948
    prospects, 107; on 1952 Stevenson
    support, 169–70; 1952 statements of
    support for Stevenson, 199–203; on
    health care in 1956 campaign, 220–
    21; 1956 Stevenson campaign
    committee, 205; 1956 Stevenson
    campaign, 210, 211–12, 213–15,
    217–19, 222, 233; 1956 Stevenson
    support, 221–22; Stevenson student
    support, 170–71; on 1956 Stevenson
    women's campaign committee, 197,
    198; congratulates Stevenson on
    good 1956 campaign, 224–25; on
    New York election of 1958, 228–29,
    229–31; Stevenson nomination at
    1960 convention, 247; Stevenson

support from DiSalle in 1960, 246; 1960 primaries, 242; 1960 election, 239–40
—, foreign affairs: on Cold War and World War III, 100–102, 102; Cuban relations, 256; European conditions in 1948, 124–27; on foreign aid, 64–65; on U.S. foreign policy, 73–74, German conditions, 33–34, 72–73; India report, 173–74; on peace agency, 239–40; on Russian trip, 61; on U.S. support in world, 153–54
—, homesteads, 27–28
—, Japanese internment, 39–40
—, Middle East, 121–22; concern about, 99–100; on Jewish state (Israel), 95–96, 104–5, 110–12, 112–13, 115–16, 118–19; on peace in, 206
—, personal: life of, 1–10; in cancer crusade, 275; on donation of "Little White House," 81–82; first presidential wife to hold government position, 7; on her health, 279; newspaper column, 3; on New York governor's mansion, 236; papers at FDR Library, 10; serves in Office of Civilian Defense, 7; to resume activity after illness, 282; death of, 8, 282; burial, 8
—, photos, 4, 25, 43, 57, 109, 148, 216, 33
—. politics: activities of, 24, 107, 108, 110, 120; in New York, 137–38; on situation in 1960, 247–48; statement of, 169–70, 170–71
—, race: on African American slang term, 31, 32; on antilynching law, 29, 48; on integration of WAACS, 43, 47–48; attempts to influence NAACP on anti-segregation amendment, 193–94; attempts to resign from board of NAACP, 94–95, 138, 212; on racial problems, 28–29; rescinds resignation from board of NAACP, 213
—, religion: controversy with Catholic Church, 135–36; Cardinal Spellman criticizes, 4; Vatican ambassador appointment, 171–72
—, Roosevelt, Franklin D.: marries, 6; on 1920 campaign, 18–19; on his papers, 79; on political success of, 98; proposes memorial at Campobello, 278–79
—, television and radio: on television and radio appearances, 123–25, 181; plans television program on civil rights, 279–80, 280–81
—, United Nations: recommends CIO pay for paintings for, 187; permanent home of, 62–63; reappointed to, 84–85; resignation from, 102–3, 105–6, 134–35, 180–81, 184–85; on U.S. representation in, 164–65; serves on, 8; seeks support for AAUN, 198–99; supports, 172–73; World Federation of UN Associations, 215
—, White House, 9, on life in, 257; reluctant to move into, 7
—, World War II: on arts and crafts during, 36–37, 37–38; on conscientious objectors, 113–14; on women workers during, 40–42
Roosevelt, Eleanor Butler Alexander (TR Jr.'s wife), 17
Roosevelt, Elliott (ER's father), 5
Roosevelt, Elliott, 14, 20, 59, 116, 236
Roosevelt, Franklin D.: death of, 59–60; election, 202; family in administration, 258; Farley relationship, 83–84; foundation to preserve papers, 162; letters to, 14–15, 19–21; marries ER, 6; memorial proposed for, 278–79; political success of, 98; papers of, 79
Roosevelt, Franklin D., Jr., 106, 107, 133, 174, 175, 236, 245, 253

Roosevelt, Hall (ER's brother), 13–14, 20

Roosevelt, Harriet Howland, 19

Roosevelt, James (ER's son), 14, 79–81, 149, 175, 236, 258

Roosevelt, John, 236

Roosevelt, Kermit (TR's son), 17

Roosevelt, Quentin (TR's son), 16, 17

Roosevelt, Sara Delano (FDR's mother), 18–19, 20, 21, 89

Roosevelt, Ted (ER's cousin), 20, 21

Roosevelt, Theodore (ER's uncle), 5, 6, 10, 14, 16, 17

Rosenberg, Anna, 93–94, 243, 253

Rosenwald, Julius, 66

Ross, Malcolm, 221

Ruegger, Paul J., 160, 161

Rusk, Dean, 126

Russell, Richard B., 30–31

Russia: postwar conditions in, 70–71

Russian refugees, 148

Russians, 120–21, 149

Sandifer, Durward V., 126, 184–85, 165

"Sandy," 184–85

Scales, Junius, 273

Schaffer, Carola, 32–34

Scheider, Mrs. Melvian T., 31

Schneiderman, Rose, 23, 24

Schuman, Robert, 126, 160

Searles, Clifton, 48–49

security risks, 39

segregation, 163, 193–94, 241

Selmes, Martha, 15

SHAPE, 168

Shelton, Capt., 53

Simsarian, Jim, 184

Smith, Alfred E., 4, 6, 18, 20, 21, 84, 236

Smith, Walter B., 113

Smith Act, 273

Snyder, John Wesley, 92, 119, 120

Sophoulis, Themistocles, 90

Southern Conference on Human Welfare (SCHW), 66

Souvestre, Marie, 6

Soviet Union, 100, 125–27

Spaak, Paul-Henri, 121, 122

Spellman, Cardinal Francis, 5; controversy with, 135, 133–34, 134–35, 135–36, 137–38; criticizes, 4

Spring-Rice, Sir Cecil Arthur, 15, 16, 17

Stalin, Joseph, 58–59, 61, 148, 151, 152

Stassen, Harold E., 175

Stephens College, 136

Sterling, Shep, 282

Stettinius, Edward R., 73

Stevenson, Adlai E., 1, 180, 182, 198, 231, 245, 246, 250, 254, 255, 260, 261, 262; and Chester Bowles, 222–23; on 1956 campaign, 210–12, 222, 223; congratulates on good campaign 196, 224–25; on convention in 1960, 247; on chances in 1960, 248; governor of Illinois candidate, 108; health advice, 221; on international experience, 169–70; on Kefauver defeat, 216–17; letters to, 108, 179, 204–5, 208–9, 210–12, 213–15, 217–19, 220, 220–21, 222–23, 224–25, 248–49; considers second nomination, 197; considers third nomination, 237; on his personal life and future, 225; photo of, 109; political advice to, 204–5; presidential withdrawal, 174; support for in 1960, 244, 246; support of, 8, 169–70, 221–22; support statements, 199–203; Wilkins criticizes, 5

Stilwell, Joseph W., 51

Stimson, Henry, 89, 90

Stokes, Thomas L., 130

subversive organizations: FBI list of, 89–90

Suez crisis, 218

Sullivan, Gail, 80

Sun Yat Sen, Madame, 161
Supreme Headquarters, Allied Powers Europe (SHAPE), 168
Swartz, Abba, 274
Swartz, Nelle, 24
Symington, Stuart, 245, 246

Taber, John, 83, 92, 93, 175
Taft, William Howard, 13
Talmadge, Herman, 30–31
television, 155–56, 156–57, 160
Thompson, Geraldine (Mrs. Lewis), 88
Tobias, Channing H., 212, 213
Todhunter School, 6
Tolstoy, Alexandra L., 147–49
Tolstoy Foundation, 147
Tractors for Freedom Committee, 270
Treaty of Versailles, 18–19
Truman, Bess, 57, 77, 78, 88, 91, 133, 172, 208, 239
Truman, Harry S, 104, 107, 174, 178, 238; annoyed by Bernard Baruch, 179; candidacy in 1948, 110, 119–20, 121–22; civil rights report of, 91; on endorsement in 1948, 122–23; defends government of, 152; letters to, 56–57, 57–59, 62–63, 63–65, 66–68, 68–72, 73–74, 75, 75–76, 75–77, 77–78, 79, 79–81, 84–85, 85, 87–88, 90, 91, 91–93, 93–94, 95–96, 97–99, 100, 102, 102–3, 105–6, 112–13, 113–14, 116, 118–19, 122–23, 124–27, 132–33, 134–35, 137–38, 153–54, 159–60, 164–65, 171–72, 173–74, 176–77, 177–78, 180, 205–6, 208, 238–39; loyalty oaths of, 82–83; on MacArthur, removal, 162; and Nobel Prize, 187–88; photo of, 57; report to, 165–69; UN appointment, 8; vice presidential nomination, 55
Truman, Margaret, 75, 77, 78, 88, 91, 133, 172, 208
Truman, Martha Ellen Young, 85

Truman Doctrine, 76, 90
Tsaldaris, Constantin, 90
Tully, Grace, 96

United Kingdom. *See* Great Britain
United Nations: headquarters location, 62–63; Franklin Roosevelt's influence felt, 56; Stevenson's support of, 202; support for, 95–96, 149–50, 172–73; U.S. representation in, 164–65
USSR, 133, 168–69

Val-Kill, 8
Vandenberg, Arthur H., 70, 72, 76, 77, 107
Vanderbilt Mansion, 63
Vatican: appointment of ambassador to, 171–72
Vaughan, Harry Hawkins, 119, 120
Vidal, Gore, 263, 264
Vietnam, 167
Vishinsky, Andrei, 121, 122, 166, 169
Voice of America, 148
Von Schaffer-bernstein, Carola, 32–34
Voorhis, Horace Jeremiah "Jerry," 255

Wagner, Robert F., 251; antilynching bill, 29; election loss, 224; letters to, 189, 191, 219, 224; New York City mayor inauguration, 191; primary victory, 189; on Senate election, 219
Wagner, Robert F. Sr., 189
Wallace, Henry A., 54, 100; candidacy concern, 93–94, 97–99; on Communists in labor unions, 86; complains, 154–55; hearing for him, 139; letters to, 35, 38–39, 44, 47, 55, 72–73, 86, 139, 154–55
Wallace, Mrs. Henry A., 55
Walter, Francis B., 177
Walton, William, 249, 251
Webb, Mrs. Vanderbilt (Aileen), 36–37, 37–38

Webber College, 190

Weston, Harold, 187

White, Lee, 274

White, Walter: on black community, 163; letters to, 26, 28–29, 29, 30–31, 42–43, 47–48, 48, 94–95, 138–39, 144, 163

White House, 257

Wilkins, Roy, 5, 138, 139, 144, 193–93, 212, 213

Williams, Aubrey, 78, 163–64

Wilson, Edith Bolling Galt, 20, 21, 32, 34;

Wilson, Milburn, 27

Wilson, Woodrow, 17, 32, 202; death of, 19, 20; 1912 election, 13; Franklin Roosevelt in administration, 14

Wiltwyck School, 281–82

Winant, John Gilbert, 71

Winthrop, Alice, 20

women: in politics, 74–75

Women's Army Auxiliary Corps (WAAC), 51–52

Women's Army Corps, 42, 47–48

Women's Trade Union League, 6

women workers in World War II, 40–42

Woodward, Ellen S., 31–32, 40, 42

Works Progress Administration (WPA), 151, 163

world citizenship, 136

World Citizenship Organization, 136

World Federation of UN Associations, 215, 248

World War II: responsibility for, 239

World War III: possibility of, 100–102, 102

Yalta Conference, 149

youth: in postwar Europe, 69